# Mediterranean
## COOKBOOK
### Fresh, fast and easy recipes

EDITOR-IN-CHIEF **MARIE-PIERRE MOINE**

LONDON, NEW YORK,
MUNICH, MELBOURNE, DELHI

DK UK
**Project Editor** Cressida Tuson
**Senior Art Editor** Sara Robin
**Managing Editor** Dawn Henderson
**Managing Art Editor** Christine Keilty
**Senior Jacket Creative** Nicola Powling
**Design Assistant** Kate Fenton
**Editorial Assistant** Elizabeth Clinton
**Pre-Production Producer** Rebecca Fallowfield
**Senior Producer** Oliver Jeffreys
**Creative Technical Support** Sonia Charbonnier
**Art Director** Peter Luff
**Publisher** Peggy Vance

DK INDIA
**Senior Editor** Charis Bhagianathan
**Senior Art Editor** Balwant Singh
**Editors** Ligi John, Divya Chandhok
**Art Editor** Anjan Dey
**Assistant Art Editor** Gazal Roongta
**Managing Editor** Alicia Ingty
**Managing Art Editor** Navidita Thapa
**Pre-Production Manager** Sunil Sharma
**DTP Designers** Rajdeep Singh, Neeraj Bhatia

NOTE: The author and publisher advocate sustainable
food choices, and every effort has been made to include
only sustainable foods in this book. Food sustainability
is, however, a shifting landscape, and so we encourage
readers to keep up to date with advice on this subject,
so that they are equipped to make their own ethical choices.

First published in Great Britain in 2014 by
Dorling Kindersley Limited
80 Strand, London WC2R 0RL

A Penguin Random House Company
2 4 6 8 10 9 7 5 3 1
001 – 192070 – Apr/2014

A CIP catalogue record for this book is available
from the British Library.

ISBN 978-1-4093-4724-8

Colour reproduction by Alta Image Ltd
Printed and bound in China by South China

Discover more at **www.dk.com**

# Contents

# regional index

To help you plan the perfect Mediterranean menu, this index lists the recipes by region and type of dish.

# introduction

I fell in love with the aromas, flavours, and sensuous frugality of the Mediterranean during holidays in the South of France when I was growing up in Paris. Faraway Provence became real the moment we'd reached Montélimar and stopped for *essence* for the Citroen DS and eagerly awaited sticky nougat for us. Our destination was a very small island. It had a lighthouse, a decrepit tower, no electricity or running water, hiding places, sandy and rocky pools, narrow paths winding through scented bush – Peter Pan would have been happy there. I learnt to smash pine cones to extract creamy nuts. I helped make salty tapenade, mashed anchovies, and rubbed garlic on leftover toast (this was waste-not-want-not for practical as well as financial reasons, food shopping being a laborious expedition *à terre* by canoe and car). Drinking water came from the well. Water for washing was restricted to a pail each a day, left in the sun to be kind to skin burning from salt, sun, and sand. I discovered the joys of winkles, the mixed blessings of sea urchins (sharp spines and intense roe), and the magic of seeing pastis become opaque when my father added water to his glass. Milk and butter always tasted pleasantly faintly sour. Three decades later the same taste surprised me at breakfast. I was in Sanlucar de Barrameda in Andalucia; the fridge had broken down and the butter had gone a

**The Mediterranean region**
This map shows how the Mediterranean got its name. The sea in the middle of the land, it is the meeting point of Europe, Asia, and Africa.

little tart overnight. I had a similar hit of Mediterranean recognition on my first trip to Istanbul, eating *baba ganoush* (formerly experienced in Grasse as *caviar d'aubergine*). Learning to make *mutabal* at the Petra Kitchen with memorably good aubergines, I recognized it as, in fact, my old favourite, aubergine purée, in its Arabic interpretation, with oodles of tahini and parsley. Even if I dislike the taste of the stuff, the sight and aroma of rakı, arak, or ouzo always take me back to hot, dry sunny days with the beautiful glittering Mediterranean in the background.

**From Morocco to Sardinia**, from Meis, the most eastern of the Greek islands, off Kas in southern Turkey, to Lebanon, on islands and along the coast on summer evenings, everywhere there are garlands of light, wafting aromas of grilling fish, aniseed, and fresh herbs, laughter and urgent voices, and gently clinking glasses. There is a shared way of life, similar values – conviviality, an enjoyment of simple, good food with family and friends. The ingredients used in dishes are similar; many recipes are related, with local variations and preferences. In this region with its long, complex history, the appreciation of a common food culture, the enthusiasm for cooking, the respect (sometimes grudging) for the recipes of others have always been a power for good relations between different people. The Mediterranean diet is healthy, based on vegetables, grains, pulses, nut, fruit, fish, some meat, simple cheeses, olives, and olive oil. Figs, grapes, and citrus are important in the economy as well as on the table. Dairy products are variations on a theme of yogurt and simple traditional cheeses, mostly goat's milk and ewe's milk.

**A word about geography.** This is a cookbook about the Mediterranean, with recipes illustrating the best of its culinary style, diversity, and traditions. The book takes a few liberties with geography (but, I hope, within the boundaries of the subject).The Mediterranean basin is often defined as the olive belt, the region where olive trees grow. The olive and olive oil industry is a major factor in the economy, food culture, and history of the lands bordering the middle sea. The olive oil countries include Portugal, which has no Mediterranean coast but is part of the essentially Mediterranean Iberian Peninsula. In this book, Iberia also includes the Basque Country (on both sides of the border). Also mentioned is the Balkans, which extends into the Mediterranean climate zone. And Roquefort cheese because it's worth it and in any case comes from the *Midi*, the old South of France, which included Provence.

**Drinking my morning tea** recently, with the radio on in the background, I was happily contemplating a possible trip to Palermo, when I was brought back to my kitchen by a news item about doctors and health experts urging the Government to persuade people to eat fresh fruit and vegetables, nuts, fish, and olive oil – to shift from "dubious drugs" to the benefits of a Mediterranean diet. This was hardly news but it was music to my ears. This proposed alternative medicine needs no spoonful of sugar to help it go down. I hope you'll enjoy cooking from this book.

Marie-Pierre Moine

**Marie-Pierre Moine**

# mezze, tapas, and antipasti

# zahlouk

### ❖ *north africa* ❖

There are a variety of cooked aubergine dips and salads throughout the Middle East. This spicy version includes tomatoes and is a classic mezze dish from Morocco, Tunisia, and Algeria.

**PREP** 20 MINS ❖ **COOK** 1 HR ❖ **SERVES** 6-8

2 medium **aubergines**
2 tbsp **olive oil**
2–3 **garlic cloves**, crushed
400g can chopped **tomatoes**, drained
1–2 tsp **harissa paste**
1–2 tsp **clear honey** or sugar
juice of 1 **lemon**
small bunch of **flat-leaf parsley**, finely chopped
small bunch of **coriander**, finely chopped
**sea salt** and freshly ground **black pepper**

1 Preheat the oven to 200°C (400°F/Gas 6). Place the aubergines on a baking tray and bake for 1 hour, or until soft when pressed with a finger. Using a sharp knife, slit the aubergines open, scoop out the warm flesh, and chop into a pulp.

2 Heat the oil in a heavy-based pan, stir in the garlic, and sauté until it begins to colour. Add the tomatoes, harissa, and honey and cook over a medium heat for 5–6 minutes, or until thick and pulpy. Toss in the aubergine pulp with the lemon juice, parsley, and most of the coriander, and season.

3 Tip the mixture into a serving bowl, sprinkle the rest of the coriander over the top, and serve warm or at room temperature with chunks of crusty bread.

variation

**Smoked zahlouk** You can prepare a smoked version of this dish by placing the aubergines directly on a gas flame until they are very soft. Hold the smoked aubergines under cold running water to remove the skin, squeeze the flesh to remove the excess water, chop to a pulp, and follow the recipe above.

# muhammara

### ❖ *middle east* ❖

This delicious medieval Arab dip is usually served with strips of toasted flatbread or thin carrot and celery pieces. Traditionally, a mortar and pestle is used to pound the ingredients to a paste, but you can also use an electric blender.

**PREP** 20 MINS ❖ **COOK** 1 HR ❖ **SERVES** 4-6

3 **red bell peppers**
2 **red chillies**
150ml (5fl oz) **olive oil**
150g (5½oz) shelled **walnuts**
2–3 tbsp **white breadcrumbs**
2 tbsp **pomegranate syrup**
juice of 1 **lemon**
1–2 tsp **clear honey**
2–3 **garlic cloves**, crushed
1–2 tsp ground **cumin**
small bunch of **flat-leaf parsley**, finely chopped
**sea salt**

1 Preheat the oven to 200°C (400°F/Gas 6). Place the peppers and chillies on a baking tray, drizzle with half the oil, and roast for about 1 hour. Turn them occasionally in the oil until the skins are slightly burnt and bursting. Remove and set aside.

2 Place the walnuts on a baking tray and roast for about 10 minutes, or until they produce a nutty aroma.

3 Place the peppers and chillies on a wooden board, peel off the skins, and remove the stalks and seeds. Roughly chop the flesh and place in a food processor with the walnuts, breadcrumbs, pomegranate syrup, lemon juice, honey, garlic, and cumin. Drizzle in the rest of the oil while whizzing, add most of the parsley, and season well with salt. Tip into a serving bowl, sprinkle over the rest of the parsley, and serve.

variation

**Creamy muhammara** Combine the basic muhammara recipe with 2–3 tablespoons of the traditional strained yogurt, *labneh*, to make a thicker version.

# tapenade

*provence*

Tapenade, which takes its name from the Provençal word for capers, *tapeno*, is the quintessential tapas of Provence. The most traditional one is made with black olives.

**PREP** 5 MINS ❖ **SERVES** 6-8

150g (5½oz) **black olives**, pitted and chopped
1 **garlic clove**, crushed
1 tbsp **capers**, drained
2 tbsp **lemon juice**
1 tsp **lemon zest**
75ml (2½fl oz) **olive oil**
freshly ground **black pepper**

1 Place the olives, garlic, capers, lemon juice, and zest in a mortar or the small bowl of a food processor. Add 1 tablespoon oil and pound or whizz, gradually adding more oil until you have a thick paste.

2 Taste, season with pepper, and serve immediately. Tapenade can be refrigerated, covered with cling film, for up to 4 days.

## variations

**Green tapenade** Use chopped green olives instead of black.
**Anchovy tapenade** For this version, add 2 tablespoons of Anchoïade (see p20) to green or black tapenade.

# marinated olives

*middle east*

These work best if made a few days in advance to allow the fruits, spices, and herbs to mingle and infuse the olives.

**PREP** 10 MINS, PLUS MARINATING
**COOK** 2 MINS ❖ **MAKES** 500ML (16FL OZ)

250g (9oz) **black or green olives**, or a mix of both
1 tsp **fennel seeds**
½ tsp **cumin seeds**
grated zest of ½ **orange**
grated zest of ½ **lemon**
2 **garlic cloves**, finely chopped
2 tsp **chilli flakes**, crushed
1 tsp dried **oregano**
1 tbsp **lemon juice**
1 tbsp **red wine vinegar**
2 tbsp **olive oil**
1 tbsp finely chopped **flat-leaf parsley**

1 If desired, pit the olives. Toast the fennel and cumin seeds in a dry pan over a low heat for 2 minutes, until aromatic.

2 Combine the olives, toasted seeds, citrus zests, garlic, chilli flakes, oregano, lemon juice, vinegar, and oil and toss to coat the olives well. Place in an airtight container. Leave to marinate at room temperature for 8 hours.

3 Shake the container occasionally to coat the ingredients while marinating. Stir in the parsley. Serve at room temperature.

## prepare ahead

Make up to 1 week in advance, omitting the parsley. Store in an airtight container and refrigerate. Add parsley up to 3 hours before serving.

## cook's tip

Warming the olives will intensify the flavours. Gently heat the marinated olives over a low heat for 5 minutes, until warmed through. Serve warm.

*how to eat*
No convivial aperitif is complete without tapenade, croutons, a glass of pale chilled rose, or a bright yellow aniseed pastis

# *essential*
# olives and olive oil

Olive trees have always been a part of the Mediterranean landscape, their branches symbols of peace and plenty. Olives and their oil are cornerstones of everyday cooking.

**Green olives** are picked before they are ripe and black olives are left to ripen on the tree. If olives are for eating rather than for making oil, they are cured to remove their unpalatable raw bitterness. The salt helps to create the olive's distinct flavour and texture. Oil is pressed from fresh ripe olives, the first cold pressing produces the best and most expensive extra virgin oil. Don't waste this liquid gold on frying – save it for dressing salads, eating with fine bread, and dribbling over cooked dishes. Keep oil away from light and use it quickly – unlike good wine it won't improve with age.

**Spain's** bright, extra virgin olive oil is fruity and robust. Use for drizzling on grilled or marinated vegetables.

**Tuscan** olive oil has a deep gold colour and with its smooth, well-rounded flavour is the best oil to use for cooking.

**Tunisia** produces a lot of robust everyday oil and some excellent extra virgin oil. This one is an organic extra virgin oil, well-rounded, with pleasant bitterness, perfect for dipping.

**Gaeta**, a favourite in Southern Italy, is a delicately meaty olive with a mild, slightly tart flavour.

**Niçoise** olives are small but packed with delicate flavour, perfect for pissaladière.

**Picholine** olives are nutty and fleshy – good for snacks and for adding to poultry dishes.

**Provence's** best oils are light, flowery, and elegant, with black olive aromas. Douse it over soft fresh bread, or use to dress grilled fish, and salade niçoise.

**Liguria** is home to this amber-coloured, sweet, and richly flavoured extra virgin oil. Use it for dipping or for making very special pesto.

**Crete** has been producing oil since antiquity. This extra virgin oil has a light green tinge and a flavour to match – fresh but ripe, and strongly fruity.

**Manzanilla** olives, a Spanish green variety, are often pitted and stuffed with almonds, anchovies, or red peppers.

**Nyons** olives are from Provence and have a rich flavour. Use them in salads.

**Kalamata** is the traditional Greek black olive, tinged with purple. Large, and with a fruity flesh, they go as well with mezze as they do in salads.

**Lucques** green olives originate from Lucca. Long and shiny, with a firm texture, they make for a great appetizer.

# taramosaláta

❖ *greece* ❖

The commercial version of this creamy fish dip – a familiar sight in many chiller cabinets – is a pale shadow of the real thing. In Greece, the basis is *tarama* – the salted, pressed roe of the grey mullet.

**PREP** 10 MINS ❖ **COOK** 20 MINS ❖ **SERVES** 4

4 slices of **dry country bread** (not sliced white)

100g (3½oz) **tarama paste** or **salted cod's roe**, skinned

2 **garlic cloves**, crushed

200ml (7fl oz) **olive oil**, plus extra for drizzling

juice of 1 **lemon**

salt

1 Roughly chop the bread and process or liquidize into crumbs. Alternatively, if the bread is very hard and stale, soak it in water and squeeze dry. Reserve.

2 Process the roe with 2 tablespoons of the reserved breadcrumbs. Add the garlic, whizz to blend, and trickle in the oil, alternating with breadcrumbs and the lemon juice diluted with its own volume of water, until the mixture is light and fluffy – it should not become grainy. Taste and add more lemon juice and salt, if needed.

3 Serve swirled onto a shallow plate, topped with a single black olive and maybe an extra drizzle of oil, with pitta bread or raw vegetables and cos lettuce leaves for scooping.

### cook's tip

The alternative thickener to breadcrumbs is mashed potato. Omit the bread and process the rest of the ingredients to a purée, then beat in the mashed flesh of 2 large cooked and skinned potatoes.

# canapés à la brousse et aux figues

❖ *provence* ❖

A true flavour of Provence, fresh figs and creamy soft ewe's cheese sweetly rounded off by aromatic honey, make a great combination for a delightful mezze dish. A quick grinding of black pepper can add a nice finishing touch.

1 Preheat the grill. Cut the baguette on the slant into slices. Arrange them in one layer on a baking tray and lightly toast them on both sides under the grill.

2 Slice the figs lengthways. Arrange on top of the toasted baguette slices. Spoon over the ewe's cheese, pressing it down a little.

3 Place under the grill for 3–4 minutes until bubbling and a little golden.

4 Drizzle with the honey and serve immediately.

### cook's tip

Cut the figs into neat slices and place on the baguette, then cover with the cheese. The topping will grill more quickly and evenly if the pieces of cheese are small.

**PREP** 10 MINS ❖ **COOK** 15 MINS ❖ **SERVES** 6

1 **baguette**

8 ripe **figs**

250g (9oz) fresh creamy **ewe's milk cheese**

6–8 tbsp clear **rosemary** or **lavender honey**

# baba ganoush

### *middle east*

No Middle Eastern mezze table is complete without a bowl of this creamy, smoky dip. It tastes delicious with warmed pitta bread, cut into strips, or just scooped up with fresh bread.

**PREP** 10 MINS, PLUS STANDING
**COOK** 25-30 MINS ❖ **SERVES** 6

oil, for greasing
900g (2lb) **aubergines**, cut in half lengthways
2 large **garlic cloves**, crushed
2 tbsp **extra virgin olive oil**
2 tbsp **plain yogurt**
3–4 tbsp **tahini**
2–3 tbsp **lemon juice**
**salt** and freshly ground **black pepper**
sprigs of **coriander**, to garnish

1 Preheat the oven to 220°C (425°F/Gas 7) and lightly grease a baking sheet. Score down the centre of each aubergine half without cutting through the skin, then place on the baking sheet, cut–sides down. Place in the oven and bake for 25–30 minutes, or until the flesh is thoroughly softened and collapsing.

2 Transfer the aubergine halves to a colander and set aside to stand for 15 minutes, or until they become cool enough to handle.

3 Scoop the aubergine flesh into a food processor or blender. Add the garlic, oil, yogurt, 3 tablespoons of tahini, and 2 tablespoons of lemon juice, and process until smooth. Taste and adjust the tahini and lemon juice, if needed, then season to taste. Garnish with coriander, and serve. Any leftovers can be kept in the fridge, covered, for up to 2 days.

### prepare ahead

The dip can be made 1 day in advance. Cover and chill until 15 minutes before required, then return to room temperature to serve.

### prepare by hand

Preheat the grill to its highest setting, then grill the aubergine halves, cut-sides down, until thoroughly softened and collapsing. Alternatively, chargrill the aubergine halves in a very hot ridged cast-iron grill pan. Instead of using a food processor or a blender, the ingredients can be pounded to a paste using a mortar and pestle.

# anchoïade

### *❖ provence ❖*

There are many versions of this powerful, versatile anchovy paste. Typically French, it has a moreish salty taste, and used sparingly it goes a long way.

**PREP** 5 MINS ❖ **SERVES** 6-8

12 **anchovy fillets** in oil or brine
2 **garlic cloves**, crushed
1 **spring onion**, white part only, chopped
90ml (3fl oz) **olive oil**
juice and grated zest of ½ small
    unwaxed **lemon**
freshly ground **black pepper**

1 Drain the anchovies. If using anchovies in oil, pat dry between layers of kitchen paper, and if in brine, rinse in cold water before patting dry.

2 Chop the anchovies. Place in the bowl of a food processor, add the garlic, spring onion, and a little oil, and whizz to make a coarse paste. If you prefer, use a mortar and pestle.

3 Trickle in the rest of the oil, a little at a time, with the motor running. Add the lemon juice and zest, and whizz until you have a coarse, thick purée.

4 Adjust the seasoning with a little pepper and serve immediately. Any leftovers can be kept in the fridge for up to 5 days.

### *how to serve*

Spread sparingly over lightly buttered toast or crostini. Use as a dip for crudités, or smear over grilled fish, such as sardine or red mullet.

# a taste of
# GREECE

Greek cuisine is the grandmother of Mediterranean cuisines. Over the centuries, as Greece colonized parts of the Mediterranean, its culinary influence developed. There was plenty of give and take, with other regions bringing in new ingredients, flavours, and types of food. Greek cookery still relies on the same core ingredients, although its modern repertoire is much more varied. Lamb remains the preferred meat animal, yogurt and cheese are made from ewe's milk and goat's milk, and vegetables include peppers and aubergines. Fruits and spices from other continents are used, while pastry and sweet, nutty dishes are shared with the Ottomans. Greece has distinctive favourite flavourings – thyme, oregano, mint, basil, garlic, onion, dill, bay leaves, and lemons. Meat is often flavoured with sweeter spices such as cinnamon and cloves. Eating is a sociable business, and sharing mezze is as convivial as it is further east or south.

**Mastic** is an important industry on the island of Chios, where the resin is harvested from slashes made in the trunks of the trees. Rare and expensive, mastic is used like starch to stabilize desserts, and to flavour liqueurs.

**Figs** have been prized in Greece for 3000 years – the favourite high-energy food for athletes in the ancient Olympic Games.

Ermoupoli on the island of Syros is a glorious sight, with the blue cupola of the cathedral high up on the hill.

**Feta** is made from ewe's milk, sometimes with up to 30 per cent goat's milk. A soft, briny cheese, it has a grainy texture and a mild, salty tang. It is delicious in salads or as a filling in hot, crisp filo pastry parcels.

**Wild greens** are leaves such as dandelion, wild asparagus, sow-thistle, wild fennel, lamb's lettuce, chicory, poppy, wild celery, and wild salsify – all distinctively aromatic.

**Red onions** are popular in salads sliced wafer thin.

**Lima beans** with fennel is a popular starter, dressed with olive oil and lemon juice.

Veg on one side, fruit on the other, stacked crates are neatly piled up with fresh produce.

**Plum tomatoes** are intensely flavoured and come in irregular shapes and sizes.

When the boats come in it's time to relax with mezze, a drink, and good conversation.

**Beetroot** mixed with yogurt, lemon juice, parsley, garlic, and pistachio, makes an excellent starter salad.

# A family gathering in Greece

Everything is very informal – most of the dishes end up together on the table. Black olives, Greek bread, and olive oil are essential props. The meal starts with a favourite chickpea soup, revithosoupa, with its warming broth redolent of rosemary, lemon, and garlic, finished off winningly with pomegranate seeds and olive oil. Grilled pork and sweet pepper kebabs are served with lemons and, of course, Greek salad. Golden baklava lozenges wait to provide a perfect sweet ending.

**Kalamata olives**

**Revithosoupa**
page 60

**Ouzo**

**Souvlakia**
page 168

**Horiatiki salata**
page 221

**Baklava**
page 310

# pasteis de bacalhau

### ✳ *portugal* ✳

Portugal's national snack, these crisp little fritters are found in every seaside bar, particularly in Lisbon. If you can't get salt cod, fresh fish fillets, smoked salmon, or haddock give good results, too.

**PREP** 10 MINS, PLUS SOAKING
**COOK** 20-30 MINS ❖ **SERVES** 4-6

500g (1lb 2oz) middle-cut
   salt cod (bacalhau)
500g (1lb 2oz) **floury potatoes**
1 large mild **onion**, grated
4 tbsp chopped **flat-leaf parsley**
freshly ground **black pepper** or **chilli flakes**
2 large **eggs**
**olive oil**, for deep-frying

1 Soak the salt cod in several changes of water for 48 hours. Drain the soaked salt cod and reserve.

2 Place the potatoes in a pan and cover with water. Bring to the boil. Cook for 20 minutes, or until the potatoes are tender.

3 In a separate pan, cook the fish in simmering water for 10 minutes. Remove the fish and reserve. Drain the potatoes and skin them as soon as they are cool enough to handle. Meanwhile, skin and bone the fish with your fingers – it is easiest with a pair of tweezers. Flake the flesh with a fork.

4 Mash the potatoes thoroughly with the onion and parsley, season with pepper, mash in the flaked fish, and beat in the eggs.

5 Pour the oil in a frying pan, filling it about half way. As soon as the surface is lightly hazed with blue, drop in a bread cube. When small bubbles form immediately around the edges and the crumb begins to brown, the oil is ready for frying.

6 Drop teaspoons of the fish mixture into the hot oil, a few at a time. Wait until they bob to the surface, turn them over, remove with a slotted spoon, and drain on a kitchen paper. Repeat until the mixture is all used up. Serve hot, with piri-piri or chilli sauce on the side.

# crevettes à la marocaine

### ✳ *provence* ✳

Originally from Morocco and also found in Provence, this easy dish tastes as good as it smells. Serve with a salad for a quick lunch, or tapas-style with wooden cocktail sticks.

**PREP** 5 MINS ❖ **COOK** 5 MINS ❖ **SERVES** 4-6

500g (1lb 2oz) uncooked shelled **gambas**
   or **large prawns** (defrosted if frozen)
4 tbsp **olive oil**
½ tsp **harissa paste** or **hot paprika**
1 tsp ground **ginger**
1 tsp ground **cumin**
½ tsp **ground coriander**
3 **garlic cloves**, crushed
1 tbsp snipped **flat-leaf parsley**
1 tbsp snipped **coriander**

1 Drain the gambas on a double layer of kitchen paper. Heat the oil in a large frying pan, tip in the spices and garlic, and stir for a minute to release the flavours.

2 Add the gambas and cook for 1–2 minutes over a medium-high heat until they turn a little pink, then turn over. Cook until the gambas are pink all over, stirring frequently. Stir in the herbs and serve hot.

# hummus
## ❖ *middle east* ❖

This chickpea and tahini dip is one of the most widely recognized of all Middle Eastern dishes. It tastes brilliant with warm pitta bread and sticks of carrot, cucumber, celery, and sweet pepper.

**PREP** 10 MINS ❖ **SERVES** 4

400g can **chickpeas**
3 tbsp **tahini**
juice of 3 **lemons**
3 **garlic cloves**, chopped
½ tsp **salt**
**pimentón** (Spanish paprika), for sprinkling
**olive oil**, to drizzle

1 Drain and rinse the chickpeas, reserving 4–6 tablespoons of the liquid from the can. Place the chickpeas in a blender or food processor with 3 tablespoons of the reserved liquid.

2 Add the tahini, lemon juice, and garlic, then blend well for a few seconds until smooth and creamy. Add a little more of the liquid from the can, if required.

3 Season to taste with salt. Transfer the hummus to a small bowl, sprinkle with paprika, and serve at room temperature. Drizzle with oil for a traditional finish.

### prepare ahead

Make the dip up to 24 hours in advance, and chill, covered, until needed. Allow the hummus to stand at room temperature for 30 minutes before serving.

### variation

**Red pepper hummus** Preheat the grill to its highest setting. Halve and deseed a small red pepper, then grill, skin-side up, for 4–5 minutes, or until the skin is lightly charred. Place in a plastic food bag until cool enough to handle, then peel away the skin. Roughly chop the pepper and add it to the blender along with the chickpeas, then follow the recipe above. Depending on the juiciness of the pepper, you may need less of the reserved liquid from the can. Add 1 teaspoon of ground cumin for a spicier flavour.

# pa amb tomàquet
## ❖ *spain* ❖

Barcelona's answer to Nice's *pan bagna*, this Catalan bread and tomato snack is moreish and popular. It is fun and very simple to prepare, but use fresh ingredients and your best olive oil.

**PREP** 5 MINS, PLUS SOAKING ❖ **COOK** 5 MINS
**SERVES** 4, OR MORE AS TAPAS

1 **baguette**
1 large **garlic clove**, halved
2 **tomatoes**, halved
**sea salt**
3–4 tbsp **extra virgin olive oil**

1 Cut off both ends of the baguette and set aside. Cut the baguette crossways into 4 segments, halve each segment lengthways, and toast.

2 Rub the cut sides of each piece of toasted bread with the cut sides of the garlic and tomatoes – the toast must be well smeared with pulp. Season with salt.

3 Drizzle over the oil. Use the ends of the baguette to press the oil, salt, and tomato pulp well into the bread. Leave to soak for at least 5 minutes before serving.

### how to serve
Serve as part of a summer brunch with Serrano ham and olives. Cut each piece crossways into 3 and serve as tapas.

# tzatziki

*✤ greece ✤*

As a dip, sauce, or side salad, this perfect combination of yogurt, cucumber, and herbs has long worked its magic in the Mediterranean regions. Try this easy recipe and you will never be tempted to buy the ready-made version.

**PREP** 10-15 MINS, PLUS SOAKING AND STANDING ✤ **SERVES** 4-6

1 large **cucumber**
**sea salt** and freshly ground **black pepper**
300ml (10fl oz) **Greek-style yogurt** or **strained yogurt**
1–2 tbsp **olive oil**
1 **garlic clove**, grated or finely chopped
few fronds of **dill** or **mint leaves**, snipped
1 tbsp **lemon juice**

1 Peel the cucumber, leaving a few narrow strips unpeeled for colour, and cut in half crossways. Cut each piece in half lengthways and scoop out the seeds with a teaspoon. Discard the seeds. Finely chop the cucumber and place in a colander.

2 Sprinkle 1 generous teaspoon of salt over the cucumber and mix in. Leave to drain for at least 20 minutes and rinse thoroughly. Press down with the palm of your hands and pat dry with kitchen paper.

3 Place the yogurt in a shallow bowl, stir in the oil and garlic, and fold in the cucumber. Stir in the dill or mint, season to taste, and add the lemon juice. You can refrigerate for up to 30 minutes. Leave to stand for 10 minutes before serving.

**prepare ahead**

You can deseed and salt the cucumber in advance for flavour and texture. Chill until needed and serve within 30 minutes of mixing with the yogurt.

# fatayer bisabanikh

*✤ middle east ✤*

Fillings for this dish can be plain or spicy, and vary from spinach or chard, to cheese, mushroom, or spiced lamb.

**PREP** 50 MINS, PLUS RISING ✤ **COOK** 35-40 MINS
**MAKES** 25-30 PASTRIES

30g (1oz) **fresh yeast** or 15g (½oz) **dried yeast**
450g (1lb) **plain flour**, plus extra for dusting
1 tsp **salt**
2 tbsp **olive oil**, plus extra for greasing

### For the filling
900g (2lb) **spinach**, stems discarded, rinsed and drained
3 tbsp **olive oil**
1 **onion**, finely grated or very finely chopped
2 **garlic cloves**, finely chopped
100g (3½oz) **pine nuts**
100g (3½oz) **walnuts**
1 tsp **sumac** (optional)
juice of 1½ **lemons**
1 **pomegranate**, seeds removed and reserved with juice
**salt** and freshly ground **black pepper**

1 For the pastry, mix the yeast with a spoonful of the flour and a little water to make a paste. Add 150ml (5fl oz) lukewarm water. Leave in a warm place for 10 minutes.

2 In a large bowl, sift the flour and salt. Make a well in the centre, add the oil and the yeast mixture, and mix. Gradually add 150ml (5fl oz) lukewarm water and mix. On a floured surface, knead the dough for 15 minutes, until shiny and elastic. Form into a ball, place in an oiled bowl, and cover with cling film. Leave in a warm place for 2 hours, or until doubled in size.

3 Chop the spinach leaves and squeeze dry. In a heavy-based pan, heat the oil over a medium heat. Add the onion and sweat for 3–4 minutes, until soft, and push to one side. Add the garlic, pine nuts, and walnuts. Increase the heat, fry until golden brown, and mix into the onion mixture. Reduce the heat, add the spinach, and cook for 2–3 minutes until wilted. Add the sumac, pomegranate seeds, and lemon juice. Season to taste. Remove from the heat and set aside.

4 Preheat the oven to 190°C (375°F/Gas 5). Divide the dough into 25–30 equal-sized balls. On a floured surface, roll out to thin discs. Place 1 teaspoon of the filling in the centre of each disc. Bring up the sides of the dough to form a three-sided packet, pinch the edges together firmly, and place on an oiled baking tray. Bake for 5 minutes, then reduce the temperature to 180°C (350°F/Gas 4). Bake for a further 15 minutes.

# wara einab
### *middle east*

Called *wara einab* in Arabic and *yalancı yaprak dolması* in Turkish, this dish is traditionally served cold as mezze with lemon wedges.

**PREP** 40 MINS ❖ **COOK** 1 HR ❖ **SERVES** 6-8

25–30 **fresh** or **preserved vine leaves**, plus a few extra for lining
2–3 tbsp **olive oil**
2 **onions**, finely chopped
3 **garlic cloves**, chopped
2 tbsp **pine nuts**
1 tsp **allspice**
1 tsp ground **cinnamon**
1–2 tsp **sugar**
225g (8oz) **short-grain rice**, well rinsed and drained
**sea salt** and freshly ground **black pepper**
small bunch of **flat-leaf parsley**, finely chopped
small bunch of **dill**, finely chopped
large bunch of **mint leaves**, finely chopped
1–2 **lemons**, cut into thin wedges, to serve

**For the cooking liquid**
150ml (5fl oz) **olive oil**
juice of 1 **lemon**
1 tsp **sugar**

1 Prepare the vine leaves (see Cook's tip), drain thoroughly, and trim off the stalks. Stack them up on a plate, cover with a clean kitchen towel to keep them moist, and set aside.

2 Heat the oil in a heavy-based pot, stir in the onions and garlic, and sauté until they begin to colour. Stir in the pine nuts, spices, and sugar for 1 minute. Add the rice, mix well to coat in the spices, and season.

3 Pour in enough cold water to just cover the rice and bring to the boil. Reduce the heat and simmer gently for 10 minutes, or until all the water has been absorbed and the rice is cooked. Toss in the herbs and set aside for the rice to cool.

4 Place a vine leaf on a plate or board and place 1 heaped teaspoon of rice at the bottom of the leaf, where the stem would have been. Fold the stem edge over the filling, then fold both of the side edges in towards the middle of the leaf so that the filling is sealed in. Roll up the leaf, place in the palm of your hand, and squeeze it lightly to fix the shape. Set aside and repeat with the remaining leaves and rice.

5 For the cooking liquid, mix together the oil, 150ml (5fl oz) cold water, lemon juice, and sugar in a small bowl. Line the bottom of a shallow pan with the extra vine leaves, then place the stuffed vine leaves on top, tightly packed side by side. Pour most of the oil mixture over the stuffed vine leaves and place a plate on top to prevent them from unravelling during cooking.

6 Simmer gently for about 1 hour, topping up with the cooking liquid, if necessary. Remove from the heat and allow the stuffed vine leaves to cool in the pan. Serve on a plate with lemon wedges or slices.

### cook's tip

To prepare fresh leaves, bring a large pot of water to the boil and dip the leaves into it for 1–2 minutes to soften. Drain and refresh under cold running water, making sure they are thoroughly drained before using.

To prepare preserved leaves, place the leaves in a deep bowl and pour boiling water over them. Leave them to soak for 15–20 minutes, using a fork to gently separate the leaves and get rid of any salty residue. Drain the leaves, rinse thoroughly, and drain again.

### *how to serve*
There are other traditional stuffed vine leaf dishes, including those filled with minced beef and rice, but these are not usually served as mezze.

# habas con jamón
### *spain*

Broad beans with ham is a popular Spanish tapas dish that tastes brilliant with crusty bread and a chilled glass of sherry.

**PREP** 10 MINS ❖ **COOK** 30 MINS
**SERVES** 6 AS A TAPAS DISH, OR 4 AS A STARTER

2 tbsp **olive oil**
1 **onion**, finely chopped
200g (7oz) **Serrano ham**, diced
2 **garlic cloves**, finely crushed
500g (1lb 2oz) **broad beans**
120ml (4fl oz) **dry white wine**
200ml (7fl oz) hot light **chicken** or **vegetable stock**
1 tbsp chopped **flat-leaf parsley**, to garnish (optional)

1 In a saucepan, heat the oil and fry the onion over a medium heat, stirring, until soft and translucent. Increase the heat slightly and add the ham and garlic. Fry until the ham begins to brown. Add the beans and the wine, and cook for a further 8–10 minutes, stirring occasionally.

2 Reduce the heat and add the stock. Stir thoroughly and leave to simmer for 10 minutes. Transfer to a warm serving dish and sprinkle with the parsley, if using. You can prepare this dish 2 days in advance – the flavours improve with reheating.

# imam bayıldı

## ✣ *turkey* ✣

Literally translated as the "imam fainted" – either from shock or pleasure – at the quantity of olive oil used in this classic stuffed aubergine dish from Turkey. Traditionally, the dish was prepared by placing the filling on top of the halved aubergines and the filling was pressed down into them.

**PREP** 15 MINS, PLUS SOAKING ✣ **COOK** 1 HR
**SERVES** 6-8

### ingredients

4 small or medium-sized, long, slim **aubergines**, stalks cut
**sea salt** and freshly ground **black pepper**
**sunflower oil**, for frying
150ml (5fl oz) **olive oil**
juice of 1 **lemon**
2 tsp **sugar**
small bunch of **flat-leaf parsley**

### for the filling

2 medium-sized **red onions**
4 **garlic cloves**, finely chopped
400g can chopped **tomatoes**
2 tsp **sugar**
1 tbsp **olive oil**
bunch of **flat-leaf parsley**, finely chopped
bunch of **dill**, finely chopped
**sea salt** and freshly ground **black pepper**

1 **For the filling**, cut the onions in half lengthways and finely slice them. Place in a bowl with the garlic. Drain the tomatoes and add to the bowl. Then add the sugar and olive oil, and mix well. Toss the parsley and dill into the onion mixture, season, and set aside.

2 **Partially peel the aubergines** in thick stripes using a sharp knife or a potato peeler. Place in a bowl of salted water for 5 minutes, then pat dry with a kitchen towel. In a pan, heat enough sunflower oil for frying and fry the aubergines over a medium heat, turning them over to make sure all the peeled areas turn golden. Fry until they soften and give when pressed with a finger.

3 **Lift the aubergines** onto kitchen paper to drain, then transfer to a chopping board. Carefully slit them open, end to end, keeping both ends and the base intact, so that the aubergines resemble canoes.

4 **Spoon the onion and tomato mixture** into the aubergine pockets, packing it tightly, until all the mixture is used up. In a deep, heavy-based pan, place the aubergines side by side. In a bowl, mix the olive oil and lemon juice, pour over the aubergines, and sprinkle over the sugar.

5 **Cover the pan** and place over a medium heat to create some steam. Reduce the heat and cook the aubergines gently for 45–50 minutes, basting occasionally, until they are soft and tender and only a little caramelized oil is left in the pan. Season and leave to cool in the pan. Serve warm.

# dolmades avgolemono

### ❖ *g r e e c e* ❖

The juices of these stuffed vine leaves are thickened with egg and lemon to make a traditional zesty avgolemono sauce.

**PREP** 25 MINS ❖ **COOK** 55-65 MINS
**MAKES** 40-50 ROLLS

500g (1lb 2oz) **vine leaves** (fresh, frozen, or brined)
6–7 tbsp **olive oil**, plus extra for greasing
1 large **mild onion**, finely chopped
2 **garlic cloves**, finely chopped
175g (6oz) **minced beef** or **lamb**
175g (6oz) **long-grain rice**
small bunch of **dill**, chopped
small bunch of **flat-leaf parsley**, chopped
zest and juice of 2 **lemons**
**salt**
**chilli flakes**
2 **eggs**, separated

1 Rinse the vine leaves if using fresh or brined, and cook in a pan of water for 3–4 minutes until tender. Remove from the heat and pat dry. In a frying pan, heat 1 tablespoon of the oil and fry the onion and garlic until soft but not browned. Add the meat and cook over a low heat until it starts to brown. Transfer to a bowl, add the rice, 4 tablespoons of oil, the herbs, lemon zest, salt, and chilli flakes, and mix.

2 Preheat the oven to 190°C (375°F/Gas 5). Grease a baking dish. Use any torn vine leaves to line the dish. Lay a leaf flat on the work surface, stalk-end towards you, and place 1 teaspoon of the stuffing on the broadest part. Fold the sides over the filling and tightly roll up from the stalk end. Tuck the loose end under and place in the dish. Repeat until all the stuffing is used.

3 Sprinkle the remaining oil over the rolls and cover with the remaining leaves. Pour in enough boiling water to submerge the rolls and cover the dish with foil. Bake for 40–50 minutes, until only 1 cup of the liquid remains. Add more boiling water, if necessary.

4 Whisk the eggs with the lemon juice in a bowl until frothy. Remove the cooked dolmades from the oven. Drain the liquid into a bowl, pour into the egg mixture, and whisk well. Transfer to a saucepan and cook over a low heat, whisking, until the sauce thickens. Pour over the dolmades and serve.

# saganaki

### ❖ *g r e e c e* ❖

Halloumi is a firm, slightly springy white cheese traditionally made from sheep and goat's milk. It tastes great served with crusty bread, and a spinach and red onion salad.

**PREP** 5 MINS ❖ **COOK** 3-5 MINS ❖ **SERVES** 4-6

2 x 250g packets **halloumi cheese**
**flour**, for dusting
120ml (4fl oz) **olive oil**, plus extra for drizzling
2 handfuls of **thyme** or **oregano leaves**
juice of 2 **lemons**
1 **lemon**, cut into wedges, to serve

1 Rinse the halloumi cheese before using to rid it of excess salt; dry well on kitchen paper. Cut the halloumi into 1cm (½in) thick slices and dust lightly with flour.

2 Heat the oil in a non-stick frying pan over a high heat and fry the cheese for 2–3 minutes on each side, or until golden brown.

3 Remove from the pan and sprinkle with the thyme and lemon juice. Serve immediately with a little oil drizzled over the cheese and with lemon wedges.

# banderillas

❖ *spain* ❖

These small skewers, which are served as tapas, are named after the darts used to needle the bull during a *corrida*.

**PREP** 15–20 MINS, PLUS STANDING
**COOK** 30–40 MINS ❖ **MAKES** 18–24 SKEWERS

1 slice of **Serrano ham**, cut into 1cm (½in) cubes

12 cooked **prawns**

12 hard-boiled **quail's eggs**

1 slice of **Manchego cheese**, cut into 1cm (½in) cubes

3 cooked deli-style **artichoke bottoms**, drained and quartered

6 **cocktail onions**

3 **pickled gherkins**, cut into chunks if large

3 **baby cherry tomatoes**, halved

12 **green olives**, pitted and stuffed with almonds, pimento, or anchovy

### For the romesco sauce

1 large **red pepper**, halved, deseeded, and halved again

2 large ripe **tomatoes**

3–4 **garlic cloves**, unpeeled

1–2 dried hot **chillies**, deseeded

3 tbsp blanched **almonds**

3 tbsp blanched **hazelnuts**

**sea salt** and freshly ground **black pepper**

90ml (3floz) **olive oil**

2 tbsp **sherry vinegar**

1 Preheat the oven to 180°C (350°F/Gas 4). For the romesco sauce, line a baking sheet with foil. Place the pepper, cut-sides down, with the tomatoes, garlic, chillies, almonds, and hazelnuts on the baking sheet. Roast for 30–40 minutes without burning.

2 Wrap the pepper in cling film and leave to cool. Peel and cut into strips. When cool enough to handle, peel and quarter the tomatoes, then peel and smash the garlic.

3 Place the chillies, almonds, hazelnuts, and garlic in a food processor. Add a little salt and whizz until chopped. Add the tomatoes and pepper strips and whizz until you have a thick chunky paste. With the motor running, add the oil in a thin stream, then add the vinegar and season. Let the sauce stand for at least 1 hour before using.

4 For each banderilla, choose 3 or 4 different ingredients, slide them onto wooden toothpicks, and lay them flat on a platter. Serve with a bowl of romesco sauce.

# labna

❖ *middle east* ❖

This fresh cheese made from strained yogurt is served as a mezze dish in the Middle East. It is good with herbs or spices sprinkled over and served with toasted flatbreads.

**PREP** 10 MINS, PLUS DRAINING ❖ **SERVES** 4

600ml (1 pint) plain **Greek-style yogurt**
½ tsp **salt**

1 Stir the yogurt and salt together until evenly combined. Spoon onto a large square of muslin, then gather together the 4 corners and tie the top of the bundle with string, to make a bag.

2 Suspend the bag over a bowl and leave for at least 12 hours for the whey to drip through.

3 Remove the strained yogurt from the muslin, shape into a ball, and serve.

**variation**

**Sweet labna** For a sweet version, drizzle with clear honey, dust with ground cinnamon, and scatter with chopped pistachios.

# almendras tostadas

❖ *spain* ❖

These delicately roasted and lightly salted almonds are traditionally served with drinks in Spain.

**PREP** 15 MINS ❖ **COOK** 15–25 MINS ❖ **SERVES** 8

500g (1lb 2oz) blanched whole **almonds**
2 tbsp **sea salt**
2 tsp **pimentón** (Spanish paprika)

1 Preheat the oven to 220°C (425°F/Gas 7). Spread the almonds out on a baking tray, and sprinkle with a little water (this will dry out, and the salt and spices will cling to the nuts). Sprinkle the almonds with the salt and the paprika, tossing to ensure that they are all well coated. Spread them out evenly again.

2 Roast the almonds for 15–25 minutes, depending on how brown you want them to be, but take care that they do not burn.

**variation**

**Spiced nuts** Use a mix of nuts, such as cashews, hazelnuts, or brazils. Substitute the pimentón for ground cumin, coriander, or cayenne pepper.

# kofte samak

❖ *Morocco* ❖

These small Moroccan fish cakes are full of flavours from North Africa and the Middle East. They can be served with a cucumber salad dressed with ground cinnamon and a little orange juice, or as a canapé with drinks before a meal.

**PREP** 10–15 MINS
**COOK** 20–25 MINS ❖ **SERVES** 4–6

1 tbsp **olive oil**
1 **garlic clove**, finely chopped
1 tbsp **coriander seeds**, crushed
1 tsp **pimentón** (Spanish paprika)
500g (1lb 2oz) firm **white fish fillets** (such as hake, snapper, sea bream, or cod), skin and bones removed
rind of ½ **preserved lemon**, pith removed and rind finely diced
4 **spring onions**, finely sliced
½ bunch of **coriander**, roughly chopped
2 tsp **harissa paste**
1 **egg**
**salt** and freshly ground **black pepper**
juice of ½ **lemon**
**vegetable oil**, for frying

1 In a small pan, heat the olive oil and fry the garlic and coriander seeds until golden brown and fragrant. Add the paprika and remove from the heat.

2 Place the fish in a food processor with the aromatic fried spices, lemon rind, spring onions, and chopped coriander. Add the harissa and egg, and season. Add half the lemon juice and process until smooth.

3 Heat the vegetable oil in large frying pan over a medium-high heat. Fry a small piece of the mixture and taste to check the seasoning. Season and add the remaining lemon juice, if required. Roll the mixture into 16 balls. Fry in small batches until golden brown on all sides. Drain on kitchen paper and serve.

**cook's tip**

To make preserved lemons, place 2 lemons in a small, tight-fitting pan. Cover with cold water. Add 3 heaped tablespoons of sea salt (to remove the bitterness from the skin). Bring the water to the boil and simmer for 10–12 minutes until the lemons are soft to the point of a knife. Remove from the hot water, and refresh under cold running water. When cool, cut in half. Using a sharp knife, remove all the flesh and pith. Trim down the lemon skin from the inside, so you are left with lozenges of lemon zest. Cover the lemon zest with olive oil. Preserved lemons can be stored in the fridge, covered, for up to 6 weeks.

# caponata

*sicily*

This wonderful Sicilian aubergine stew is prepared Arabic-style, with raisins and a sweet vinegar sauce. It can be served as an antipasto, a side dish, or a pasta sauce.

**PREP** 10 MINS ❖ **COOK** 30 MINS ❖ **SERVES** 4-5

3 tbsp **olive oil**
400g (14oz) **aubergines**, diced into 1in (2.5cm) cubes
1 large mild **onion**, thinly sliced
3 **celery sticks**, sliced
1 heaped tbsp **capers**, rinsed and drained
2 tbsp **green olives**, blanched, drained, pitted, and halved
1 tbsp **raisins**
2 tsp **honey** or caster sugar
2 tbsp **red wine vinegar**
sea salt and freshly ground **black pepper**
1 large **tomato**, blanched, peeled, deseeded, and finely chopped
1 tbsp **pine nuts** (optional)
2 tsp finely grated, unwaxed **lemon zest**
1 tbsp snipped **flat-leaf parsley**

1 Heat the oil in a large frying pan or sauté pan. Add the aubergines, fry for 6–8 minutes until brown and softened. Stir in the onion and celery, and cook for 3 minutes.

2 Add the capers, olives, raisins, honey, and vinegar. Stir, season, bring to a simmer, and cover with a lid. Cook, stirring occasionally, for 10–15 minutes, until just cooked through.

3 Add the tomato and 2–3 tablespoons water, and the pine nuts, if using. Cook for 2–3 minutes without the lid. Leave to cool a little, then stir in the lemon zest and parsley, and adjust the seasoning. Serve warm or at room temperature.

# falafel

*middle east*

Dried chickpeas, soaked in advance, will give the best flavour to this classic dish from Lebanon, Jordan, and Syria.

**PREP** 25 MINS, PLUS SOAKING AND STANDING
**COOK** 15 MINS ❖ **MAKES** 12

225g (8oz) **dried chickpeas**, soaked overnight in cold water
1 tbsp **tahini**
1 **garlic clove**, crushed
1 tsp **salt**
1 tsp ground **cumin**
1 tsp **turmeric**
1 tsp ground **coriander**
½ tsp **cayenne pepper**
2 tbsp finely chopped **flat-leaf parsley**
juice of 1 small **lemon**
**vegetable oil**, for frying

1 Drain the soaked chickpeas and place them in a food processor with the remaining ingredients. Process until finely chopped but not puréed.

2 Transfer the mixture to a bowl and set aside for at least 30 minutes (and up to 8 hours), covered, in the fridge.

3 Wet your hands and shape the mixture into 12 balls. Press down slightly to flatten.

4 Heat 5cm (2in) of oil in a deep pan or wok. Fry the balls in batches for 3–4 minutes, or until lightly golden. Drain on kitchen paper and serve immediately.

# pittule pugliese

*❖ italy ❖*

Fast food for party goers, these crisp little puffballs – a rough translation of the name in the Puglian dialect – are made with a yeasted batter flavoured with capers and olives.

**PREP** 20 MINS, PLUS RISING ❖ **COOK** 20 MINS
**MAKES** ABOUT 30 BALLS

500g (1lb 2oz) **strong bread flour**
**salt**
25g (scant 1oz) **fresh yeast**
 or 1 tsp **dried yeast**
2 tbsp **capers**, drained
2 tbsp chopped **black olives**
**olive oil**, for frying

1 Sift the flour into a warm bowl with 1 teaspoon salt and rub in the fresh yeast. If using dried yeast, follow the packet instructions. Work in about 300ml (10 fl oz) warm water to make a soft dough. Working with the heel of your hand, knead the dough well. Form into a ball, cover with a damp cloth or cling film, and set in a warm place to rise for 1–2 hours, until doubled in size.

2 Mix the dough with 4–5 tablespoons of warm water, working it well with your hands until you have a thick and slightly lumpy batter – wetter than a bread dough but not as wet as a coating batter. Beat in the capers and olives, and set aside for 15 minutes to develop the gluten.

3 Dust your hands well with flour, pick up some of the batter, and squeeze it in your fist – it should hold its shape without dropping.

4 In a medium frying pan, heat enough oil to submerge the fritters. As soon as the surface is faintly hazed with blue, use 2 wet teaspoons to drop blobs of the dough into the hot oil – only add as many as will cover the surface of the oil. Cook until the fritters puff and brown, then flip over to cook the other side. Remove and transfer to kitchen paper to drain. Repeat until all the dough is used up.

## cook's tip

To use your hand instead of the teaspoons, as they do in Puglia, scoop up a handful of the batter, close the hand to make a fist, and squeeze the dough through the tunnel of your fingers, slicing each dollop with a knife before dropping into the hot oil.

# brandade de morue

*❖ provence ❖*

This dish of creamed salt cod is popular in Mediterranean countries, and is a favourite in the south of France.

**PREP** 20 MINS, PLUS SOAKING AND STANDING
**COOK** 20 MINS ❖ **SERVES** 4

450g (1lb) **salt cod**
2 **garlic cloves**, crushed
200ml (7fl oz) **olive oil**, plus extra to drizzle
100ml (3½fl oz) boiled **milk**
2 tbsp chopped **flat-leaf parsley**
freshly ground **black pepper**
triangles of **bread**, fried in olive oil, to serve
**black olives**, to serve

1 Soak the fish in a bowl of cold water for 24 hours, changing the water 3–4 times.

2 Drain the cod and place in a large shallow pan, then cover it with cold water and bring to a gentle simmer. Cook for 10 minutes, then remove the pan from the heat and leave the cod to sit in the water for a further 10 minutes before draining.

3 Remove the skin and bones from the fish, then flake the flesh into a bowl and pound to a paste with the garlic.

4 Place a pan over a gentle heat and put in the fish paste. Beat in sufficient oil and milk, a little at a time, to make a creamy white mixture that holds its shape.

5 Serve hot, with a drizzle of oil and some pepper, alongside fried bread triangles and black olives.

## cook's tip

The oil and milk must be beaten very gradually into the cod or the mixture will separate. Should this happen, transfer the mixture to a bowl and whisk vigorously to bring it back together.

# soups

# gazpacho
### *andalucia*

This chilled, no-cook Spanish soup is extremely popular during the summer months when temperatures are high. You can also include soaked stale bread cubes to add substance and texture.

**PREP** 15 MINS, PLUS CHILLING ❖ **SERVES** 4

1kg (2¼ lb) **tomatoes**, plus extra to serve

1 small **cucumber**, peeled and finely chopped, plus extra to serve

1 small **red pepper**, deseeded and chopped, plus extra to serve

2 **garlic cloves**, crushed

4 tbsp **sherry vinegar**

**salt** and freshly ground **black pepper**

120ml (4fl oz) **extra virgin olive oil**, plus extra to serve

1 **hard-boiled egg**, white and yolk separated and chopped, to serve

1 Bring a kettle of water to the boil. Place the tomatoes in a heatproof bowl, pour over enough boiling water to cover, and leave for 20 seconds, or until the skins split. Drain and cool under cold running water. Gently peel off the skins, cut the tomatoes in half, deseed, and chop the flesh.

2 Place the tomato flesh, cucumber, red pepper, garlic, and vinegar in a food processor or blender. Season to taste and process until smooth. Pour in the oil and process again. Dilute with a little cold water if too thick. Transfer the soup to a serving bowl, cover with cling film, and chill for at least 1 hour.

3 When ready to serve, finely chop the extra cucumber and red pepper. Place the cucumber, pepper, and egg yolk and white in individual bowls and arrange on the table, along with a bottle of olive oil. Ladle the soup into bowls and serve, letting each diner add their own garnish.

# salmorejo
### *andalucia*

This thick purée from Cordoba is served chilled, garnished with Serrano ham and hard-boiled egg, as a soup or a dip, with chunks of bread.

**PREP** 15 MINS, PLUS SOAKING AND CHILLING ❖ **SERVES** 4

115g (4oz) **stale white bread**, crusts removed, torn into bite-sized pieces

3 tbsp **olive oil**, plus extra to drizzle

2 tbsp **red wine vinegar**

1 **onion**, roughly chopped

3 **garlic cloves**

1 **red pepper**, deseeded and chopped

5 **tomatoes**, skinned and deseeded

1 **cucumber**, peeled, deseeded, and chopped

**salt** and freshly ground **black pepper**

2 **hard-boiled eggs**, chopped

2 slices **Serrano ham**, cut into strips

1 Place the bread into a bowl. Add the oil and vinegar, mix well, and set aside to soak for 10 minutes.

2 Place the onion, garlic, red pepper, tomatoes, and most of the cucumber in a blender or food processor with 90ml (3fl oz) cold water, and blend to a purée. Add the bread mixture, blend again, then season to taste.

3 Chill for at least 30 minutes, pour into serving bowls, and top with hard-boiled eggs, strips of ham, and the remaining cucumber. Serve, drizzled with a little oil.

# caldo verde

### ❖ *p o r t u g a l* ❖

This clean, simple, and fresh-flavoured soup is one of the best-loved dishes in Portugal's culinary repertoire. The main ingredient is a dark green brassica galegas, rather like Italy's cavolo nero.

**PREP** 10 MINS ❖ **COOK** 30 MINS ❖ **SERVES** 4-6

500g (1lb 2oz) **Portuguese galegas, curly kale, spring greens,** or **cavolo nero**

4 large **floury potatoes**, peeled and cut into chunks

1 **onion**, finely chopped

**salt**

2 tbsp **extra virgin olive oil**, plus extra to serve

**piri-piri** or **chilli sauce**, to serve

1 Trim the cabbage, removing the central stalk, if necessary, and shred the leaves as finely as possible. It is easier if you roll the leaves up into little bundles and cut firmly right across the grain. Set aside.

2 Place the potatoes and onion in a large pan with 2 litres (3½ pints) of cold water. Bring to the boil, add some salt, and cook for 20 minutes, or until the potatoes are perfectly tender.

3 Mash the potatoes a little into the broth to thicken the juice, check for salt, and stir in the oil. Bring the broth back to the boil and sprinkle in the shredded cabbage by the handful, stirring to allow the heat to reach the greens immediately. Bring to the boil and cook for 3–4 minutes, just long enough to soften the cabbage but not to cook it to a mush.

4 Ladle into bowls, add the oil and piri-piri, and serve steaming hot.

**variation**

**Caldo verde with chorizo** Include a few slices of chorizo or any other smoked pork sausage for a more substantial dish.

### *how to serve*

Serve this soup as a light supper or midday meal, with chunks of Portugal's dense, golden cornmeal bread, *broa*, and Portuguese red wine.

# acquacotta di funghi
## ❖ *italy* ❖

Porcini, Italy's favourite drying mushrooms, are combined with prosciutto in a clear, water-and-wine broth that allows the flavour of the funghi to shine through.

**PREP** 10 MINS, PLUS SOAKING
**COOK** 30 MINS ❖ **SERVES** 4-6

75g (2½oz) dried **porcini mushrooms**
2 tbsp diced **prosciutto**
2 **celery stalks**, finely sliced
1–2 sprigs of **thyme**
150ml (5fl oz) **white wine**
300ml (10fl oz) hot **chicken** or **vegetable stock**
**salt** and freshly ground **black pepper**
**flat-leaf parsley**, chopped, for sprinkling

1 Pick over the porcini mushrooms (they can be a little gritty) and set aside to soak in enough warm water to cover – about 150ml (5fl oz) – for 1–2 hours.

2 Transfer the mushrooms with a slotted spoon to a large saucepan and strain in the soaking water. Add the remaining ingredients, along with the stock and bring gently to the boil. Reduce the heat and simmer gently for 20–30 minutes, until the mushrooms are perfectly soft and the broth is well flavoured. Season to taste. Remove the thyme sprigs before serving. Garnish with a sprinkle of chopped parsley.

### cook's tip

If using fresh porcini or any other type of fresh mushrooms, allow 500g (1lb 2oz). There is no need to soak, just slice them finely and fry gently in a little butter until most of the liquid in the funghi evaporates before you add the wine.

# zuppa di lenticchie e finocchio
## ❖ *italy* ❖

Unlike other pulses, lentils do not need preliminary soaking, making them a great fast-food option. Choose the brownish green tender-skinned lentils of Castelluccio in Umbria, or Puy lentils from France, for their nutty flavour.

**PREP** 10 MINS ❖ **COOK** 30-40 MINS
**SERVES** 4-6

350g (12oz) **small brown lentils**, cleaned
1 **fennel bulb**, trimmed and diced (reserve some fronds)
1 medium **potato**, peeled and diced
2–3 **garlic cloves**, roughly chopped
1 tsp **fennel pollen**, crushed **fennel seeds**, or finely chopped fresh **fennel fronds**, plus extra for garnish
6 **black peppercorns**, crushed
½ tsp **salt**
1.5 litres (2¾ pints) **vegetable stock**
100ml (3½fl oz) **peppery extra virgin olive oil**

1 In a large pan, add all the ingredients, except the oil, to the stock and bring to the boil. Reduce the heat, cover the pan loosely with a lid, and simmer for 30–40 minutes, until the lentils are absolutely tender and the potato has collapsed into the soup. Top up with boiling water as needed.

2 Stir in half the oil and boil for 1–2 minutes to thicken the juices. Check the seasoning and ladle into warm bowls. Finish each portion with a swirl of oil and a sprinkle of finely chopped fennel fronds.

# pisto manchego
### ❖ *spain* ❖

This Spanish dish, similar to the French ratatouille, goes particularly well with spicy chorizo. It can also be served as a starter.

**PREP** 10 MINS ❖ **COOK** 30 MINS ❖ **SERVES** 4–6

2 tbsp **olive oil**
1 **garlic clove**, chopped
2 **onions**, finely chopped
2 **green peppers**, deseeded and sliced
1 **red pepper**, deseeded and sliced
3 **courgettes**, cut into chunks
250g (9oz) ripe **tomatoes**, skinned and quartered
½ tsp **sugar**
1 tbsp **red wine vinegar**
**salt** and freshly ground **black pepper**
2 tbsp chopped **parsley**

1 Heat the oil in a pan over a medium heat. Add the garlic and onions, and fry, stirring frequently, for 5 minutes, or until the onions are soft and translucent.

2 Add the green and red peppers and continue to cook, stirring, for 5 minutes. Add the courgettes, cook for a further 5 minutes, then add the tomatoes, sugar, and vinegar and continue to cook for 15 minutes, stirring occasionally.

3 Season to taste, transfer to a warm serving dish, and scatter with parsley.

### *how to serve*
To serve this dish as a starter, top with slices of fried chorizo and chopped hard-boiled eggs.

# tarator
### ❖ *balkans* ❖

There are many regional variations of this popular summer soup in the eastern Mediterranean. If it gets too thick, float in a few ice cubes just before serving.

**PREP** 10 MINS, PLUS STANDING AND DRAINING
❖ **SERVES** 4–6

4 tbsp fresh **white bread**, crust removed, torn or cut into small pieces
2–3 **garlic cloves**, crushed
4 tbsp chopped fresh **walnuts**
300ml (10fl oz) light **chicken stock**
**sea salt** and freshly ground **black pepper**
1 **cucumber**
2 tbsp **olive oil**
3 tbsp chopped **flat-leaf parsley**
few sprigs of **dill** or **mint leaves**, snipped, plus extra to garnish
300ml (10fl oz) **Greek-style yogurt**
1 tbsp **lemon juice**

1 Blend together the bread, garlic, walnuts, and chicken stock. Season to taste, and refrigerate for at least 2 hours or longer to allow the flavours to combine.

2 Peel the cucumber, cut in half crossways, and cut each piece in half lengthways. Scoop out the seeds with a teaspoon, discard, and finely chop the cucumber. Place in a colander and sprinkle over 1 teaspoon of salt, mix in, drain for at least 20 minutes, and rinse thoroughly. Press down with the palm of your hands and pat dry with kitchen paper.

3 Place the cucumber in a food processor, add the oil, parsley, dill, and yogurt. Whizz, trickle in the prepared stock, and continue whizzing until blended. Adjust the seasoning, if necessary.

4 Refrigerate for at least 2 hours. Just before serving, stir in the lemon juice and reserved herbs.

**variation**

**Tarator soup with tahini** Add 1 tablespoon of tahini and white wine vinegar along with the stock.

# sopa de pedra

*portugal*

This oddly named soup, literally translated as "stone soup", appeals to the Portuguese sense of humour and is popular on rural menus throughout the land.

**PREP** 10 MINS, PLUS SOAKING
**COOK** 2 HRS ❖ **SERVES** 4–6

500g (1lb 2oz) dried **red kidney beans**, soaked overnight

about 125g (4½oz) **pork skin**, rolled and sliced

1 link of **chouriço nero, morcela**, or **black pudding** (optional)

1 thick slice of **streaky bacon**, diced small

2 large **onions**, finely sliced

1 whole **garlic head**, separated into cloves and peeled

1 **bay leaf**

½ tsp **white peppercorns**, crushed

**salt**

3–4 large **waxy potatoes**, peeled and diced

generous handful of **coriander leaves**

1 smooth rounded **river pebble** of noticeable size, to serve (optional)

1 Drain the beans and transfer them to a large saucepan filled with enough water to cover. Bring to the boil and drain the beans again.

2 Add the pork skin, sausages, if using, bacon, onions, garlic, and bay leaf and pour in enough water to cover well. Bring to the boil, skim off any grey foam that rises, and season with the peppercorns and salt.

3 Reduce the heat and keep the soup bubbling gently for 1–2 hours, or as long as it takes to tenderize the beans. If you need to add more water, make sure it is boiling. Remove and reserve the sausage, if using. Add the potatoes and bubble for another 15–20 minutes, until tender. Chop the coriander and stir it in.

4 Place the stone, if using, in a warm tureen, then transfer the broth to it. Neatly slice the sausage and return it to the broth. For a more substantial dish, place thick slices of bread in the soup plates before you spoon in the broth.

**cook's tip**

In summer, the soup is made with fresh borlotti beans – the mature seeds of the runner bean left to develop in the pod, which do not need soaking. Other pork bits, trotters, or spare rib, can replace the pork skin.

# soupe au pistou

*provence*

Provence's answer to minestrone, this hearty soup is originally from Nice. It makes a great vegetarian supper followed by salad and cheese.

**PREP** 20-35 MINS ❖ **COOK** 40-50 MINS
**SERVES** 8-10

250g (9oz) uncooked small **white haricot beans**, rinsed and drained

**coarse sea salt** and freshly ground **black pepper**

2 tbsp **olive oil**

1 large sweet **white onion**, thinly sliced

2 large **tomatoes**, chopped

large handful of fresh **green beans**, topped and tailed

2 **courgettes**, thickly sliced

2 **carrots**, thickly sliced

1 small **fennel bulb**, chopped

2 **leeks**, cut into rounds

120g (4¼oz) small **macaroni** or **vermicelli**

**Parmesan cheese** shavings, to garnish

**basil**, chopped, to garnish

## For the pistou sauce

2–3 **garlic cloves**, peeled and crushed

2 large handfuls of **basil**, torn

1 medium to large **tomato**, blanched, skinned, deseeded, and chopped

125ml (4½fl oz) **fruity olive oil**

1–2 tbsp grated **Parmesan** or **pecorino cheese**

1 Place the beans in a large stewing pot. Bring to the boil, add a pinch of salt, and bubble for 10 minutes. Drain, rinse under cold running water, and set aside.

2 For the sauce, pound the garlic, a pinch of salt, and basil in a mortar and pestle. Add the tomato and pound to a purée. Add the oil, a trickle at a time, and pound between additions, working in the same direction. Add the cheese and mix. Season to taste, cover with cling film, and set aside.

3 In a pan, add oil and the onion, and cook on a medium heat, until pale and soft. Add the tomatoes, stir, and tip in the remaining vegetables. Pour in 1.2 litres (2 pints) cold water, season, and bring to a simmer. Partly cover and cook gently for 30–40 minutes, until the beans are tender. Skim 1–2 times. Add the macaroni and cook for 5–8 minutes, uncovered. Season to taste.

4 Remove from the heat. Stir the pistou sauce into the soup and garnish with Parmesan and basil. Serve hot.

# stracciatella alla romana

*italy*

This elegant pick-me-up enjoyed in Rome is made by swirling raw egg beaten with grated Parmesan cheese into boiling chicken broth so that it forms fine threads.

**PREP** 10 MINS ❖ **COOK** 10 MINS ❖ **SERVES** 4-5

2 litres (3½ pints) hot **chicken stock**

salt

4–5 **eggs**

2 tbsp finely grated **Parmesan cheese**

1 tsp freshly grated **nutmeg**

grated zest of 1 **lemon**

2 tbsp finely chopped **flat-leaf parsley**

1 In a large pan, bring the chicken stock to the boil and bubble up until reduced by one-third. Season to taste with salt.

2 In a bowl, whisk the eggs with the Parmesan, nutmeg, and lemon zest, until well-blended.

3 Reduce the heat to a steady simmer and whisk in the egg mixture. Continue to whisk for a further 1–2 minutes as the egg forms fine pasta-like threads. Taste and add more cheese and seasoning, if you like. Garnish with parsley. You could also add diced prosciutto, finely chopped parsley, and a few scraps of deseeded peperoncino to the soup, if you like.

# harira
### ✦ *north africa* ✦

Variations of this traditional lamb, chickpea, and lentil soup from Morocco and Tunisia can be found throughout the Middle East. Thick and hearty, it is generally served with thick, crusty bread, flatbread, or rustic cornmeal rolls.

**PREP** 10 MINS  ✦  **COOK** 1½ HRS
**SERVES** 4

2–3 tbsp **olive oil**
2 **onions**, chopped
2 **celery sticks**, trimmed and diced
2 small **carrots**, peeled and diced
2–3 **garlic cloves**, crushed
2 tsp **cumin seeds**
2 tsp **coriander seeds**
450g (1lb) **lean lamb**, cut into bite-sized cubes
2 tsp ground **turmeric**
2 tsp **paprika**
2 tsp ground **cinnamon**
2 tsp **sugar**
2 **bay leaves**
2 tbsp **tomato paste**
1 litre (1¾ pints) hot **lamb** or **chicken stock**
400g can chopped **tomatoes**, drained
100g (3½oz) **brown** or **green lentils**, thoroughly rinsed
400g can **chickpeas**, drained and rinsed
**sea salt** and freshly ground **black pepper**
small bunch of **flat-leaf parsley**, coarsely chopped
small bunch of **coriander**, coarsely chopped
1 **lemon**, cut into quarters, to serve

1 Heat the oil in a large, deep heavy-based saucepan. Stir in the onions, celery, and carrots, and cook until the onions begin to colour.

2 Add the garlic and cumin and coriander seeds, then toss in the lamb. Add the spices, sugar, and bay leaves, and stir in the tomato paste. Pour in the stock, bring the liquid to the boil, reduce the heat, and simmer with the lid on for about 1 hour.

3 Add the tomatoes, lentils, and chickpeas, and cook gently for a further 30 minutes, until the lentils are soft and the soup is almost as thick as a stew. Season and toss in most of the parsley and chopped coriander.

4 Garnish with the remaining parsley and coriander, and serve the soup with the lemon wedges to squeeze over and plenty of bread to mop up.

# minestrone
### ✦ *italy* ✦

This substantial soup makes a great lunch or supper dish, and you can add whatever vegetables are in season.

**PREP** 20 MINS, PLUS SOAKING
**COOK** 1¾ HRS  ✦  **SERVES** 4-6

100g (3½oz) dried **white cannellini beans**
2 tbsp **olive oil**
2 **celery sticks**, finely chopped
2 **carrots**, finely chopped
1 **onion**, finely chopped
400g can chopped **tomatoes**
750ml (1¼ pints) **chicken** or **vegetable stock**
**salt** and freshly ground **black pepper**
60g (2oz) small **short-cut pasta**
4 tbsp chopped **flat-leaf parsley**
40g (1½oz) **Parmesan cheese**, finely grated

1 Place the cannellini beans in a large bowl, cover with cold water, and leave for at least 6 hours or overnight.

2 Drain the beans, place in a large saucepan, cover with cold water, and bring to the boil over a high heat, skimming the surface as necessary. Boil for 10 minutes, then reduce the heat to low, partially cover the pan, and leave the beans to simmer for 1 hour, or until just tender. Drain well and set aside.

3 Heat the oil in the rinsed-out pan over a medium heat. Add the celery, carrots, and onion, and fry, stirring occasionally, for 5 minutes, or until tender. Stir in the beans, the tomatoes with their juice, the stock, and season to taste. Bring to the boil, stirring, then cover and leave to simmer for 20 minutes.

4 Add the pasta and simmer for 10–15 minutes more, or until cooked but still tender to the bite. Stir in the parsley and half the Parmesan, then adjust the seasoning. Serve hot, sprinkled with the remaining Parmesan.

### prepare ahead

Steps 1 and 2 can be done 1 day before. Soak the beans before starting the recipe. The soup may be frozen for up to 1 month before the pasta is added in step 4.

# a taste of
# TUSCANY

When in Tuscany, expect simple hearty dishes, well cooked and plainly presented. Start your meal with antipasti of cured prosciutto or salame, crostini laden with pâté, olives, and your host's favourite olive oil with unsalted white bread. The best-loved lunch is white bean ribollita guaranteed to satisfy the bean-loving Tuscan tastebuds. Pasta is often dressed with a gamey ragù of hare or wild boar, maybe with truffles or dried mushrooms. Fish is served along the coast. Meat main courses are dark, deep-flavoured, and good matches for the region's great red wines. The best-known steak dish to come from Italy is named after Florence. Bistecca alla Fiorentina is thick T-bone steak from Chianina or Maremmana cattle, seared over charcoals with olive oil and rosemary. Less hefty is thinly sliced tagliata steak served with rocket. Spinach is the favourite green vegetable. Desserts are low-key and on the small side – dried biscuits, panforte, or castagnaccio.

**Finocchiona** and other cured meats are made with secret cocktails of flavourings, often including dried fennel flowers.

Cured hams and sausages, antipasti vegetables, and assorted cheeses compete for space in a small gastronomia.

The skyline which launched millions of photographs still takes your breath away when you visit Florence.

**Florence fennel** looks as lovely as it tastes. The bulb is eaten raw or cooked, the leaves can be added to salads, and the dried seeds and flowers taste a little like aniseed.

Picking white grapes in Tuscany.

**Chestnuts** have long been used here for their flour and to dry for winter stores. Nectar from the flowers produces a particularly delicious honey. Every October there is a chestnut festival in Marradi to the north east of Florence.

**Pecorino**, little ewe's milk cheeses, are matured for at least two months and gradually develop an attractive, light pungent sharpness.

**Unsalted breads** are made to accompany strong flavours – salty ham, leafy olive oil, plenty of garlic, and mature cheese.

# An autumn supper in Tuscany

Tuscan people like top-quality food simply served. Supper starts with
a glass of local red wine, olives, chunks of warm fresh bread, and a first
course of crostini with a generous topping of spiced puréed chicken
livers. The pasta may be pappardelle anointed with a little aromatic
ragù. Beef is a popular main course, with a side dish of tomatoes.
Dessert might be a dense nutty cake made with chestnut flour,
accompanied with a small glass of vin santo.

**Crostini di
fegatini**
page 266

**Pappardelle al ragù**
page 103

**Spezzatino
di manzo
alla toscana**
page 160

**Castagnaccio**
page 300

# zuppa di pasta e ceci
### ❖ *italy* ❖

No need for meat in this simple combination of pulses and vegetables finished with crispy fried pasta. Do not be tempted to use stock rather than the water or you will lose the delicate flavours of the chickpeas.

**PREP** 10 MINS, PLUS SOAKING
**COOK** 2-3 HRS ❖ **SERVES** 6

350g (12oz) dried **chickpeas**, soaked overnight in cold water

1 medium **onion**, chopped

1-2 **celery sticks**, diced

1-2 **bay leaves**

6 **black peppercorns** or 1 small **dried chilli**

about 150ml (5fl oz) **olive oil**

**sea salt**

250g (9oz) fresh **tagliatelle** or other ribbon pasta

1 Drain the chickpeas and transfer to a large saucepan with the onion, celery, bay leaves, and peppercorns, and twice its own volume of cold water. Do not add salt or the chickpeas will not soften properly. Bring to the boil, reduce the heat, cover loosely with the lid, and simmer gently for 2-3 hours. Add boiling water as needed and cook until the chickpeas are perfectly tender. Stir in half the oil and bring to the boil to thicken the broth.

2 Heat the rest of the oil in a small frying pan and drop in one-third of the pasta ribbons. Fry for 1-2 minutes, then remove with a slotted spoon as soon as the pasta puffs up and browns.

3 Stir the rest of the pasta into the soupy chickpeas and bring to the boil. Add more boiling water to ensure plenty of broth. Cook for 5-6 minutes, or until the pasta is soft. Remove the bay leaves. Ladle into bowls and top with crisp pasta ribbons.

### cook's tip

The crisped pasta looks and tastes just like bacon – a useful tip if you do not want to include meat in pasta dishes.

# zuppa di fave
### ❖ *italy* ❖

This fortifying winter dish prepared with dried broad beans, or *fave*, is the traditional midday meal of Puglia. It is eaten as a scooping purée with bread in much the same way as Middle Eastern hummus.

**PREP** 10 MINS, PLUS SOAKING
**COOK** 3-4 HRS ❖ **SERVES** 4-6

250g (9oz) dried, split skinned **broad beans** (fave), soaked overnight

1 large **potato**, peeled and diced

**sea salt**

125ml (4½fl oz) **olive oil**

500g (1lb 2oz) **chicory**, **endive**, or **broccoli florets**

1-2 **garlic cloves**, sliced

crushed **peperoncini** or **chilli flakes**

1 Drain the beans, discard the soaking water, and place them in a large saucepan with 1.5 litres (2¾ pints) of cold water.

2 Bring the water to the boil, skim off the grey foam that rises, and keep skimming until the foam is almost gone. Add the potato and a generous pinch of salt. Return the pan to the boil, then reduce the heat, cover loosely, and cook gently for 3-4 hours, stirring regularly and scraping the bottom of the pan, until the beans are completely mushy and soft, adding boiling water as necessary. If there is any excess water, remove the lid and continue to cook until the water has evaporated – ensure that the beans do not stick to the bottom of the pan.

3 Beat in half the oil, taste, and add more salt, if required. The result should be a thick, soft cream without any lumps, somewhere between a soup and a scooping purée.

4 Meanwhile, rinse the greens, leaving them damp, and cut into thin ribbons. Place in a pan with the remaining oil and garlic, cook, and sprinkle with salt and the peperoncini. Cover loosely, reduce the heat, and cook gently for 5-8 minutes, or until perfectly tender. Set aside.

5 To serve, gently reheat the purée (diluted with extra boiling water or left thick, as desired), ladle into warm bowls, and garnish each portion with a tablespoonful of greens.

# revithosoupa

*❖ greece ❖*

This aromatic soup, a winter dish from the Ionian island of Corfu, is flavoured with the rosemary that grows wild on the hillsides.

**PREP** 10 MINS, PLUS SOAKING
**COOK** 1½–2 HRS ❖ **SERVES** 4-6

350g (12oz) dried **chickpeas**, soaked overnight

½ **garlic bulb** or 6 large **cloves**

2–3 sprigs of **rosemary**

3–4 tbsp **olive oil**

½ tsp **black peppercorns**, roughly crushed

1 medium **potato**, peeled and diced

**lemon juice**, to taste

**salt**

1 tbsp **pomegranate seeds**, to serve (optional)

1 Drain the chickpeas and place them in a large pan with twice as much cold water. Bring to the boil and skim off the grey foam that rises.

2 Add the garlic, rosemary, oil, and peppercorns, and bring to the boil. Turn down the heat, cover loosely, and simmer for 1–1½ hours, or until the chickpeas are soft. If they are old and hard, they will take longer. Keep the broth bubbling throughout; do not add salt or let the temperature drop, otherwise the chickpeas won't soften. Add more boiling water, if necessary.

3 When the chickpeas are tender, add the potato, return to the boil, and simmer for another 10 minutes, or until the potato softens to a mush and thickens the broth. Add the lemon juice and salt, ladle into bowls, and serve each portion with pomegranate seeds, if desired.

**cook's tip**

Use ready-cooked or canned chickpeas, proceed as above, but chop the garlic first, add the potato at the beginning, and shorten the boiling time to 20 minutes.

*how to serve*

To serve as a main course, accompany with chunks of sourdough bread and a salad of cos lettuce leaves and sliced mild onion.

# ribollita

❖ *t u s c a n y* ❖

This classic Tuscan bean soup is named after the traditional method of reboiling soup from the day before. You can keep adding to it and recooking it, and it's ideal for using leftovers.

**PREP** 15 MINS ❖ **COOK** 1¼ HRS ❖ **SERVES** 4-6

4 tbsp **extra virgin olive oil**, plus extra to drizzle

1 **onion**, chopped

2 **carrots**, peeled and sliced

1 **leek**, trimmed and sliced

**salt** and freshly ground **black pepper**

2 **garlic cloves**, chopped

400g can chopped **tomatoes**

1 tbsp **tomato purée**

900ml (1½ pints) hot **chicken stock**

400g can **borlotti beans**, **flageolet beans**, or **cannellini beans**, drained and rinsed

250g (9oz) **baby spinach leaves** or **spring greens**, shredded

8 slices of **ciabatta bread**

grated **Parmesan cheese**, to serve

1 Heat the oil in a large heavy-based pan over a low heat. Add the onion, carrots, and leek, and cook for 10 minutes, until softened but not coloured. Season, stir in the garlic, and cook for 1 minute. Add the tomatoes, tomato purée, and stock and season once more to taste.

2 In a bowl, mash half the beans with a fork and add to the pan. Bring to the boil, lower the heat, and simmer for 30 minutes. Add the remaining beans and spinach and leave to simmer for a further 30 minutes.

3 Toast the bread until golden, place 2 pieces in each soup bowl, and drizzle with oil. To serve, spoon the soup into the bowls, top with a sprinkling of Parmesan cheese, and drizzle with a little more oil.

# sopa de pescado con hinojo

❖ *s p a i n* ❖

This rustic fish soup – robustly flavoured with brandy, orange, and fennel – is simple to prepare and sure to please.

**PREP** 10 MINS ❖ **COOK** 1 HR ❖ **SERVES** 4-6

30g (1oz) **butter**

3 tbsp **olive oil**

1 large **fennel bulb**, finely chopped

2 **garlic cloves**, crushed

1 small **leek**, sliced

4 ripe **plum tomatoes**, chopped

3 tbsp **brandy**

¼ tsp **saffron threads**, infused in a little hot water

zest of ½ **orange**

1 **bay leaf**

1.7 litres (3 pints) hot **fish stock**

300g (10oz) **potatoes**, peeled, diced, and parboiled for 5 minutes

4 tbsp **dry white wine**

500g (1lb 2oz) **fresh black mussels**, scrubbed and debearded

**salt** and freshly ground **black pepper**

500g (1lb 2oz) **monkfish** or firm **white fish**, cut into bite-sized pieces

6 large raw **prawns**

**flat-leaf parsley**, chopped, to garnish

1 Heat the butter with 2 tablespoons of the oil in a deep-sided pan. Stir in the fennel, garlic, and leek, and fry over a medium heat, stirring, for 5 minutes, until softened.

2 Stir in the tomatoes, add the brandy, and boil for 2 minutes, or until the juices are reduced. Stir in the saffron, orange zest, bay leaf, stock, and potatoes. Bring to the boil, reduce the heat, and skim off any foam. Cover and simmer for 20 minutes, until the potatoes are tender. Remove the bay leaf.

3 Heat the remaining oil and the wine in a deep pan until boiling. Add the mussels, cover, and cook on a high heat for 2–3 minutes, shaking the pan often. Discard any unopened mussels. Strain, reserve the liquid, and set the mussels aside. Add the liquid to the soup and season to taste. Bring to the boil, add the monkfish pieces and prawns, then reduce the heat, cover, and simmer for 5 minutes. Add the mussels to the pan and bring almost to the boil. Serve sprinkled with the parsley.

# chorba bil hout

## *middle east*

In the Middle East, fish is generally grilled, fried, or baked. It only appears in a few classic stews and soups, such as this North African recipe, which is popular in the coastal regions of Morocco, Tunisia, Libya, and Egypt.

**PREP** 10 MINS ❖ **COOK** 20 MINS ❖ **SERVES** 4-6

2–3 tbsp **olive oil**

1 **onion**, finely chopped

2–3 **garlic cloves**, finely chopped

2–3 tsp **harissa paste**

small bunch of **flat-leaf parsley**, finely chopped

1.2 litres (2 pints) hot **fish stock**

150ml (5fl oz) **white wine** (optional)

400g can chopped **tomatoes**, drained

1kg (2¼lb) fresh firm-fleshed **fish fillets**, such as cod, haddock, ling, grouper, sea bass, or snapper, cut into bite-sized chunks

**salt** and freshly ground **black pepper**

small bunch of **coriander**, coarsely chopped, to garnish

1 Heat the oil in a large, deep, heavy-based pan and stir in the onion and garlic, until they begin to colour. Add the harissa and parsley, and pour in the fish stock. Bring to the boil, reduce the heat, and simmer, uncovered, for 10 minutes to let the flavours mingle.

2 Add the wine, if using, and the tomatoes. Gently stir in the fish chunks and bring to the boil again. Reduce the heat, season to taste, and simmer uncovered for about 5 minutes to make sure the fish is cooked through. Scatter the chopped coriander over the top and serve immediately with lots of bread to dip into the stock.

### variation

**Chorba bil hout with shellfish** Prepare this soup using shellfish, such as prawns, mussels, and squid, or a combination or fish and shellfish. Cook for 1–4 minutes, depending on the combination. Prepare the soup with more wine and less stock, or with fino sherry instead of wine.

# zuppa di cozze

## *italy*

Mussels, cultivated since ancient times in the Bay of Taranto in the far south of Italy, are cooked in a wine-laced fish broth, flavoured with capers and oregano, and finished with basil.

**PREP** 10 MINS ❖ **COOK** 10-20 MINS
**SERVES** 4-6

1.35kg (3lb) large **mussels** in shells

150ml (5fl oz) **dry white wine**

2–3 tbsp **olive oil**

1 medium **onion**, finely chopped

1 **garlic clove**, finely chopped

1 litre (1¾ pints) hot **fish stock**

500g (1lb 2oz) ripe **tomatoes**, skinned and diced

1–2 **bay leaves**

1 tbsp crumbled **fresh** or **dried oregano**

1 tsp **capers**, drained

**salt**

bunch of **basil**, shredded, to serve

1 Scrub the mussels and trim off the beards. They will close themselves tightly – but if they do not, they are dead and should not be used.

2 In a large soup pan, bring the wine to the boil and pack in the mussels. Cover and steam for 2–3 minutes, giving the pan a shake to move the shellfish around, until all the shells are open. Reject any that remains shut and reserve the ones in their shells. Strain the broth through a fine sieve to remove the grit and set aside.

3 In the same pan, heat the oil and fry the onion and garlic until soft but not browned. Add the stock and the reserved broth, tomatoes, bay leaves, and oregano, and bring to the boil. Simmer for 5 minutes, then tip in the mussels and capers. Reheat and season with salt.

4 Sprinkle with the basil and serve in deep soup bowls with plenty of bread for mopping.

# chorba al-adas

*⋄ middle east ⋄*

Thick lentil soups flavoured with cumin are common everyday fare in the Middle East, but this particular combination of lentils and rice topped with fried onions is a great favourite in Lebanon and Syria.

**PREP** 10 MINS ⋄ **COOK** 1 HR 10 MINS
**SERVES** 6-8

2 litres (3½ pints) hot **chicken** or **lamb stock**
200g (7oz) **red lentils**, rinsed and drained
100g (3½oz) **short-grain** or **pudding rice**, rinsed and drained
1–2 tsp **cumin seeds**
2 tbsp **olive oil**
knob of **butter**
2 **onions**, halved and finely sliced
1 tsp ground **coriander**
1 tsp ground **cumin**
salt and freshly ground **black pepper**
4–6 tbsp thick, creamy **yogurt**, to serve
1–2 **lemons**, cut into wedges, to serve

1 Pour the stock into a deep saucepan and bring to the boil. Add the lentils, rice, and cumin seeds, and boil for a further 3–4 minutes. Reduce the heat and simmer uncovered for about an hour, until the lentils and rice have cooked to a thick pulp.

2 In the meantime, heat the oil and butter in a pan, then stir in the onions for 4–5 minutes, until soft and golden brown. Stir in the ground coriander and cumin, and season with a little salt. Set aside.

3 Beat the pulped lentils and rice with a wooden spoon or a whisk, or blend in a food processor, until the mixture is creamy. Season well, spoon into individual bowls, and sprinkle the fried onions over the top. Serve immediately with a dollop of yogurt and wedges of lemon.

# tortellini in brodo

*⋄ italy ⋄*

A speciality of the city of Bologna in Emilia-Romagna, these little crescent-shaped pasta envelopes with a delicate cream-enriched meat filling are poached in a strong meat broth and served as the main dish of the evening meal.

**PREP** 30 MINS, PLUS RESTING
**COOK** 5-10 MINS ⋄ **SERVES** 4-6

350g (12oz) **pasta flour** or **"00" flour**, plus extra for dusting
½ tsp **salt**
3 **eggs**, beaten
1.5 litres (2¾ pints) hot **beef consommé**

### For the filling
250g (9oz) **chicken breast fillet**
150ml (5fl oz) or 1 glass **white wine**
salt and freshly ground **black pepper**
**black peppercorns**
1 **bay leaf**
50ml (1¾fl oz) **single cream**
2 tbsp grated **Parmesan cheese**
½ tsp freshly grated **nutmeg**
1 **egg**, beaten
1–2 tbsp **breadcrumbs**

1 Toss the flour with the salt in a bowl and work in enough egg to make a soft, pliable dough. Form into a ball, cover with cling film, and leave to rest for 30 minutes.

2 For the filling, poach the chicken gently in the wine with salt, peppercorns, and bay leaf for 5 minutes, or until firm. Remove the bay leaf and drain. Strain and reserve the liquid. Mince or pound the chicken finely with the cream, cheese, and nutmeg. Make a stiff paste with the egg and breadcrumbs. Add 1–2 spoonfuls of the chicken liquor to moisten the mixture. Set aside to cool.

3 Cut the dough in half. On a well-floured surface, roll out the dough with a floured rolling pin until fine enough to see the surface through the sheet. Cut out circles of the dough with a wine glass. Place a little filling on one side of each circle, wet the edge, and close to make a half moon. Join the two little wings to make a ring, pinching them together with damp fingers.

4 Bring the consommé to the boil, reduce the heat a little, and slip in the tortellini. Poach gently, allowing 4–5 minutes to cook the pasta and heat the filling through.

# zuppa di polpettine
❖ *italy* ❖

A strong beef or chicken broth enriched with little meatballs is traditionally served before the pasta and the roast in a southern Italian Christmas feast.

**PREP** 20–30 MINS ❖ **COOK** 10 MINS ❖ **SERVES** 6

400g (14oz) lean **minced meat**

175g (6oz) fresh **breadcrumbs**

1 **garlic clove**, finely chopped

2 tbsp finely chopped **flat-leaf parsley**, plus extra to garnish

2 large **eggs**, beaten

a little **milk**

**salt** and freshly ground **black pepper**

2–3 heaped tbsp **plain flour**

1.5 litres (2¾ pints) hot **strong chicken** or **beef broth**

1 Work the minced meat with the breadcrumbs, garlic, parsley, and eggs to a soft paste – you may need a little milk or more breadcrumbs. Season.

2 Spread the flour on a plate. With damp hands, pinch off little pieces of the paste and form into balls no bigger than a marble. Season the flour and roll the balls through it to coat and reserve.

3 Bring the broth gently to the boil and slip in the meatballs. Reduce the heat to a steady simmer and poach the meatballs until firm, for about 10 minutes. Garnish with parsley.

**cook's tip**

Meatballs prepared as above can be fried rather than poached and finished in a tomato sauce.

# sopa de cuarto de hora
❖ *spain* ❖

This simple soup is prepared with a ready-made broth in Spain – leftovers from one of the bean soups popular at midday, flavoured with diced Serrano ham and parsley, and fortified with hard-boiled egg.

**PREP** 5 MINS ❖ **COOK** 25 MINS ❖ **SERVES** 4

1 litre (1¾ pints) hot **chicken** or **beef broth**

2 tbsp **rice**

4 tbsp diced **Serrano ham**

2 **eggs**, hard-boiled and chopped

1 tbsp finely chopped **flat-leaf parsley**

1 tbsp finely chopped **mint** (optional)

1 In a large pan, bring the broth, rice, and ham to the boil. Reduce the heat and simmer for 15 minutes, or until the rice is nearly tender.

2 Add the eggs and simmer for a further 1 minute. Remove from the heat, then stir in the parsley and mint, if using. Serve piping hot.

**cook's tip**

You can cut down the preparation time by using leftover rice. You can also replace the rice with soup pasta – vermicelli, ditalini, or alphabet pasta if making for children.

# melokhia and chicken soup

## ❖ *egypt* ❖

One of Egypt's national dishes but also enjoyed in Libya and Jordan, this soup contains melokhia, a leafy plant from the mallow family.

**PREP** 30 MINS ❖ **COOK** 1 HR ❖ **SERVES** 4-6

1 **onion**, cut into bite-sized slices, plus
   2 **onions**, quartered
seeds of 1 **pomegranate**
2 tbsp **white wine vinegar**
450g (1lb) **fresh melokhia leaves** or
   225g (8oz) **dried melokhia leaves**,
   or 100g (3½oz) **fresh kale** or **spinach leaves**
1 small **chicken**
2 **carrots**, peeled and each cut into thirds
2 **garlic cloves**, crushed in their skins
4-5 **cloves**
3-4 **cardamom pods**
**salt** and freshly ground **black pepper**

1 Place the onion slices and pomegranate seeds in a bowl and toss in the vinegar. Cover and marinate for 1 hour.

2 If using dried melokhia leaves, crush them by hand and place in a bowl. Pour over just enough boiling water to cover and set aside to soak for 20 minutes, or until they have doubled in size.

3 Place the chicken in a deep pan and cover with just enough water. Add the quartered onions, carrots, garlic cloves, and cardamom pods, and season. Bring the water to the boil, then reduce the heat and simmer for about 30 minutes.

4 Stir in the melokhia leaves and simmer for a further 30 minutes. Lift the chicken out of the stock, skin it, and tear the flesh into thin strips. Strain and season the stock, and return the chicken to the pot.

5 Ladle the soup into bowls. Top each bowl with a spoonful of the marinated onions and pomegranate seeds and serve the stew with plenty of bread to dip into the stock.

# düğün çorbası

## ❖ *turkey* ❖

Yogurt-based soups are very popular in Turkey, particularly in the winter. Often they are prepared with rice or pulses and herbs, but this recipe is for the traditional "wedding soup", which is prepared with chunks of lamb.

**PREP** 10 MINS ❖ **COOK** 2 HRS ❖ **SERVES** 4-6

500g (1lb 2oz) **lamb** on the bone
2 **carrots**, peeled and roughly chopped
2 **potatoes**, peeled and roughly chopped
1 **cinnamon stick**
**salt** and freshly ground **black pepper**
3 tbsp thick, strained **yogurt**
3 tbsp **flour**
1 **egg yolk**
juice of ½ **lemon**
2 tbsp **butter**
1 tsp finely chopped **dried red chillies**
   or **pimentón** (Spanish paprika)

1 Place the lamb in a deep pan with the carrots, potatoes, and cinnamon stick. Pour in 2 litres (3½ pints) cold water and bring to the boil. Skim any scum off the surface, then reduce the heat. Simmer for about 1½ hours, until the meat is so tender that it almost falls off the bone.

2 Lift the meat out of the pan and place on a wooden board. Remove the meat from the bone and chop into small pieces. Strain the stock and discard the carrot and potato. Pour the stock back into the pan, season, and bring to the boil.

3 In a deep bowl, beat the yogurt with the flour. Add the egg and lemon juice, and beat well. Pour in about 250ml (9fl oz) of the hot stock, beating all the time. Reduce the heat and pour the yogurt mixture into the stock, beating all the time. Add the meat and heat it through, but do not bring to the boil.

4 In a small pan, melt the butter and stir in the chillies. Ladle the soup into individual bowls and drizzle the melted butter over each one.

# eggs

# meshweya with hard-boiled eggs
### ❖ *t u n i s i a* ❖

This egg and roasted vegetable salad often features on Tunisian menus. It is served as a starter or light lunch.

**PREP** 20 MINS ❖ **COOK** 30 MINS ❖ **SERVES** 4

1 large **mild onion**, halved
2 **red peppers**, halved
4 large **tomatoes**
4 **hard-boiled eggs**
1 tbsp **capers**, rinsed and drained
85g (3oz) canned **tuna** in oil, drained and flaked (optional)
4 **anchovies**, drained and chopped (optional)
3–4 tbsp **olive oil**
¼ tsp **harissa paste**
juice and 1 tsp finely grated zest of 1 small **unwaxed lemon**
**salt** and freshly ground **black pepper**

1 Preheat the oven to 240°C (475°F/Gas 9). Line a baking sheet with foil. Place the onion and peppers, cut-sides down, on the baking sheet along with the tomatoes. Roast the vegetables for 8–10 minutes, until the skin of the tomatoes chars a little and loosens. Remove the tomatoes and return the onion and peppers to the oven. Peel and quarter the tomatoes and set aside.

2 Roast the peppers for a further 8–10 minutes, until charred and softened. Remove from the oven, wrap in cling film, and leave to cool. When cool enough to handle, peel, deseed, and quarter each halved pepper. Roast the onion for a further 1–2 minutes, until soft and a little charred. When cool enough to handle, peel and cut each half into 4 wedges.

3 Arrange the vegetables on individual plates or on a serving dish. Slice the eggs, lengthways, into 4 wedges and add to the vegetables. Scatter over the capers and flaked tuna and/or anchovies, if using. Mix the oil, harissa, lemon juice, and zest in a small cup. Season well and drizzle over the salad. Serve immediately.

# œufs mimosa à la niçoise
### ❖ *p r o v e n c e* ❖

This old-fashioned starter looks very good as part of a buffet or in the centre of a tomato salad. It goes well with a simple green leaf salad on the side.

**PREP** 10 MINS ❖ **COOK** 10 MINS ❖ **SERVES** 4

4 **hard-boiled eggs**, shelled
1 tbsp **black olive tapenade** (see p14)
1 tbsp **mayonnaise** or **aïoli** (see p152)
1 tsp finely grated zest of 1 **unwaxed lemon**
1 tbsp finely chopped **flat-leaf parsley**
4 small **anchovy fillets** in oil, drained and patted dry
freshly ground **black pepper**

1 Halve the eggs lengthways. Carefully scoop out the yolks of 4 of the egg halves with a teaspoon and place in a bowl. Place the remaining yolks on a saucer. Make sure the halved egg whites can sit straight on a flat surface – cut off a little of the underside to flatten, if necessary.

2 Mash the 4 egg yolks with a fork, add the tapenade, mayonnaise, lemon zest, and 2 teaspoons of the chopped parsley, and mix well.

3 Using the teaspoon, divide the tapenade mixture between the halved eggs and place on a serving dish.

4 Flatten the anchovy fillets with the back of a knife into long strips. Cut lengthways and crossways to make 16 small strips. Arrange 2 anchovy strips on the top of each filled halved egg.

5 Push the reserved yolks through a sieve or grater over the dish. Scatter over the rest of the parsley, season with the pepper, and serve immediately.

# beid bi tom

### ❖ *middle east* ❖

Boiled, fried, or scrambled egg dishes are very popular in the Middle East, where they are served for breakfast, as street snacks in busy markets, or as a late-night snack at home. This recipe is often served in Lebanon, Syria, and Jordan.

**PREP** 5 MINS ❖ **COOK** 6-8 MINS ❖ **SERVES** 4

2 tbsp **olive oil**

knob of **butter**, plus extra to serve

2–3 **garlic cloves**, crushed

1–2 tsp **sumac**

8 **eggs**

1 tsp **dried mint**

salt

1 In a heavy-based frying pan, heat the oil and the butter. Add the garlic and sumac, and cook for 1–2 minutes, until it begins to colour. Crack the eggs into a bowl and pour into the pan.

2 Sprinkle the mint over the eggs and cover the pan with a lid. Reduce the heat and cook until the whites are just set.

3 Sprinkle a little salt over the eggs, divide into 4 portions, and serve with toasted and buttered flat or leavened bread.

### cook's tip

These fried eggs can be flavoured with dried chillies and coriander or cumin seeds. Other street variations include frying the eggs with slices of cumin-flavoured cured sausage or slices of fenugreek-flavoured cured beef, which are often combined with tomatoes and flat-leaf parsley or coriander.

### *how to serve*

You can serve this fried eggs dish on toasted flatbread or with chunks of fresh, crusty bread as a delicious breakfast or snack option.

# beid hamine
### ❖ *egypt* ❖

Hard-boiled eggs flavoured with spices and herbs, coloured with saffron, or cooked slowly with onion skins (as in this dish) are a great favourite on picnics and pilgrimages in the Middle East.

**PREP** 5 MINS ❖ **COOK** 6 HRS ❖ **SERVES** 4

skins of 3–4 **onions**
4 large **eggs**
1 tbsp **sunflower** or **olive oil**
**harissa paste**, to serve

1 Place half the onion skins in the base of a heavy-based saucepan. Place the eggs on top and cover with the rest of the onion skins. Add enough water to cover the eggs and skins, bring to the boil, then reduce the heat and simmer for 15 minutes.

2 Add more boiling water to fill up the pan and bring to the boil. Reduce the heat, drizzle the oil into the water, and cover. Simmer for about 6 hours, but check occasionally to make sure there is enough water in the pot. Add more boiling water, if required.

3 Peel the eggs and cut in half lengthways to reveal the creamy yolks surrounded by brown-coloured whites. Dip in a little harissa paste, or serve with a bean and onion salad and flat-leaf parsley.

# uova alla sarda
### ❖ *sardinia* ❖

This is a quick and easy Sardinian dish. The eggs are treated like stuffed sardines, or *sarda*, and topped with a crisp little hat.

**PREP** 15 MINS ❖ **COOK** 15-20 MINS
**SERVES** 4

4 large **eggs**
4 tbsp **olive oil**
2 **garlic cloves**, finely chopped
2 tbsp chopped **flat-leaf parsley**
1 tbsp **wine vinegar**
**salt** and freshly ground **black pepper**
4 tbsp fresh **breadcrumbs**

1 Place the eggs in a heavy-based pan. Add enough water to cover them, bring to the boil, and simmer for 8–10 minutes. Rinse them under cold water to loosen the shells. Peel the eggs, cut in half lengthways, and arrange, cut-sides up, in a serving dish.

2 Heat half the oil in a small frying pan, add the garlic and parsley, and fry until the garlic softens and browns a little. Add the vinegar, boil for a minute to form an emulsion with the oil, then season and tip the contents of the pan over the eggs.

3 Reheat the pan with the remaining oil, stir in the breadcrumbs, and fry gently, stirring, until crisp and golden. Top the eggs with the breadcrumbs.

### cook's tip

For extra crunch, include a few chopped almonds with the breadcrumbs.

*how to eat*
In the Middle East, hard-boiled eggs are often shelled and dipped in a mixture of ground nuts and spices, or shelled and fried in oil and cumin and sprinkled with salt.

# uova e carciofi
*italy*

This is a simple supper dish of eggs scrambled with artichoke hearts softened in olive oil with onion and parsley. In Italy, when artichokes are in season, you can buy the hearts ready prepared.

**PREP** 20 MINS ❖ **COOK** 15 MINS ❖ **SERVES** 2-4

4 medium-sized **artichokes**

½ **lemon**, roughly chopped

3–4 tbsp **olive oil**

2–3 **spring onions**, sliced

2 tbsp chopped **flat-leaf parsley**, plus extra to serve

**salt** and freshly ground **black pepper**

4–6 **eggs**

1–2 tbsp grated **pecorino** or Parmesan cheese

1 To prepare the artichoke hearts, trim off the stalks by making a nick in the stem near the base of the leaves and giving it a sharp twist. Pull out the tougher fibres from the centre as the stem comes away. Cut off the top two-thirds of the leaves, revealing the pale heart closed over the feathery choke. Using a sharp-edged teaspoon, scoop out the choke. Trim off the tough tips of the remaining leaves, then chop the hearts into bite-sized pieces. As you work, toss these into a bowl of cold water with chopped lemon to prevent them from browning.

2 Heat the oil in a small frying pan, add the spring onions, parsley, and artichoke pieces, season, and fry for 2–3 minutes. Add about 150ml (5fl oz) cold water, bring to the boil, and cover loosely with a lid. Simmer gently for about 10 minutes, removing the lid for the last 2–3 minutes, until the artichoke pieces are tender and the juices reduced to an oily slick.

3 Beat the eggs with the cheese and stir into the pan, stirring continuously over a low heat, until the egg is just set. Serve straight from the pan with plenty of bread for mopping.

### cook's tip

Choose your artichokes as if they were fresh flowers, which indeed they are. The stems should be juicy and the leaves bright and firm, with no sign of browning. If not using immediately, store them in a cool place with the stems in water. Once cooked, they won't keep for long.

# omelette basquaise

*pyrenees*

*Basquaise* describes dishes prepared in the style of the French Basque region, in the southwest corner of the country near the Spanish border. Expect tomatoes and sweet red peppers with a touch of heat.

**PREP** 5 MINS ❖ **COOK** 10-15 MINS ❖ **SERVES** 4

8 large **eggs**

coarse **sea salt** and freshly ground **black pepper**

**piperade sauce** (see p78)

3–4 tbsp **olive oil**

1 Break 4 eggs into two bowls, 2 eggs in each. Whisk with a fork until fluffy. Season lightly.

2 Divide the piperade sauce between the bowls and whisk well.

3 Oil two frying pans and place over a moderately high heat. Preheat the grill.

4 Once the pans are hot, pour in the contents of the bowls, reduce the heat a little, and cook until the bottom of each omelette is set, stirring frequently.

5 Place under the grill for 2–3 minutes, until lightly set and just coloured. Serve immediately with crusty bread. If you like, you can fold over each omelette before slipping them onto plates.

# shakshouka

*middle east*

There are many interpretations of *shakshouka*, but it is primarily a pepper and tomato dish to which eggs are added. Known as *menemen* in Turkey, this particular dish is popular in Syria, Lebanon, and Jordan.

**PREP** 10 MINS ❖ **COOK** 15 MINS ❖ **SERVES** 4

2 tbsp **olive oil**

1 **onion**, halved and finely sliced

2 **red** or **green bell peppers**, finely sliced

2 **garlic cloves**, finely chopped

1 **red chilli**, deseeded and finely chopped

1 tsp **sugar**

400g can chopped **tomatoes**

**salt** and freshly ground **black pepper**

4 large **eggs**

small bunch of **flat-leaf parsley**, finely chopped

1 Heat the oil in a heavy-based frying pan and fry the onion and peppers for 2–3 minutes, until soft. Toss in the garlic and chilli, and fry until the vegetables begin to colour.

2 Add the sugar and tomatoes, and cook over a medium heat for 3–4 minutes, until the mixture is slightly pulpy. Season well.

3 Using a wooden spoon, make 4 indentations in the tomato mixture and crack an egg into each one. Reduce the heat, cover the pan, and cook until the whites are set. Scatter over the parsley and serve with fresh crusty bread.

# piperade sauce
### ❖ *pyrenees* ❖

This aromatic red sauce, which takes its name from *piper* or sweet pepper, exemplifies the taste of the French Basque country. You can leave out the cured ham if you wish.

**PREP** 10 MINS ❖ **COOK** 10-15 MINS ❖ **SERVES** 4

2 tbsp **olive oil**

1 large **sweet white onion**, chopped

1 large **sweet red pepper**, deseeded, white parts removed, cut into small strips

2 **garlic cloves**, crushed

coarse **sea salt** and freshly ground **black pepper**

½ tsp **Piment d'Espelette**, **chilli powder**, or **hot pimentón** (Spanish paprika)

8 ripe **cherry tomatoes**, halved or quartered

thick slice of **cured ham**, such as Bayonne or Serrano, cut into small pieces

1–2 tbsp **sweet vermouth** or a pinch of **caster sugar**

1 Heat the oil in a frying pan, add the onion, and fry over a medium heat for 2–3 minutes, until pale and softened.

2 Add the red pepper and garlic. Season and add the Piment d'Espelette.

3 Stir in the tomatoes, ham, and the vermouth. Cook until the pepper and tomatoes are softened and the sauce is thick and mushy, stirring frequently. Add a little water if the sauce starts drying out. Taste and adjust the seasoning. Serve hot or at room temperature. You can also keep the sauce for 2–3 days in the fridge in a covered bowl.

# arroz a la cubana
### ❖ *spain* ❖

Cuban rice, named for the fried bananas served on the side, is loved by Spanish children as much for its pretty colours as for the sweet-salty combination of flavours. Leftover paella makes a particularly good version.

**PREP** 10 MINS ❖ **COOK** 10 MINS
**SERVES** 4

about 300g (10oz) ready-cooked **rice**

3–4 tbsp **olive oil**

4–8 **eggs**

4 small **bananas**, skinned and halved lengthways

500g (1lb 2oz) **fresh** or **canned tomatoes**

1 thick slice of **onion**, chopped

1 **garlic clove**, chopped

1 fresh **red chilli**, deseeded and chopped (optional)

1 Heat the rice through in a low oven or microwave and transfer to a warm serving dish.

2 Heat the oil in a large frying pan. Crack the eggs in and fry sunny-side up. Remove with a slotted spoon, arrange on top of the rice, and keep warm.

3 In the same pan, fry the bananas just enough to caramelize them a little. Remove and arrange them with the eggs.

4 Meanwhile, liquidize the tomatoes, onion, and garlic with the chilli, if using. Pour the tomato mix into the same frying pan and bubble up for 1–2 minutes to concentrate the juices and develop the flavours. Serve the rice with its toppings, and the tomato sauce on the side.

### *how to serve*

Use this sauce as a filling for Omelette basquaise (see p77), a sauce for rice, pasta, or ham, a topping for crostini, or a dip for sautéed prawns.

# huevos a la flamenca
### *spain*

This traditional Andalucian egg dish is comfort food at its best. Just like a full English breakfast, it can be enjoyed at any time of the day.

**PREP** 10 MINS ❖ **COOK** 30-35 MINS ❖ **SERVES** 4

3 tbsp **olive oil**

1 large **white onion**, finely chopped

1 **red pepper**, finely chopped

2 **garlic cloves**, crushed

1 tbsp **smoked pimentón** (Spanish paprika)

450g (1lb) ripe **tomatoes**, blanched, skinned, deseeded, and chopped

**salt** and freshly ground **black pepper**

2 slices of **Serrano ham**, cut into small pieces, and 2 slices halved

2 slices of **chorizo**, cut into small pieces, and 4 whole slices

4 generous tbsp **frozen peas**, defrosted

4 large **eggs**

4 tbsp **breadcrumbs** made from day-old bread

3 tbsp finely chopped **flat-leaf parsley**

1 Preheat the oven to 200°C (400°F/Gas 6). Heat 2 tablespoons of the oil in a frying pan over a medium heat. Add the onion and red pepper, and fry for 8–10 minutes, stirring frequently, until soft. Stir in the garlic and paprika, cook for a further 1–2 minutes, then tip in the tomatoes and cook for 10 minutes, stirring often. Season to taste.

2 Spoon the mixture into 4 ramekins. Stir in the chopped ham and chorizo, and the peas. Crack an egg on top of each. Place the slices of ham and chorizo on top.

3 Place the ramekins on a baking tray and bake for about 10 minutes, until the whites are set but the yolks are still runny.

4 Meanwhile, fry the breadcrumbs in the remaining oil until crisp and golden brown. Remove from the heat and stir in the parsley.

5 When the eggs are cooked, remove the ramekins from the oven and sprinkle over the breadcrumb mixture. Serve hot.

### variation

**Huevos a la flamenca with asparagus**
Add blanched green asparagus tips to the ramekins before baking.

# uova piemontese
### *italy*

The best way with Italy's prized white truffle, *Tuber magnato*, is to combine it with something soft and buttery and let the flavour speak for itself. The white, or Alba, truffle should be heated minimally.

**PREP** 5 MINS ❖ **COOK** 10 MINS ❖ **SERVES** 2

1 smallish **white Piedmont truffle** or **black summer truffle** (*T. aestivum*)

4 **eggs**

1 tbsp grated **Parmesan cheese**

**salt** and freshly ground **black pepper**

50g (1¾oz) **unsalted butter**

1 Clean the truffle gently with a soft brush and wipe it with a damp cloth. In a bowl, beat the eggs with the Parmesan and seasoning.

2 Melt the butter in a small frying pan. As soon as it foams but before it browns, add the eggs and turn them gently, then cook until they set in soft curds.

3 Using a straight-edged cutter or a sharp knife, shave or grate the truffle onto the eggs when they are just setting and scrambled. The truffle should fall in fine transparent ribbons on the hot egg, releasing delicate perfume. Transfer to warm plates and serve with crusty country bread and a glass of red wine.

# tortilla de primavera

*◆ spain ◆*

This variation of a traditional thick Spanish omelette includes broccoli and peas. Serve as tapas with a dressed salad or sandwiched between chunks of crusty bread.

**PREP** 15 MINS ◆ **COOK** 45 MINS ◆ **SERVES** 4

salt and freshly ground black pepper
115g (4oz) fresh or frozen peas
115g (4oz) broccoli florets
6 tbsp olive oil
350g (12oz) floury potatoes, such as King Edward, peeled and cut into 2cm (¾in) cubes
2 small red onions, finely chopped
6 eggs

1 Bring a large pan of lightly salted water to the boil over a high heat. Add the peas and boil for 5 minutes, or until just tender. Transfer the peas to a bowl of cold water. Return the pan to the boil, add the broccoli, and boil for 4 minutes, or until just tender. Remove the florets and add to the peas, then drain both vegetables well and set aside.

2 Heat 4 tablespoons oil in a 23cm (9in) non-stick pan over a medium heat. Add the potatoes and onions and cook for 10–15 minutes until the potatoes are tender.

3 In a bowl, beat and season the eggs. Add the potatoes, onions, peas, and broccoli and stir. Discard the excess oil from the pan.

4 Heat the remaining oil in the pan over a high heat. Add the egg mixture, reduce the heat to low, and smooth the surface. Cook for 20–25 minutes until the top of the omelette begins to set. Slide the tortilla onto a plate, place a second plate on top, and invert. Slide back into the pan and cook for 5 minutes, until both sides are set. Leave for 5 minutes before serving, cut in wedges.

# tortilla de habas

*◆ spain ◆*

This juicy tortilla is made with broad beans instead of potatoes and is flavoured with marjoram, a herb that works well with all members of the bean family. To serve as tapas, cut into bite-sized cubes.

**PREP** 5 MINS ◆ **COOK** 10-15 MINS
**SERVES** 4-6

500g (1lb 2oz) broad beans, shelled
4 tbsp olive oil
2 tbsp white wine or dry sherry
4 large eggs
salt and freshly ground black pepper
1 tsp fresh marjoram leaves

1 Slip the beans out of their skins, unless they are very tiny and the skins are unwrinkled and tender. Heat 1 tablespoon of the oil in a small frying pan and stir in the beans, and turn them. Add the wine, allow the alcohol to evaporate, then cover the pan and leave to simmer gently for 5–6 minutes, until the beans are just soft and the liquid has almost evaporated. Leave to cool.

2 In a bowl, beat the eggs with seasoning and marjoram leaves, then add the beans and stir.

3 Reheat the pan with the remaining oil. Tip in the egg-bean mixture and cook gently as a thick pancake, neatening the edges with a spatula and lifting up the edges to let the uncooked egg run underneath.

4 Cook until the top is beginning to set and the base is golden brown. Then slide the tortilla onto a plate, remove the pan from the heat, place a second plate on top, and invert so that the cooked side is on top. Slide back into the pan and cook for 2–3 minutes more on a low heat, until the tortilla is firm but still juicy in the middle. Serve warm or cool.

**cook's tip**

At the beginning of the season, when the pods are still tender and the beans only just beginning to form, use the whole pods sliced into short lengths following the curve of the beans.

# *essential*
# peppers

Red peppers arrived in the Mediterranean from the Americas at the end of the 15th cenutry and soon flourished around the Mediterranean, particularly in Spain and Turkey.

**All peppers** belong to the *capsicum* genus, a huge family ranging from large, sweet red bell peppers to tiny fiery chillies. In a Mediterranean context, peppers are an everyday vegetable used raw, roasted, stuffed, smoked, and pickled. They are also a discreetly used condiment. Green peppers are unripe, with a herby flavour. Ripe peppers are red, and sometimes yellow or orange. Red, long, and narrow peppers indicate a sweet flavour and a palatable thin skin – these are best for eating raw in salads.

**Red, yellow, and orange bell peppers** are best for stuffing, as they can stand upright. The red variety has a slightly sweeter and deeper flavour.

**Ñora peppers**, small, squashed, and dried, are a Spanish institution. They are mostly used for Romesco sauce and pimentón (Spanish paprika).

**Peperoncino** is a mild chilli pepper with thin skin and a great flavour – very popular pickled.

**Nardello** has a lovely flavour and can be very sweet. It is perfect for frying – serve with sausages, fish, green lentils, couscous, or chickpeas.

**Padrón** is a Spanish favourite, served fried, with sea salt. They are usually mild but can be on the fiery side.

**Large red peppers** can have a thick skin and not much flavour when raw. They are best for roasting and taste much better when peeled. They are also good split lengthways and stuffed.

# frittata di menta
*italy*

Mint is a popular herb in southern Italy where the Middle Eastern influence is strong. It flavours this Italian version of the Spanish tortilla beautifully.

**PREP** 5 MINS ❖ **COOK** 10-15 MINS ❖ **SERVES** 4

8 large **eggs**
3 tbsp grated **pecorino** or **Parmesan cheese**
**salt** and freshly ground **black pepper**
3–4 tbsp **olive oil**
1 small **onion**, finely chopped
generous handful of **mint leaves**, roughly torn

1 Beat the eggs with the cheese and season. Set aside.

2 Heat 2 tablespoons of the oil in a frying pan. Add the onion, salt lightly to get the juices running, and fry gently until just soft – do not let it brown. Stir in the mint and cook for another minute.

3 Remove the pan from the heat and allow the mixture to cool. In a bowl, mix the onion and mint with the eggs.

4 Reheat the pan with the remaining oil. As soon as the oil is lightly smoking, pour in the egg mixture.

5 As soon as the first layer sets, pull the edges to the middle, then leave to cook gently, running a palette knife round the rim to loosen the edge. Shake the pan to keep the base from burning.

6 As soon as the top begins to look set, remove the pan from the heat. Slide the tortilla onto a plate, place a second plate on top, and invert so that the cooked side is on top. Slide the tortilla back into the pan and cook for a further 1–2 minutes.

*how to prepare*
To bake the frittata, pour the egg mixture into a shallow earthenware dish – the size of an omelette pan – and bake at 180°C (350°F/Gas 4) for 20–30 minutes, until firm to the touch.

# çılbır
*turkey*

Simple and satisfying, this delicious egg dish is a Turkish classic served with the ubiquitous garlic-flavoured yogurt. It can be enjoyed as a snack, as a hot mezze dish, or as a supper dish with a salad.

**PREP** 5 MINS ❖ **COOK** 10 MINS ❖ **SERVES** 4

500g (1lb 2oz) thick, creamy **yogurt**
2 **garlic cloves**, finely chopped
**salt** and freshly ground **black pepper**
2–3 tbsp **white wine vinegar**
4 large **eggs**
1–2 tbsp **butter**
1 tsp **pimentón** (Spanish paprika) or **dried red chillies**, finely chopped
a few **dried sage leaves**, crumbled

1 In a bowl, beat the yogurt with the garlic. Season to taste. Spoon the yogurt into a serving dish or individual plates, spreading it flat to create a thick base for the eggs.

2 Fill a pan with 850ml (1½ pints) water, add the vinegar, and bring to a rolling boil. Stir the water with a spoon to create a mini whirlpool in the centre. Crack one egg into a small bowl and gently slip it into the water. As the egg spins and the white sets around the yolk, stir the water again for the next one. Poach each egg for 2–3 minutes, so that the yolks are still soft. Drain the eggs using a slotted spoon and place on top of the yogurt base.

3 Quickly melt the butter in a small pan. Stir in the paprika and sage leaves, then spoon over the eggs and sprinkle a little salt over the top. Serve immediately with chunks of crusty bread to mop up the egg.

# eggah bi eish wa kousa
### ❖ *middle east* ❖

Arab omelettes, called *eggah*, are thick and packed with flavour, similar to the traditional Spanish *tortilla*. This recipe is popular in Syria and Lebanon, but there are variations throughout the Middle East.

**PREP** 25 MINS  ❖  **COOK** 50 MINS  ❖  **SERVES** 4-6

2 **courgettes**, thinly sliced on the diagonal
**salt** and freshly ground **black pepper**
2 tbsp **olive oil**
1 tbsp **butter**
1 **onion**, halved and finely sliced
small bunch of **mint**, finely chopped
8 **eggs**
2–3 slices of **bread**, crusts removed, soaked in a little milk
small bunch of **flat-leaf parsley**, finely chopped
1 **lemon**, cut into wedges

1 Preheat the oven to 180°C (350°F/Gas 4). Sprinkle the courgettes with a little salt to draw out the juices. Set aside for about 15 minutes, then rinse and pat dry.

2 In a heavy-based frying pan, heat the oil with most of the butter. Stir in the onion and cook until soft and beginning to colour. Add the courgettes and fry until the onions and courgettes are golden. Toss in the mint, then leave the mixture to cool.

3 In a bowl, crack the eggs and beat them lightly. Squeeze the bread dry, crumble with your fingers, and add to the eggs. Beat well, stir in the courgette and onion mixture, and season well.

4 Grease a heavy-based ovenproof dish with the remaining butter, tip in the courgette mixture, and bake for about 30 minutes, until risen and nicely browned on top.

5 Divide into 4 portions and serve garnished with parsley and lemon wedges to squeeze over.

# kayiania
### ❖ *greece* ❖

This juicy egg cake, a breakfast and supper dish in the Peloponnese, is flavoured with dill and melted cubes of salty *kefalotiri*, a cheese made with ewe's or goat's milk.

**PREP** 15 MINS  ❖  **COOK** 15 MINS  ❖  **SERVES** 4-5

4 tbsp **olive oil**
2 large ripe, firm **tomatoes**, thickly sliced
1 **garlic clove**, chopped
100g (3½oz) **kefalotiri**, **mozzarella**, or **taleggio cheese**, diced
6 large **eggs**
1 tbsp chopped **dill**
**salt** and freshly ground **black pepper**

1 Heat the oil in a small frying pan. Spread the tomato slices in an even layer over the surface, sprinkle with garlic, and cook gently until the tomato is soft and slightly dry. Top with the cheese but do not stir.

2 Meanwhile, beat the eggs with dill and a little seasoning. As soon as the cheese has melted a little, pour over the egg, turn up the heat, cover loosely, and cook until the top begins to look set. Flip the cake over and cook the other side. You can also slip the pan under the grill.

### cook's tip

You can skin the tomatoes, if you prefer, by scalding them in boiling water first to loosen the skins. For a more substantial dish, the Greeks include slices of fried *loukanika*, an all-pork sausage.

# brik with eggs

### ❖ *tunisia* ❖

Little filled pastries are called "brik" in Tunisia, "briouat" in Morocco, and "bourek" in Algeria and other regions of the Middle East. In this recipe from Tunisia, the pastry triangles are filled with tuna and egg.

**PREP** 30 MINS ❖ **COOK** 2 MINS ❖ **SERVES** 4

1 tbsp **olive oil**
1 **onion**, finely chopped
6–8 **anchovy fillets**
bunch of **flat-leaf parsley**, finely chopped
200g can **tuna**, rinsed and drained
**salt** and freshly ground **black pepper**
2 sheets of **filo pastry** or *ouarka*, cut into 4
   20cm (8in) squares
4 small **eggs**
**sunflower oil**, for frying
1 **lemon**, cut into quarters, to serve

1 Heat the olive oil in a frying pan, stir in the onion, and cook for 2 minutes, until soft. Add the anchovies and fry until they melt into the oil, then add the parsley and toss in the tuna. Cook the mixture over a low heat for 4–5 minutes, until it resembles a thick paste. Season well and leave to cool.

2 Place all 4 filo squares on a work surface, then spoon a quarter of the mixture into the middle of one half of each square. Indent the mixture with the back of a spoon to make a well. Crack an egg into the well and fold the other filo half over the filling to form a triangle. Do not move or burst the egg. Fold the edges over and seal with a little water.

3 Heat the sunflower oil in a heavy-based pan, filling it about half way. Slip 1–2 pastries into the oil and cook for about 30 seconds on each side, until crisp and golden brown. Lift out of the pan using a slotted spoon and drain on kitchen paper. Serve the pastries while they are hot and the yolk is still runny, with a wedge of lemon to squeeze over them.

# avga tiropita

### ❖ *greece* ❖

A popular midday snack on the islands, these deep-fried pasties are made with a robust olive oil pastry dough. They are stuffed with softly scrambled eggs and flavoured with parsley and mint.

**PREP** 20–30 MINS, PLUS RESTING
**COOK** 30 MINS ❖ **SERVES** 4-6

### For the pastry
250g (9oz) **plain flour**
pinch of **salt**
1 tbsp **olive oil**

### For the filling
1 tbsp **olive oil**, plus extra for frying
2 tbsp finely chopped **onion**
2 large **eggs**, beaten
100g (3½oz) **feta cheese**, crumbled
1 tbsp finely chopped **mint**
2 tbsp finely chopped **flat-leaf parsley**
**salt** and freshly ground **black pepper**

1 For the pastry, sift the flour and salt into a bowl. Make a well in the centre and pour in the oil. Add about 4 tablespoons of warm water and bring the mixture together to from a soft, pliable dough. Knead with the heel of your hand until the dough is smooth and elastic. Cover with a clean cloth and leave in a cool place for 30 minutes.

2 For the filling, heat the oil in a small frying pan and fry the onion over a low heat for 5–6 minutes, until just soft. Stir in the eggs, cheese, and herbs, and season. Cook until the egg sets in soft curds. Remove from the heat and leave to cool.

3 Roll out the pastry thinly. Using a coffee saucer as template, cut out circles from the dough. Place a teaspoon of the filling on one half of each circle, leaving a border around the edge. Dampen the edges with water and bring them together to seal and form into the pasty shape.

4 In a frying pan, heat the oil to a depth of 7.5cm (3in). Fry the pasties in two batches, for 2 minutes on each side, until golden brown.

### cook's tip
You can also use layers of ready-prepared filo. If you prefer to bake the pasties, brush the tops with a little milk and bake at 180°C (350°F/Gas 4) for 12–15 minutes, until the pastry is crisp and browned.

# pasta, rice,
# and pulses

# trofie al pesto
### ✤ italy ✤

The original pasta of Genoa, trofie is often dressed with pesto and is particularly good with green beans and, surprisingly, diced potato.

**PREP** 10 MINS ✤ **COOK** 15–20 MINS
**SERVES** 4-6

sea salt and freshly ground **black pepper**
200g (7oz) small **green beans**, topped, tailed, and cut into 3cm (1½in) segments
2 **waxy potatoes**, peeled and diced
450g–500g (1lb–1lb 2oz) **dried trofie**
handful of small **basil leaves**, to garnish
2 tbsp Parmesan shavings, to garnish

### For pesto genovese
3–4 **garlic cloves**
5–6 tbsp **pine nuts**
3–4 large handfuls of **basil leaves**, torn
2 tbsp coarsely grated **Parmesan** or **pecorino cheese**
4–6 tbsp **fruity olive oil**

1 For the pesto, crush the garlic using a mortar and pestle. Add the pine nuts and pound well until creamy. Add the basil and a little salt. Pound until you get a rough, fragrant purée. Add the cheese and pound until mixed. Work in the oil, a little at a time, working in the same direction, until you get a thick, sloshy, bright green sauce. Season and cover with cling film.

2 Bring a large saucepan filled with water to the boil over a high heat. Season with salt, add the beans, and boil for 4–6 minutes, until just tender. Remove the beans with a slotted spoon, refresh under cold running water, then drain and set aside.

3 Add the potatoes to the saucepan and return to the boil. Add the trofie and cook, as per the packet instructions, until al dente. Meanwhile, put the pesto in a serving bowl and pour over with 3 tablespoons of the boiling cooking liquid.

4 Drain the pasta and potato. Tip into the bowl with the pesto, add the beans, and toss gently. Adjust the seasoning with pepper, and scatter over the basil and Parmesan.

### variations

**Pesto genovese with almonds and mint** Replace the pine nuts with slivered almonds, and the basil with fresh mint leaves.

**Pesto genovese with coriander** Add fresh coriander instead of the basil.

# penne primavera
### ✤ italy ✤

Depending on availability, almost any spring vegetable can be used in this Italian-style pasta dish, such as green peas, courgette, and cauliflower. Serve with hot crusty garlic rolls for a filling meal.

**PREP** 20 MINS ✤ **COOK** 25 MINS ✤ **SERVES** 4-6

450g (1lb) **dried penne**
**salt** and freshly ground **black pepper**
350g (12oz) **broccoli florets**
175g (6oz) **asparagus tips**
115g (4oz) **mangetout**, tips and strings removed
2 large **carrots**, cut into juliennes
2 tbsp chopped **basil** or **oregano**

### For the vinaigrette
175ml (6fl oz) **olive oil**
6 tbsp **wine vinegar**
1 tbsp Dijon mustard
1 **garlic clove**, finely chopped

1 Cook the penne in plenty of lightly salted boiling water for 10–12 minutes, or according to the packet instructions.

2 Meanwhile, steam the vegetables for 5–6 minutes, or until tender but still crisp. Drain the vegetables thoroughly, place in a large bowl, and add the basil.

3 For the vinaigrette, place all the ingredients in a small bowl and beat with a fork. Season to taste. Pour the vinaigrette over the vegetables and herbs. Drain the penne thoroughly. Add the pasta to the vegetables and toss gently to combine.

### variation

**Creamy pasta primavera** In place of the vinaigrette, add 200g (7oz) crème fraîche and 1 teaspoon of wholegrain mustard to the vegetables and pasta. Vary the vegetables used according to what is available: peas, courgettes, baby carrots, or sugar snap peas are all ideal. You can also change the pasta shape used – try rigatoni or fusilli.

# spaghetti aglio olio e peperoncino
### ❖ *sicily* ❖

This vibrant Sicilian sauce is ready in minutes and often dresses spaghetti, arguably the star of Italian pasta. If managing the long spaghetti strands is a worry, rejoice in the fact that they used to be even longer!

**PREP** 10 MINS ❖ **COOK** 10 MINS ❖ **SERVES** 4

salt and freshly ground **black pepper**
400g (14oz) **dried spaghetti**
100ml (3½fl oz) **olive oil**
2 **garlic cloves**, crushed
1 small **red chilli**, deseeded and finely chopped
3 tbsp snipped **flat-leaf parsley**
freshly grated **ricotta salata**, **pecorino**, **feta**, or **Parmesan cheese**, to serve (optional)

1 Bring a large saucepan of lightly salted water to the boil, then add the spaghetti and cook until al dente, or according to the packet instructions.

2 Meanwhile, heat 5 tablespoons of the oil in a large sauté pan or non-stick frying pan and cook the garlic and chilli over a low heat, stirring frequently, until the garlic turns golden. Add 4 tablespoons of spaghetti water. Remove from the heat, stir, and set aside until the spaghetti is cooked.

3 Drain the spaghetti into a colander. On a high heat, stir the garlic sauce until emulsified and tip in the spaghetti. Stir in the remaining oil and the parsley. Toss until thoroughly coated. Adjust the seasoning. Serve immediately, with grated ricotta salata or other cheese, if you like.

### variation

**Sicilian spaghetti with anchovies** Omit the chilli and add 1 tablespoon of finely chopped drained anchovy fillets. You can also replace the parsley with other herbs, or add a mixture of herbs – basil, dill, coriander, and a little thyme or oregano.

# fettuccine alfredo
### ❖ *italy* ❖

A simple supper made with a few good-quality ingredients, this dish was named by a Roman restaurateur, Alfredo Di Lelio.

**PREP** 5 MINS ❖ **COOK** 15 MINS ❖ **SERVES** 4

salt and freshly ground **black pepper**
600g (1lb 5oz) **fresh fettucine**, or 450g (1lb) **dried fettucine**
115g (4oz) **unsalted butter**, cut into cubes
250ml (9fl oz) **double cream**
75g (2½oz) grated **Parmesan cheese**, plus extra shavings to serve

1 Bring a large saucepan of lightly salted water to the boil, then add the pasta. Simmer for 1–2 minutes if using fresh fettucine, or 10–12 minutes if using dried, or until the pasta is al dente. Drain well, return to the pan, and cover to keep warm.

2 In a separate large pan, melt the butter, then add the cream and heat until hot but not boiling. Reduce the heat to low, add the cooked pasta and the grated Parmesan, and season to taste with pepper. Gently toss the pasta to coat and serve immediately, scattered with Parmesan shavings.

### variation

**Alfredo light** For a lighter version of this dish, omit the butter and cream, and toss the hot pasta in 4 tablespoons of extra virgin olive oil and 115g (4oz) of freshly grated Parmesan cheese.

# fideua

*✣ s p a i n ✣*

This Catalan noodle paella, with a tasty mixture of seafood, is hearty and filling. For extra zing, add a little garlic to the dish. Serve with chunks of crusty bread to mop up the juices.

**PREP** 15 MINS ❖ **COOK** 25 MINS ❖ **SERVES** 4

pinch of **saffron threads**

750ml (1¼ pints) hot **fish stock**

2–3 tbsp **olive oil**

1 **onion**, finely chopped

2 **garlic cloves**, crushed

3 ripe **tomatoes**, skinned, deseeded, and chopped

1 tsp **sweet** or **smoked pimentón**

300g (10oz) **dried spaghetti** or **linguine**, broken into 5cm (2in) lengths

225g (8oz) **raw prawns**, peeled and deveined

8 small **scallops**, cut in half

12 **clams** or **mussels**

225g (8oz) **firm white fish**, such as cod, haddock, or monkfish, cut into 2cm (¾in) pieces

140g (5oz) frozen **peas**

**salt** and freshly ground **black pepper**

2 tbsp chopped **flat-leaf parsley**

1 Place the saffron threads in a small bowl and add 2 tablespoons of the fish stock. Set aside.

2 Heat the oil in a large frying pan or paella pan over a medium heat. Add the onion and garlic, and fry for 5–8 minutes, or until soft and translucent, stirring frequently. Add the tomatoes and pimentón, and cook for a further 5 minutes. Add the saffron with its soaking liquid and half the remaining stock, increase the heat, and bring to the boil.

3 Add the spaghetti, reduce the heat, and simmer, uncovered, stirring occasionally for 5 minutes. Add the prawns, scallops, clams, white fish, and peas, and cook for a further 5 minutes, or until the pasta and fish are cooked through. If the mixture begins to dry out too much, add a little more stock. Season to taste, sprinkle with the parsley, and serve hot, straight from the pan.

# orecchiette con cime di rape

*❖ italy ❖*

A speciality of Puglia, here orecchiette are tossed in an aromatic green sauce made by cooking broccoli in olive oil and wine.

**PREP** 10 MINS ❖ **COOK** 25 MINS ❖ **SERVES** 6–8

1kg (2¼lb) **sprouting broccoli, broccoli florets,** or **turnip tops**
5–6 tbsp **olive oil**
2–3 **garlic cloves,** finely chopped
2–3 **anchovy fillets,** drained and chopped
150ml (5fl oz) **white wine**
2–3 **peperoncini** or **dried chillies,** deseeded and torn
500g packet **orecchiette**
**salt**

1 Prepare the broccoli sprouts by trimming the ends of the stalks and stripping out any stringy leaves. Rinse and chop into short lengths, keeping the flower bunches intact.

2 In a large pan, heat the oil gently with the garlic and fry for 1–2 minutes, until soft but not brown, then mash in the anchovies. Add the broccoli, wine, peperoncini, and a splash of water, bring to the boil, cover, and simmer for about 20 minutes, until the broccoli is soft and the juices are reduced to an oily dressing. Taste and add salt, if you like.

3 Meanwhile, bring a large pan of salted water to the boil, add the orecchiette, and cook for about 15 minutes, until the pasta is al dente. Drain and stir into the broccoli sauce. Mix everything together with a spoon and cook gently for a further 5 minutes to finish softening the pasta and allow it to soak up the oil.

**cook's tip**

To prepare your own fresh orecchiette, you will need *grano duro* flour or fine-ground semolina, a little salt, and enough hot water to work the dry ingredients into a softish dough. Knead the dough into a smooth rope, cut off hazelnut-sized pieces, and use the back of a knife to stretch each piece into a little hat, then turn the hat inside out on your thumb to make a cap. The more you practise, the easier it is.

# spaghetti mare e monti

*❖ italy ❖*

The ingredients, as the name of this well-known, low-fat pasta dish suggests, come from the sea (*mare*) and the mountains (*monti*). The dried porcini mushrooms, although little in quantity, pack in a strong flavour.

**PREP** 15 MINS, PLUS SOAKING
**COOK** 20 MINS ❖ **SERVES** 4

15g (½oz) **dried porcini mushrooms,** rinsed
6 ripe **plum tomatoes**
2 tbsp **extra virgin olive oil**
150g (5½oz) **baby button mushrooms**
2 **garlic cloves,** finely chopped
1 **bay leaf**
150ml (5fl oz) **white wine**
225g (8oz) raw **prawns,** peeled and deveined
**salt** and freshly ground **black pepper**
400g (14oz) **dried spaghetti**

1 Place the porcini in a bowl and pour over 150ml (5fl oz) boiling water. Leave to soak for 30 minutes. Remove the mushrooms with a slotted spoon and chop, then strain the soaking liquid through a fine sieve and reserve.

2 Meanwhile, place the tomatoes in a heatproof bowl. Score the skin of each with the point of a sharp knife, then pour over enough boiling water to cover. Leave for 30 seconds, then drain, peel, deseed, and roughly chop.

3 Heat the oil in a large frying pan. Add the porcini and button mushrooms and fry, stirring, until golden. Add the garlic and cook for 30 seconds. Pour in the reserved porcini soaking liquid, add the bay leaf, and cook over a high heat until the liquid is reduced to a glaze. Reduce the heat to low.

4 Pour in the wine and tomatoes, and simmer for 7–8 minutes, or until the liquid is slightly reduced and the tomatoes break down. Remove the bay leaf, add the prawns, and cook for 3–5 minutes, or until cooked through. Season to taste.

5 Meanwhile, cook the spaghetti in plenty of lightly salted boiling water for 10 minutes, or according to the packet instructions. Drain thoroughly, then return to the pan. Add the sauce, toss to combine, and serve at once.

# ravioli alla fiorentina
*✦ italy ✦*

Little egg-pasta envelopes stuffed with fresh white ricotta and finely chopped
spinach are finished with a simple dressing of melted butter and sage leaves.
The elegant Florentines love their spinach and can't live without butter and cream.

**PREP** 20 MINS, PLUS RESTING ✦ **COOK** 1¼ HRS
**SERVES** 6-8

### ingredients

**for the pasta**
200g (7oz) Italian "00" flour
pinch of salt
3 eggs
1 tbsp olive oil

**for the filling**
350g (12oz) young spinach leaves
200g (7oz) cream cheese or ricotta
1 tbsp grated Parmesan cheese
1 egg
½ tsp freshly grated nutmeg
salt and freshly ground black pepper

**to serve**
50g (2oz) melted butter
2–3 tbsp olive oil
a dozen sage leaves

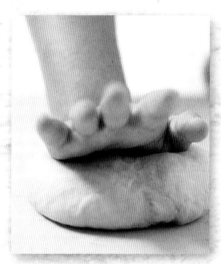 

1 **Sift the flour and salt** onto a work surface, and make a well in the middle. Beat the eggs with the oil and pour into the well. Work together the ingredients to form a soft, sticky dough. Knead well for about 10 minutes, until smooth and elastic. Wrap in oiled cling film and leave to rest for 30 minutes.

2 **For the filling**, rinse the spinach, place in a large pan over a high heat, cover, and cook in its water with a little salt, shaking the pan, for 2–3 minutes, until the leaves wilt. Drain in a colander, pressing out the water. Cool, squeeze, and chop finely. Mash the cream cheese with the Parmesan and egg, mash in the spinach, and season with nutmeg, salt, and pepper.

3 **Cut the dough in half** and roll out one half to a 3mm (⅛in) thick rectangle. Place teaspoonfuls of filling in mounds, 4cm (1½in) apart. Roll out the other half to a slightly larger rectangle. Brush a little water between the mounds and place the second sheet loosely over the top. Press down the pasta between the mounds with your fingertips to seal.

4 **Using a pasta wheel** or sharp knife, cut between the mounds to make squares. Transfer to a lightly-floured kitchen towel and leave to dry for 40–60 minutes. Heat a medium-sized serving or gratin dish to warm. Melt the butter and use a trickle to grease the dish. Reserve the remaining butter.

5 **Bring a large pan of salted water to the boil** and cook the ravioli in batches for 4–5 minutes – they're ready when they float to the surface. Remove with a slotted spoon, drain on kitchen paper, and place in the gratin dish, trickle with a little melted butter, and cover with foil to keep warm.

6 **In a small frying pan**, heat just enough olive oil to cover the base of the pan and drop in 4–5 sage leaves at a time, allowing them to fry for 25–30 seconds until just transparent – do not let them brown. Add the remaining butter to the pan and bubble up. Top the ravioli with the crisp sage leaves and hot oil and butter just before serving.

# spaghetti frutti di mare

*italy*

Use the season's freshest seafood for this delicious spaghetti dish. While preparing the mussels, tap and discard any that do not close. Cooking the mussels and squid with wine and lemon fills them with flavour.

**PREP** 25 MINS ❖ **COOK** 20 MINS ❖ **SERVES** 4

3 tbsp **olive oil**
1 small **onion**, finely chopped
2 **garlic cloves**, finely chopped
500ml (16fl oz) chunky **passata**
¼ tsp **chilli flakes**
450g (1lb) **mussels**, cleaned
450g (1lb) **baby squid**, cleaned and tubes sliced into rings
4 tbsp **dry white wine**
½ **lemon**, sliced
450g (1lb) **dried spaghetti**
**salt** and freshly ground **black pepper**
12 large raw **prawns**, peeled and deveined
3 tbsp chopped **flat-leaf parsley**

1 Heat the oil in a large saucepan and fry the onion and garlic over a low heat, stirring, for 3–4 minutes, or until softened but not brown. Add the passata and chilli flakes, then simmer for 1 minute.

2 Meanwhile, place the mussels and squid in a large pan with the wine and lemon slices, cover tightly, and bring to the boil. Cook for 3–4 minutes, or until the shells have opened, shaking the pan occasionally. Remove from the heat, strain the liquid through a fine sieve, and reserve. Discard the lemon slices and any unopened shells. Reserve a few mussels in their shells for garnishing; remove the rest from their shells.

3 Cook the spaghetti in a large pan of lightly salted boiling water until al dente, or according to the packet instructions.

4 Meanwhile, add the reserved shellfish liquid to the sauce and simmer, uncovered, for 2–3 minutes, or until slightly reduced. Add the prawns and simmer, stirring, for 2 minutes, or until just pink. Add the shellfish, stir in the parsley, and season to taste.

5 Drain the pasta thoroughly, return to the pan, and toss in the seafood and sauce. Tip into a large serving bowl, place the reserved mussels in their shells on the side, and serve.

# linguine alle vongole

*italy*

Versions of this popular combination of thin linguine and clams are cooked all along the Italian Mediterranean and Adriatic coasts. Serve with crusty ciabatta as a substantial starter or lunch dish.

**PREP** 5 MINS ❖ **COOK** 20 MINS ❖ **SERVES** 4

2 tbsp **olive oil**
1 **onion**, finely chopped
2 **garlic cloves**, finely chopped
400g can chopped **tomatoes**
2 tbsp **sun-dried tomato purée**
120ml (4fl oz) **dry white wine**
2 x 140g jars **clams** in natural juice, strained, with the juice reserved
**salt** and freshly ground **black pepper**
350g (12oz) **dried linguine**
4 tbsp finely chopped **flat-leaf parsley**, plus extra to garnish

1 Heat the oil in a large saucepan over a medium heat. Add the onion and garlic and fry, stirring frequently, for 5 minutes, or until softened. Add the tomatoes with the juices, tomato purée, wine, and reserved clam juice. Season to taste, then bring to the boil, stirring. Reduce the heat to low, partially cover the pan and simmer for 10–15 minutes, stirring occasionally.

2 Meanwhile, bring a large pan of lightly salted water to the boil over a high heat. Add the linguine, stir, and boil for 10 minutes, until al dente or according to the packet instructions. Drain the pasta into a large colander and shake to remove any excess water.

3 Add the clams and parsley to the sauce and simmer for a futher 1–2 minutes to heat through. Season to taste.

4 Add the linguine to the sauce and use two forks to toss and combine all the ingredients so that the pasta is well coated and the clams evenly distributed. Sprinkle with extra parsley and serve immediately.

**cook's tip**

The tomato sauce in step 1 can be made a day in advance and reheated before adding the clams and parsley.

# spaghetti puttanesca
*italy*

This spicy pasta dish made with store cupboard ingredients is popular all over Italy. Serve it with a simple spinach salad and some crusty bread for a quick supper.

**PREP** 15 MINS ❖ **COOK** 25 MINS ❖ **SERVES** 4

4 tbsp **extra virgin olive oil**

2 **garlic cloves**, finely chopped

½ fresh **red chilli**, deseeded and finely chopped

6 canned **anchovies**, drained and finely chopped

115g (4oz) **black olives**, pitted and chopped

1–2 tbsp **capers**, rinsed and drained

450g (1lb) **tomatoes**, skinned, deseeded, and chopped

450g (1lb) **dried spaghetti**

salt

chopped **flat-leaf parsley** or oregano, to serve

**Parmesan cheese**, grated, to serve

1 Heat the oil in a saucepan, add the garlic and chilli, and cook gently for 2 minutes, or until the garlic is slightly coloured. Add the anchovies, olives, capers, and tomatoes. Stir, breaking down the anchovies to a paste.

2 Reduce the heat and simmer, uncovered, for 10–15 minutes, or until the sauce has thickened, stirring frequently.

3 Cook the spaghetti in plenty of lightly salted boiling water for 10 minutes until al dente, or according to the packet instructions. Drain.

4 Toss the spaghetti with the sauce, and serve sprinkled with parsley and Parmesan cheese.

**variation**

**Spaghetti all'arrabiata** Make as given in the recipe, but omit the olives, capers, and anchovies. Use 1 whole fresh red chilli instead of ½ and replace the parsley with the same quantity of basil leaves.

# tagliatelle all'amatriciana

*italy*

This fresh tomato pasta sauce, flavoured with tiny cubes of pancetta, gets its spicy kick from a finely chopped hot red chilli.

**PREP** 20 MINS ❖ **COOK** 25 MINS ❖ **SERVES** 4

900g (2lb) ripe **tomatoes**

2 tbsp **extra virgin olive oil**

115g (4oz) **pancetta**, cut into cubes

1 **onion**, finely chopped

1 **celery stick**, finely chopped

2 **garlic cloves**, crushed

1 **hot red chilli**, deseeded and finely chopped

**salt** and freshly ground **black pepper**

600g (1lb 5oz) **fresh tagliatelle** or 450g (1lb) **dried tagliatelle**

1 Place the tomatoes in a heatproof bowl. Score each with the point of a sharp knife, then pour over enough boiling water to cover them. Leave the tomatoes for 30 seconds, or until the skins start to split. Drain, leave to cool a little, then peel and roughly chop.

2 Heat the oil in a heavy-based non-stick saucepan and cook the pancetta over a medium-high heat for 2–3 minutes, or until beginning to brown. Remove from the pan with a slotted spoon, leaving the fat behind, and transfer to a small plate. Reduce the heat.

3 Add the onion and celery to the pan, and cook for 5–6 minutes, or until softened. Stir in the garlic and chilli, and cook for a further 1 minute, then add the tomatoes, and season to taste. Simmer gently, stirring occasionally, for 15 minutes, or until the sauce is well reduced and thick.

4 Meanwhile, in a large pan filled with lightly salted boiling water, add the pasta and cook for 1–2 minutes if using

fresh tagliatelle, or 10–12 minutes if using dried, or until the pasta is al dente. Drain well.

5 Tip the pasta back into the pan, add the pancetta, and pour in the sauce. Gently toss together, season to taste, and serve immediately.

## cook's tip

If you can't find ripe, full-flavoured tomatoes, use two 400g cans of plum tomatoes with their juice instead. Taste the sauce, and if it needs a little more flavour, stir in 1 tablespoon of sun-dried tomato paste.

# pappardelle al ragù
### ✦ *italy* ✦

Perfect for the winter, this meaty, slow-simmered sauce goes well with spaghetti or tagliatelle, but can also be used in a lasagne. The milk helps to thicken the sauce, while also making it quite rich.

**PREP** 15 MINS ✦ **COOK** 2 HRS ✦ **SERVES** 4

30g (1oz) **butter**
2 tbsp **olive oil**
100g (3½oz) **pancetta**, diced
1 small **onion**, finely chopped
1 **celery stick**, finely chopped
1 **carrot**, finely chopped
2 **garlic cloves**, crushed
400g (14oz) **lean beef steak**, minced

100ml (3½fl oz) hot **beef stock**, plus more if needed
2 tbsp **tomato purée**
400g can chopped **tomatoes**
**salt** and freshly ground **black pepper**
75ml (2½fl oz) **milk**, warmed
450g (1lb) **dried pappardelle**
**Parmesan cheese**, grated, to serve

1 Melt the butter with the oil in a deep, heavy-based saucepan and fry the pancetta for 1–2 minutes. Add the onion, celery, carrot, and garlic, and continue to fry, stirring occasionally, for 10 minutes, or until softened but not browned.

2 Stir in the meat, breaking up any lumps, then cook for a further 10 minutes, or until evenly coloured, stirring frequently. Add the stock, tomato purée, and tomatoes, season to taste, then bring to the boil.

3 Reduce the heat to very low, cover the pan, and simmer very gently for 1½ hours. Stir occasionally to prevent sticking, adding more stock, if necessary. Stir in the milk, cover, and simmer for a further 30 minutes.

4 Bring a large pan of lightly salted water to the boil. Add the pappardelle and simmer for 8–10 minutes, or until al dente. Drain well, spoon the meat sauce over, and serve with freshly grated Parmesan.

### variation

**Pappardelle alla bolognese** For a richer sauce, cook the vegetables and pancetta in step 1. Replace half the minced steak with 200g (7oz) of lean pork mince and 100g (3½oz) of dried macaroni, and continue with the recipe as above.

# pasta alla carbonara
### ❖ *italy* ❖

A popular Italian classic, here the heat from the drained pasta cooks the eggs, which mixes with the Parmesan cheese to make a creamy sauce.

**PREP** 10 MINS ❖ **COOK** 10 MINS ❖ **SERVES** 4-6

salt and freshly ground black pepper

450g (1lb) dried pasta, such as tagliatelle, spaghetti, or linguine

4 tbsp olive oil

175g (6oz) pancetta or cured unsmoked bacon rashers, rind removed and finely chopped

2 garlic cloves, crushed

5 large eggs

75g (2½oz) Parmesan cheese, grated, plus extra to serve

75g (2½oz) pecorino cheese, grated, plus extra to serve

a few sprigs of thyme, to garnish

1 Bring a large saucepan of salted water to the boil. Add the pasta, bring to the boil, and cook for 10 minutes, until al dente or according to the packet instructions.

2 Meanwhile, heat half the oil in a large frying pan over a medium heat. Add the pancetta and garlic, and fry, stirring, for 5–8 minutes, or until the pancetta is crispy.

3 In a bowl, beat the eggs and cheeses together, and add pepper to taste. Drain the pasta well and return to the pan. Add the egg mixture, pancetta, and the remaining oil, and stir until the pasta is coated. Serve while still hot, sprinkled with the extra cheese and garnished with sprigs of thyme.

# lasagne al sugo di funghi
### ❖ *italy* ❖

This baked lasagne and mushroom recipe comes from Le Marche in central Italy, where wild mushrooms, including porcini, are plentiful.

**PREP** 20 MINS ❖ **COOK** 40 MINS ❖ **SERVES** 5

250g (9oz) wild or cultivated mushrooms or 50g (1¾oz) dried porcini, soaked and drained

50g (1¾oz) unsalted butter

2 tbsp plain flour

600ml (1 pint) full-fat milk

4 tbsp diced prosciutto

250g (9oz) dried lasagne

salt and freshly ground black pepper

2 tbsp olive oil, plus extra for greasing

4 tbsp mascarpone or double cream

4 tbsp grated Parmesan or pecorino cheese

1 egg, whisked

1 Clean the mushrooms and wipe over the caps – do not rinse. Depending on the size, slice or dice them. In a heavy-based saucepan, melt half the butter, add the mushrooms, and fry until they lose most of their moisture. Remove and set aside.

2 In the same pan, melt the remaining butter, then stir in the flour and fry gently until the mixture looks sandy, but do not let it darken. Gradually whisk in the milk, until you have a smooth sauce – it is easier if you heat the milk first. Boil and stir for 10 minutes, until thick enough to coat the back of a wooden spoon. Remove a ladleful of the sauce and reserve. Stir the mushrooms and prosciutto into the remaining sauce.

3 Meanwhile, cook the lasagne in plenty of boiling salted water for 6–7 minutes, until it begins to soften but is still al dente. Tip the pasta sheets into a colander, pass briefly under cold running water to stop it from cooking further, and drain. Separate out the sheets, leaving them a little moist.

4 Preheat the oven to 180°C (350°F/Gas4). Lightly oil the base of a medium-sized gratin dish and line with about one-third of the pasta. Spread with half the mushroom sauce and top with another layer of pasta. Repeat the layering. Whisk the reserved sauce with mascarpone, cheese, and egg. Top the pasta with the sauce and sprinkle with the reserved cheese and a trickle of oil. Bake for 10–15 minutes, until brown and bubbling.

# a taste of
# SICILY

Practically in the centre of the Mediterranean, blessed with strong sun and rich volcanic soil, the island of Sicily attracted endless waves of colonists and settlers in the 2000 years before it became part of the Italian nation. All played their part in developing the distinctive cuisine. The influence of early Greek visitors is felt strongest on the east coast around Catania – fish, olives, broad beans, pistachios, and fresh vegetables. In the 10th and 11th centuries, the Arabs brought with them irrigation, resulting in bountiful varied crops, particularly the essential citrus fruit. With them also came an enduring fondness for saffron, spices, aubergines, rice and couscous, apricots, dried fruit, and very sweet concoctions. The Spaniards brought produce from the brand new world they had discovered – maize, peppers, and tomatoes. These thrive in Sicily, as well as excellent hard durum wheat – great for pasta.

**Capers**, tiny buds and larger milder berries, preserved in salt from the region's seaside salt-flats, add a pleasant astringent note to caponata and lemony dressings.

**Sardines**, the island's most popular fish, shimmering whole on market stalls, are also sold de-boned ready to be stuffed, rolled, and baked.

Piazza della Republica in Marsala

**Saffron** strands add colour and flavour to pasta and other dishes.

**Prawns** are a favourite seafood, with their firm sweet flesh. The redder they are, the more highly prized.

**Ricotta**, both fresh and creamy soft, is delicious with pistachios and other nuts, or matured with a strong flavour to add to sauces.

**Sundried plum tomatoes** are often sold halved, still plump, and intensely flavoured.

**Watermelon**, with its ability to store water, is much in demand in hot, dry summers as a refreshing thirst quencher

**Sumptuous vegetables** like this Romanesco broccoli don't travel far to market and arrive there at the peak of their freshness.

Ballarò market in Palermo is packed with bright, tempting produce and echoes with the cries of stall holders.

**Dried mullet roe**, may not be unique to the island, but it is the roe of choice for most Italians.

# Lunch in Catania

There is no rushing over lunch in Sicily. It is a substantial, structured meal whatever the temperature outside. There is wine and water on the table, bread, olive oil, and toasted almonds. Pasta with aubergine sauce is followed by grilled swordfish with a zingy sauce, with capers and lemon wedges on the side, sliced tomatoes, new potatoes, and chopped black olives. For dessert, there are small cannoli filled with ricotta, coffee granita, and grapes to pick at.

**Pasta alla norma**
page 110

**Tomato salad**

**Capers**

**Pesce spada in salmoriglio**
page 138

**Granita di caffé expresso**
page 290

**Toasted almonds**

**Cannoli**
page 302

# pasta alla norma
*❖ sicily ❖*

Named after Bellini's famous opera, this popular Sicilian pasta dish is often made with penne. The aubergine sauce is traditionally finished off with ricotta salata, a tangy, dried variation of ricotta.

**PREP** 15 MINS, PLUS DRAINING
**COOK** 20-25 MINS ❖ **SERVES** 4

2 medium **aubergines**, cut into
  2cm (¾in) cubes

**salt** and freshly ground **black pepper**

3–4 tbsp **olive oil**

1 tsp fresh **oregano** or ½ tsp dried oregano

1–2 **garlic cloves**, crushed

½ tsp **chilli powder**

2 large **tomatoes**, blanched, peeled,
  deseeded, and finely chopped or
  ½ x 400g can chopped tomatoes

2–3 tbsp snipped **basil**, plus extra to garnish

350–400g (12–14oz) **dried penne**

125–150g (4½–5½oz) grated **ricotta salata**,
  **pecorino**, **feta**, or **Parmesan cheese**

1 Place the aubergines in a colander. Sprinkle a generous teaspoon of salt over the aubergines, mix, and cover with a weighted plate. Drain for 30 minutes. Rinse thoroughly, place in a clean kitchen towel, roll up, and press down to extract as much moisture as possible.

2 Bring a pan of lightly salted water to the boil for the penne. Meanwhile, heat 2 tablespoons of the oil in a large sauté or non-stick frying pan until very hot. Spread the aubergine in the pan, stir, and cook for 3 minutes. Add the oregano, garlic, and chilli powder. Season lightly and cook for 3–5 minutes, stirring frequently.

3 Stir in the tomatoes and basil. Add a little oil, stir, and cook for 2 minutes. Reduce the heat, partly cover, and simmer very gently for 10–15 minutes, stirring occasionally.

4 Meanwhile, cook the penne in the boiling water until al dente, or according to the packet instructions. Drain and tip into the pan with the aubergines and tomatoes. Toss for 1–2 minutes until well coated. Remove from the heat, add a little oil, stir in the cheese, and toss well. Garnish with the basil and season with plenty of black pepper.

# ziti al forno con salsiccia e pomodoro
*❖ italy ❖*

Ziti are small, dried pasta tubes like straight macaroni, but slightly larger in size. Here they are baked in a rich, meaty sauce.

**PREP** 20 MINS ❖ **COOK** 50 MINS ❖ **SERVES** 4

500g (1lb 2oz) **Italian sausages**, pricked
  with a fork

2 large **onions**, coarsely chopped

2 **garlic cloves**, finely chopped

2 x 400g can chopped **tomatoes**

2 tbsp chopped **basil**

**salt** and freshly ground **black pepper**

500g (1lb 2oz) **ziti**

125g (4½oz) **mozzarella cheese**, shredded

**basil leaves**, to garnish

1 Bring a saucepan of water to the boil. Place the sausages in the pan and simmer for 2 minutes, or until the casings become pale. Drain and allow to cool, then remove the casings and break up the meat.

2 In a large, deep frying pan, cook the sausagemeat for 5 minutes. Add the onions and garlic, and cook for a further 3 minutes, or until soft. Stir in the tomatoes and basil, and season to taste. Simmer for 10 minutes, or until the sauce has thickened, stirring occasionally.

3 Meanwhile, preheat the oven to 180°C (350°F/Gas 4). Bring a large pan of salted water to the boil and add the ziti. Drain the ziti 3 minutes before the time recommended on the packet, then return them to the pan.

5 Mix most of the sausage and tomato sauce with the ziti. Divide between 4 heatproof serving dishes, or place in 1 large 33 x 23cm (13 x 9in) casserole dish, then spoon the reserved sauce on top. Sprinkle with the cheese.

6 Bake for 20 minutes, or until the sauce bubbles and the cheese is melted and golden. Serve hot, garnished with basil leaves.

# cannelloni con spinacio e ricotta

*italy*

Fresh Napoli sauce adds a slightly tangy quality to this filling tri-coloured pasta dish. Use store-bought béchamel sauce to save time.

**PREP** 25 MINS ❖ **COOK** 35 MINS
**SERVES** 4

450g (1lb) cooked **spinach**
250g (9oz) **ricotta cheese**
1 **egg**, beaten
60g (2oz) **Parmesan cheese**, grated
pinch of freshly grated **nutmeg**
**salt** and freshly ground **black pepper**
16 dried **cannelloni tubes**
**oil**, for greasing
600ml (1 pint) **béchamel sauce**

### For the Napoli sauce
1 tbsp **extra virgin olive oil**
1 small **red onion**, finely chopped
1 **celery stick**, finely chopped
2 **garlic cloves**, crushed
400g can chopped **tomatoes**
75ml (2½fl oz) hot **vegetable stock**
handful of **basil leaves**, torn

1 Drain the spinach well, squeeze out any extra water, then chop roughly. Place the ricotta in a bowl and mix in the beaten egg and half the Parmesan. Add the spinach, then season to taste with nutmeg, salt, and pepper. Spoon the filling into the cannelloni tubes and place them in a lightly oiled baking dish.

2 For the Napoli sauce, heat the oil in a saucepan and gently cook the onion for 5–6 minutes, or until beginning to soften. Add the celery and garlic, cook for 2 minutes, then stir in the tomatoes and stock, and simmer for 15 minutes, or until the vegetables are soft and the sauce has reduced a little. Stir in the basil.

3 Preheat the oven to 190°C (375°F/Gas 5). Pour the béchamel sauce over the cannelloni tubes, then spoon the Napoli sauce on top. Sprinkle over the remaining Parmesan. Bake for 35 minutes, or until the top is golden and bubbling, and the cannelloni are cooked. Serve with a baby leaf salad.

**variation**

**Spinach and mushroom cannelloni**
Replace the ricotta in the filling with 200g (7oz) mushrooms, chopped and fried, and 60g (2oz) diced ham.

# pastitsio makaronia

*❖ greece ❖*

This layered casserole of pasta and meat sauce topped with a thick white sauce belongs to the same culinary grouping as Italy's lasagne and Greece's national dish, moussaka.

**PREP** 10 MINS ❖ **COOK** 1 HR ❖ **SERVES** 4-6

350g (12oz) dried large **tubular pasta**, such as tubetti, penne, rigatoni, or ziti
**salt** and freshly ground **black pepper**
**olive oil** or **butter**, for dressing and greasing
2–3 tbsp grated **hard cheese**

### For the meat sauce
2–3 tbsp **olive oil**
2 medium **onions**, chopped
2–3 **garlic cloves**, chopped
500g (1lb 2oz) **minced lamb** or **beef**
1 glass **red wine**

500g (1lb 2oz) fresh or canned **tomatoes**, skinned and chopped
2 tbsp **tomato paste**
1–2 **bay leaves**
short **cinnamon stick**
**sugar** (optional)

### For the topping
600ml (1 pint) **full-fat milk**
2 **eggs**, plus 1 yolk
4 tbsp grated **hard cheese**
freshly grated **nutmeg**
2–3 tbsp grated **cheese**, such as graviera and kefalotiri, to garnish
2–3 tbsp **fresh breadcrumbs**, to garnish

1 For the meat sauce, heat the oil in a large pan and gently fry the onions and garlic until soft– but do not brown. Add the meat and mash into the hot juices until it is no longer pink. Add the wine and boil for 1–2 minutes, until the steam no longer smells of alcohol. Add the tomatoes, tomato paste, bay leaves, and cinnamon, and leave to simmer gently for 30 minutes, until the meat is tender and the sauce reduced. Taste and season with salt, pepper, and sugar, if you like. Set aside.

2 Cook the pasta in salted boiling water for 15–18 minutes, until al dente. Drain, toss with a little oil and cheese, and set aside.

3 For the topping, whisk the milk with the eggs, hard cheese, nutmeg, salt, and pepper. Set aside.

4 Preheat the oven to 180°C (350°F/Gas 4). Grease the base of a 25 x 25cm (10 x 10in) gratin dish and spread in half the macaroni. Remove the bay leaf and the cinnamon stick from the meat sauce.

5 Cover the macaroni with the sauce and top with the remaining macaroni, smoothing into the corners and patting it down. Drizzle over the milk-egg mixture.

6 Bake for 30–45 minutes, until the top is firm and golden. Sprinkle with the cheese mixed with the breadcrumbs, dot with a few scraps of butter or a drizzle of oil, and slip under the grill to bubble and brown the top. Serve immediately.

# risotto primavera

*italy*

Full of spring flavours, you can mix and match vegetables, such as French beans or broccoli, depending on what you have to hand. If you are not cooking for vegetarians, use chicken stock instead of vegetable stock.

**PREP** 15 MINS ❖ **COOK** 1 HR ❖ **SERVES** 4-6

2 tbsp **olive oil**, plus extra for frying
50g (1¾oz) **butter**
1 **onion**, finely chopped
**salt** and freshly ground **black pepper**
3 **garlic cloves**, finely chopped
300g (10oz) **arborio rice** or **carnaroli rice**
250ml (9fl oz) **white wine**
900ml (1½ pints) hot **vegetable stock**
125g (4½oz) fresh or frozen **broad beans**

bunch of **asparagus spears**, trimmed and chopped into bite-sized pieces
2 small **courgettes**, diced
30g (1oz) grated **Parmesan cheese**, plus extra to serve

1 Heat the oil and half the butter in a large heavy-based pan over a medium heat. Add the onion and cook for 3–4 minutes until soft. Season, then add the garlic and cook for a minute.

2 Stir through the rice and turn it in the oily butter so all the grains are coated. Cook for a few seconds. Increase the heat, add the wine, and bubble for 1–2 minutes until it has been absorbed. Add a ladleful of hot stock at a time (keeping the rest simmering in a saucepan) and stir, cooking until it has been absorbed. Continue doing this for 30–40 minutes, or until the rice is cooked to al dente and is creamy.

3 Meanwhile, add the broad beans to a large pan of boiling salted water, and cook for 3–4 minutes. Drain well and set aside. Heat a little oil in a separate frying pan over a medium heat, add the asparagus and courgettes, and cook for 2–3 minutes until they just begin to colour. Stir all the vegetables into the risotto, dot the remaining butter all over, and stir it in. Then stir in the Parmesan and season to taste. Serve with more Parmesan and a lightly dressed wild rocket and tomato salad on the side.

# risi bisi
### ❖ *italy* ❖

Rice counts as a "pasta" course in Italy, and is served after the antipasto, before the meat dish. Italians like their rice as chewy and al dente as their pasta. This classic dish of rice and peas is great comfort food.

**PREP** 5 MINS ❖ **COOK** 25-30 MINS ❖ **SERVES** 4

2 tbsp **olive oil** or 50g (1¾oz) **unsalted butter**, plus extra butter to serve

1 medium **onion**, finely chopped

250g (9oz) **risotto rice** (arborio, roma, or carnaroli)

200ml (7fl oz) **white wine**

600ml (1 pint) hot **chicken** or **vegetable stock**

250g (9oz) shelled **peas**, fresh or frozen

**salt** and freshly ground **black pepper**

grated **Parmesan** or **Grana Padano cheese**, to garnish

1 Heat the oil or butter in a medium saucepan. Add the onion and fry, until soft and golden. Stir in the rice and fry gently until the grains are transparent.

2 Add the wine and boil to evaporate the alcohol. Add enough stock to cover the rice generously and allow to boil. Add the peas, season, and boil again. Reduce the heat, cover loosely with a lid, and simmer for 15–18 minutes, adding more hot stock or water if it becomes dry.

3 When the grains become soft but still retain a nutty little heart, remove the pan from the heat. The peas should have lost their emerald green colour. Finish with butter, pepper, and grated cheese.

# fonduta with vegetables
### ❖ *italy* ❖

This nourishing vegetarian dish is a variation of the Italian classic from northern Italy, where polenta is favoured over pasta.

**PREP** 5 MINS ❖ **COOK** 25 MINS ❖ **SERVES** 4

175g (6oz) **polenta**

2 tbsp **butter**

175g (6oz) **fontina cheese**, coarsely grated

125ml (4½fl oz) **milk**

3 large **egg yolks**

pinch of freshly ground **white pepper**

sliced **mushrooms**, to serve

**baby carrots**, to serve

1 To prepare the polenta, bring 1 litre (1¾ pints) water to the boil in a medium saucepan. In a small bowl, combine the polenta with 240ml (8fl oz) water. Stir the polenta mixture into the boiling water and cook, stirring constantly, for 5 minutes, or until thickened. Reduce the heat to low, cover, and cook for 5 minutes. Remove from the heat.

2 Meanwhile, place the butter in a heatproof bowl over a pan of gently simmering water. When the butter has melted, add the cheese and milk. Cook, stirring constantly, until the cheese melts, then add the egg yolks and continue cooking and stirring until the mixture is smooth. Season to taste with pepper.

3 Spoon a quarter of the polenta onto 4 serving plates and form a mound. Using the back of a spoon, make an indentation in each mound. Pour the cheese sauce into each indentation and serve the vegetables alongside.

## cook's tip

When cooking with a bowl over a pan of simmering water, make sure the bottom of the bowl does not touch the water. This ensures very gentle cooking without direct heat, which is ideal for melting chocolate, cooking egg sauces, and (as in this case) melting cheese without overcooking it. Overcooking the cheese would toughen it and prevent it combining with the other ingredients to form a smooth sauce.

# riso con tartufi alla piemontese
### ❖ *italy* ❖

This simple dish of rice cooked in chicken stock is the perfect background for a fresh white truffle. If you can't get the prized *Tuber magnato* (white truffle), use any of the lesser varieties, black or white.

**PREP** 5 MINS ❖ **COOK** 30-40 MINS
**SERVES** 6 8

500g (1lb 2oz) **risotto rice** (arborio, roma, or carnaroli)

about 1 litre (2 pints) hot **chicken stock**, plus extra if required

50g (1¾oz) **unsalted butter**

50g (1¾oz) grated **Parmesan cheese**

1 fresh **truffle** (30–50g/1oz–1¾oz), brushed and wiped

**salt** and freshly ground **black pepper**

1 Rinse the rice with cold water and measure the volume. Measure twice the volume of stock into a large pan, bring to the boil, and add the rice.

2 Meanwhile, preheat the oven to 180°C (350°F/Gas 4). Tip the boiling stock with the rice into an ovenproof casserole with a lid or gratin dish. Cover tightly and bake for 30–40 minutes, until the stock has dried and the rice is tender.

3 Stir half the butter and half the Parmesan into the rice. Scoop off the top layer and set it aside. Using a sharp knife or truffle-grater, grate the truffle onto the rice in fine silky ribbons. Cover with the rest of the rice and dot with the remaining butter and the rest of the Parmesan, then bake for another 10 minutes to crisp the top and develop the fragrance. Taste and adjust the seasoning.

### cook's tip

Use any of the other high value truffles including Italy's lesser white *bianchetto*, *Tuber borchii*; and the two popular French truffles, the Perigord black, *T. melanosporum*, and its cheaper lookalike, *T. aestivum*, the summer truffle.

# polenta al forno
### ❖ *italy* ❖

In this dish from northeast Italy, where cornmeal porridge replaces wheat-based pasta as the staple grain food, slow-cooked polenta is baked between layers of fontina, a cooked-curd Alpine cheese that melts to buttery smoothness.

**PREP** 10 MINS ❖ **COOK** 50 MINS ❖ **SERVES** 8

**salt** and freshly ground **white peppercorns**

300g (10oz) coarse-ground **polenta**

50g (1¾oz) **butter**

250g (9oz) **fontina cheese**, or taleggio, thinly sliced

1 In a saucepan, bring 1.5 litres (2¾ pints) of lightly salted water to the boil. Add the polenta, stirring continuously. Boil for 2–3 minutes, stirring, until the cornmeal begins to splutter. Reduce the heat to a gentle simmer, cover, and leave for 25–30 minutes, until you have a thick, smooth porridge, stirring occasionally. Add more boiling water if necessary. Remove from the heat, beat in half the butter, and season with pepper.

2 Preheat the oven to 220°C (425°F/Gas 7). Rinse a medium gratin dish, leaving it damp. Spread in one-third of the polenta, top with half the fontina, then spread another layer of polenta, top with the rest of the fontina, and smooth the remaining polenta over the top. Dot with the remaining butter. Bake for 15–20 minutes until the cheese has melted and the top is brown and bubbling. Season to taste.

### *how to serve*

Serve as they do in northern Italy, as a dish on its own. For a light lunch, serve with a salad of mustardy leaves – endive, escarole, and chicory.

# malfatti alla fiorentina

*tuscany*

These nutmeg-flavoured bread-dumplings or gnocchi make an elegant Tuscan antipasto. They are shaped using floured hands, which makes them ill-formed – *malfatti* – because you can't really make them look perfect.

**PREP** 25 MINS, PLUS CHILLING
**COOK** 8-10 MINS ❖ **SERVES** 4

2 large handfuls of **spinach leaves**, rinsed
**salt** and freshly ground **black pepper**
4 tbsp **fresh white breadcrumbs**
250g (9oz) **ricotta** or any fresh **curd cheese**
3 large **egg yolks**
50g (1¾oz) grated **Parmesan cheese**
½ tsp **nutmeg**
2–3 tbsp **plain flour**, for dusting
**butter**, for greasing, plus extra to finish
2–3 **sage leaves**, shredded

1 In a lidded pan, place the spinach and add enough water to cover. Cook the spinach, add a little salt, and shake over the heat until the leaves wilt. Drain thoroughly in a sieve, squeezing out any excess water, and chop finely. Allow to cool.

2 In a large bowl, mix the spinach with the breadcrumbs, ricotta, egg yolks, and Parmesan, and season generously with nutmeg, salt, and pepper. Refrigerate for 1–2 hours or overnight. On a floured surface, using lightly floured hands, form the mixture into small pointed sausage shapes. Freeze them, if not using immediately.

3 Bring a pan of salted water to the boil. Lower in a batch of the gnocchi a few at a time without allowing the temperature to drop below a fast simmer. Poach them gently until they bob to the surface. Remove with a slotted spoon and arrange in a lightly greased serving dish. Keep them warm under a damp cloth while you finish poaching.

4 Infuse the melted butter with the sage and drizzle over the gnocchi. Finish with a few more sage leaves crisped in a little more butter, if you like.

### cook's tip

The secret is to make sure the spinach and curd cheese are really dry – squeeze out all the moisture before mixing with the rest of the ingredients. If it is still too wet to work, add more breadcrumbs.

# arancini

*italy*

Crispy on the outside and soft and creamy on the inside, these tasty risotto balls can be served with roast chicken, ham, or pork. They can also be eaten hot or cold as a party nibble with a tomato or sweet chilli dipping sauce.

**PREP** 15 MINS ❖ **COOK** 20-25 MINS
**SERVES** 4-6

175g (6oz) **risotto rice** (arborio, roma, or carnaroli)
1 **vegetable stock cube**
60g (2oz) **Gruyère cheese**, grated
2 tbsp **pesto**
60g (2oz) **dried breadcrumbs**
**oil**, for frying
**basil leaves**, to garnish (optional)

1 Place the rice and stock cube in a saucepan and pour in 900ml (1½ pints) of cold water. Place over a high heat and bring to the boil. Cover and simmer for 15 minutes, or until the rice is just tender. Drain the rice thoroughly, then stir in the cheese and pesto, and allow to cool.

2 Using dampened hands, roll the rice into walnut-sized balls. Roll in the breadcrumbs to coat well.

3 In a frying pan, pour oil to a depth of 1cm (½in) and heat. Fry the balls for 5–10 minutes, or until crisp and golden on the outside. Drain on kitchen paper and serve with basil leaves, if you like. Alternatively, the balls can be deep-fried for 2–3 minutes, or until golden.

### prepare ahead

The balls can be made up to 24 hours in advance and stored in an airtight container in the fridge until required.

# essential herbs

## Close your eyes and imagine a pestle crushing basil leaves, a heap of just-chopped parsley and mint, or warm rosemary foccacia.

**From Andalucia** to the Levant, aromatic herbs make a sensual contribution to a basically frugal everyday diet. Wild or cultivated, herbs grow vigorous and fragrant in the Mediterranean climate and cooks use them knowingly but generously. They pick or buy just the amount they need, then chop or grind them at the last minute. A good trick is to start sparingly, then add more herbs at the end of the cooking time to liven up aromas and flavours. If fresh herbs don't stay fresh long, dried herbs also soon lose their scent, particularly if home dried. If you buy dried herbs, buy small amounts and discard them before the best-by date, unless your nose tells you otherwise.

**Lavender** is excellent used fresh in desserts, custards, and ice cream or dried with chicken, lamb, and oily fish for the sweet balsamic flavour.

**Fennel fronds** are good for stuffing fish or chopped into salads and grain dishes.

**Basil** ranges from sweetly peppery (Greek) to strongly peppery (purple). Don't cook too long, and add more fresh leaves at the last minute.

**Dill** has a fresh aniseed flavour. Use it with fish, rice, salad, and yogurt.

**Rosemary** is strongly aromatic, with a clean, woody flavour – great with lamb, pies, and baking. Use sparingly, as it can overpower gentler seasonings.

**Mint** is good fresh, steamed, or brewed, with salads, potatoes, peas, bulgur wheat, and fruit.

**Marjoram**, sweeter than oregano, has a subtle flavour. Good with pasta, eggs, and chicken.

**Thyme** (common and lemon) is versatile. Dry well and enhance roast vegetables, poultry, and fish.

**Savory** is pleasantly pungent. Use for stuffings, grilled meats, and barbecues.

**Oregano** is pungent – think pizzas and Middle Eastern pies and breads.

**Parsley** is a necessity for tabbouleh and best chopped just before using.

**Sage**, a favourite in Italy and the Eastern Mediterranean, has a pinewood, peppery flavour great with buttery risotto, creamy veal or chicken, soft fresh cheese, and olive oil.

**Coriander** has a powerful, earthy flavour – great with yogurt and a good all-rounder used in moderation.

**Bay leaves**, bruised or crushed, release a slightly bitter woody fragrance. They partner well with other herbs and are great in marinades, meat and vegetable stews, and with baked fish.

## ful medames

### *middle east*

Prepared with Egyptian brown beans, this peasant dish is thought to have originated in ancient Egypt, but is also a traditional staple in Lebanon, Syria, and Jordan. Vegetables or lentils can also be added.

**PREP** 10 MINS, PLUS SOAKING ❖ **COOK** 45 MINS
**SERVES** 4-6

250g (9oz) **brown beans**, soaked overnight

2–3 tbsp **olive oil**

2 **garlic cloves**, crushed

1–2 tsp **cumin seeds**, dry-roasted and crushed

juice of 1 **lemon**

**salt** and freshly ground **black pepper**

1 **red onion**, cut into bite-sized slices

200g (7oz) **feta cheese**, diced or crumbled

bunch of **flat-leaf parsley**, roughly chopped

1 Drain the beans and place in a deep pan. Pour over enough cold water to cover the beans well. Bring to the boil, reduce the heat, and simmer for about 45 minutes, until the beans are tender, but not soft or mushy.

2 Drain the beans and, while they are still warm, tip them into a serving bowl. Add the oil, garlic, and cumin seeds, and mix well. Toss in the lemon juice and season. Serve immediately, accompanied by bowls of red onion, feta, and parsley.

## mujaddara

### *middle east*

This classic dish of rice, lentils, and crispy onions is a great favourite in Lebanon, Jordan, and Syria. It is usually prepared with white rice and red or brown lentils, but there are brown rice versions too.

**PREP** 10 MINS ❖ **COOK** 30 MINS ❖ **SERVES** 4-6

225g (8oz) dried **brown lentils**, well rinsed

3–4 tbsp **olive oil**

2 **onions**, finely chopped, plus 2 **onions**, finely sliced

1 tsp **sugar**

1 tsp **coriander seeds**

2 tsp **cumin seeds**

225g (8oz) long- or medium-grain **white rice**, well rinsed

**salt** and freshly ground **black pepper**

1 scant tsp ground **cinnamon**

3–4 tbsp **sunflower oil**

bunch of **flat-leaf parsley**, roughly chopped

1 Bring a saucepan of water to the boil and add the lentils. Boil for 10 minutes, or until the lentils are tender but still firm. Drain and refresh under cold running water.

2 Heat the olive oil in a heavy-based saucepan and stir in the chopped onions with the sugar for 3–4 minutes, until the onions begin to turn golden. Stir in the coriander and cumin seeds, and toss in the lentils and rice, making sure the grains are coated in the spicy onion mixture. Pour in just enough cold water to cover, season, and bring to the boil. Reduce the heat and simmer gently for about 15 minutes, until the water has been absorbed. Turn off the heat, cover the pan with a clean kitchen towel, and place a lid on top. Steam for a further 10 minutes.

3 Meanwhile, heat the sunflower oil in a shallow pan and stir in the sliced onions. Fry the onions until brown and crispy, then drain on kitchen paper.

4 Toss the rice and lentils with a fork and place the mixture in a serving dish. Sprinkle over the cinnamon and spoon the crispy onions over the top. Garnish with the parsley and serve immediately with a bowl of yogurt, or as an accompaniment to grilled or roasted dishes.

### *how to serve*

A popular street dish, ful medames is often spooned with falafel or meatballs into pitta pouches, or enjoyed with mezze or grilled meat and poultry.

# nohutlu pilav
### ❖ *turkey* ❖

This classic Turkish pilaf was a great favourite amongst the Ottoman sultans and noblemen, who enjoyed it at the end of a meal and ate it with spoons from a single communal dish.

**PREP** 45 MINS, PLUS SOAKING
**COOK** 30 MINS ❖ **SERVES** 4

60g (2oz) dried **chickpeas**, soaked overnight
25g (scant 1oz) **butter**
1 tbsp **olive** or **sunflower oil**
1 **onion**, finely chopped
225g (8oz) long-grain **rice**, well rinsed
600ml (1 pint) hot **chicken stock**
**salt** and freshly ground **black pepper**

1 Drain the chickpeas and place them in a saucepan. Pour over enough cold water to cover them well. Bring to the boil, reduce the heat, and simmer for 45 minutes, until the chickpeas are tender. Drain well.

2 Melt the butter with the oil in a heavy-based pan. Stir in the onion and cook until it softens. Add the rice and chickpeas and cover with 600ml (1 pint) of hot stock or water. Season and bring the liquid to the boil. Reduce the heat and simmer for 10–15 minutes, until almost all the liquid has been absorbed.

3 Turn off the heat, cover the pan with a clean kitchen towel, and place a lid on top. Leave the rice to steam for 10 minutes. Fluff up the rice with a fork and serve with yogurt, or as an accompaniment to stews and any grilled or roasted meat, poultry, or fish dish.

# makhlouta
### ❖ *middle east* ❖

This hearty dish of pulses combined with grains varies throughout the eastern Mediterranean. It is particularly popular amongst the Palestinian communities of Syria and Jordan.

**PREP** 20 MINS ❖ **COOK** 30 MINS ❖ **SERVES** 4-6

115g (4oz) **brown lentils**, rinsed and drained
115g (4oz) **bulgur wheat**, rinsed and drained
1–2 tbsp **olive oil**
knob of **butter**
2 **onions**, finely chopped
2–3 **garlic cloves**, finely chopped
1 tsp **sugar**
2 tsp **cumin seeds**
2 tsp **coriander seeds**
small handful of dried **sage leaves**, crumbled
400g can **kidney beans**, rinsed and drained
400g can **chickpeas**, rinsed and drained
**salt** and freshly ground **black pepper**
1 tsp **paprika**

small bunch of **flat-leaf parsley**, finely chopped, plus a bunch of **leafy parsley stalks**, to garnish
1 **lemon**, cut into wedges

1 Place the lentils in a pan of boiling water, reduce the heat, and simmer for about 20 minutes, until they are tender. Drain and refresh under cold running water.

2 Tip the bulgur wheat into a bowl and pour in just enough boiling water to cover the grains by about 1cm (½in). Cover and leave to swell for about 15 minutes.

3 Heat the oil and butter in a wide, shallow, heavy-based pan and fry the onions for 2 minutes, until soft. Toss in the garlic and sugar with the spices and sage leaves, and cook over a medium heat for 3–4 minutes, until the onions begin to brown.

4 Toss in the beans and chickpeas and cook for 1–2 minutes, followed by the lentils and bulgur wheat. Keep tossing until all the grains and pulses are heated through and season well.

5 Tip the makhlouta onto a serving dish, dust with paprika, and garnish with the chopped parsley. Serve immediately with lemon wedges to squeeze over, a dollop of yogurt, and parsley stalks to chew on.

# kesksou

### ❖ *Morocco* ❖

Technically, couscous is a form of pasta as it is made from semolina flour and water, but it is eaten like a grain. It is Morocco's national dish and is enjoyed throughout North Africa and parts of the eastern Mediterranean.

**PREP** 20 MINS ❖ **COOK** 20 MINS ❖ **SERVES** 4-6

350g (12oz) **couscous**, rinsed and drained
½ tsp **salt**
2 tbsp **sunflower** or **olive oil**
40g (1¼oz) **butter**
2 tbsp flaked **almonds**

1 Preheat the oven to 180°C (350°F/Gas 4). Tip the couscous into an ovenproof dish. Stir the salt into 400ml (14fl oz) of warm water and pour over the couscous. Leave for 10–15 minutes to absorb the water.

2 Using your fingers, rub the oil into the grains to break up the lumps and aerate them. Cut 25g (scant 1oz) of the butter into small cubes, scatter over the couscous, and cover with a piece of foil or dampened greaseproof paper. Place in the oven for 15–20 minutes to heat through.

3 Melt the remaining butter in a heavy-based pan and stir in the almonds until they begin to turn golden brown. Remove and drain the almonds on kitchen paper.

4 Remove the couscous from the oven, then fluff up the grains using a fork. Tip into a serving dish, piling it high like a pyramid, and scatter the almonds over and around it. Serve warm as an accompaniment to tagines and grilled or roasted dishes.

# couscous royale

### ❖ *Morocco* ❖

This richly spiced dish does take some time to prepare, but makes for a colourful Moroccan feast.

**PREP** 10 MINS, PLUS MARINATING
**COOK** 1 HR 20 MINS ❖ **SERVES** 6

450g (1lb) **couscous**
2 tbsp **olive oil**
600g (1lb 5oz) lean **lamb leg**, cut into chunks
6 **chicken drumsticks** and **thighs**
1 large **red onion**, sliced
2 **garlic cloves**, finely chopped
1 **red pepper**, deseeded and diced
1 **aubergine**, diced
4 tsp **harissa paste**
1 tbsp **paprika**
1 tsp ground **turmeric**
2 **courgettes**, sliced
200ml (7fl oz) hot **chicken stock**
400g can **chickpeas**, drained
400g can chopped **tomatoes**
175g (6oz) **chorizo** or cooked **merguez sausage**, thickly sliced
**salt** and freshly ground **black pepper**
large sprig of **thyme**
1 **bay leaf**
chopped **coriander**, to garnish

1 In a pan, cook the couscous according to the packet instructions. Set aside.

2 Heat the oil in a flameproof casserole and brown the lamb and chicken in batches, turning. Remove and drain. Add the onion, garlic, red pepper, and aubergine and fry, stirring, for 3–4 minutes. Stir in the harissa, paprika, and turmeric, and cook for 1 minute.

3 Add the lamb and chicken, courgettes, stock, chickpeas, tomatoes, and chorizo, and season. Bring to the boil, add the thyme and bay leaf, reduce the heat to low, cover, and simmer for 1 hour, or until the meats are tender. Strain the liquid into a wide pan and bring to the boil until reduced. Reserve.

4 Stir the meats and vegetables into the couscous. Pour the reserved liquid over and serve sprinkled with coriander.

# cuscuzu siciliana

*sicily*

While traditional Arab couscous is usually eaten with vegetables and (sometimes) meat, this Sicilian version is partnered with fish and is a speciality of the southern port of Trapani.

**PREP** 30 MINS ❖ **COOK** 20 MINS ❖ **SERVES** 6–8

750g (1lb 10oz) instant **couscous**

**For the fish broth**
1kg (2¼lb) **bony soup-fish**
1 large **onion**, cut into chunks
1 large **carrot**, cut into chunks
2–3 **bay leaves**

short **cinnamon stick**
½ tsp **black peppercorns**
large pinch of **saffron**

**For the fish**
4–5 tbsp **extra virgin olive oil**
1 large **onion**, finely chopped
about 750g (1lb 10oz) ripe **tomatoes**, skinned and chopped
2 tbsp **tomato purée**
4–5 **garlic cloves**, finely chopped
2–3 **peperoncini** or **dried chillies**
500g (1lb 2oz) **calamari**, cleaned and sliced
250g (9oz) **prawns** or **shrimps** (optional)
1kg (2¼lb) assorted **white fish**, cut into chunks
1–2 tbsp **pistachios**, toasted and chopped (optional)

1 Soak the couscous in warm water until the grains are fluffy.

2 Make the fish broth with soup-fish, onion, carrot, bay leaves, cinnamon, peppercorns, saffron, and 2 lites (3½ pints) water. Bring to the boil, then simmer for 20 minutes. Drain and discard the solids.

3 Heat the oil in a pan and fry the onion on a medium heat until soft. Add the tomatoes, tomato purée, garlic, and chillies, and cook until soft, squishing down with a spoon. Add the broth and boil for 10 minutes. Add the calamari and boil. Add the prawns, if using, and fish, boil, and cook for 5–6 minutes, until the fish turns opaque. Season to taste.

4 Ladle some broth over the couscous on a large plate and top with the fish. Garnish with a dusting of pistachios, if using.

# fish and
# shellfish

# samak kibbeh
### *middle east*

The tradition of kibbeh-making extends to fish in the eastern Mediterranean, particularly in Syria and Lebanon. Kibbeh, or "ball-shaped" in Arabic, are popularly served as a main course or as a mezze dish.

**PREP** 30 MINS ❖ **COOK** 12 MINS ❖ **SERVES** 4-6

175g (6oz) **fine bulgur wheat**, rinsed and drained
1 **onion**, finely chopped
450g (1lb) boneless, **firm-fleshed fish fillets**, such as sea bass, cod, or haddock
1–2 tsp ground **turmeric**
small bunch of **coriander**, finely chopped
**salt** and freshly ground **black pepper**
**flour**, for dusting
**sunflower oil**, for frying
1 **lemon**, cut into wedges, to serve

### For the filling
1–2 tbsp **olive oil**
2 **onions**, finely chopped
1 tsp ground **cinnamon**
zest of 1 small **orange**
3–4 dried **sage leaves**, finely crumbled

1 For the filling, heat the olive oil in a small frying pan. Stir in the onions, and cook for 4–5 minutes, until they begin to colour. Add the cinnamon, orange zest, and sage leaves, and season well. Remove from the heat and set aside to cool.

2 For the kibbeh, tip the bulgur into a bowl and pour over enough boiling water to just cover. Place a kitchen towel over the bowl and leave the bulgur for about 10 minutes to absorb the water and expand. Squeeze the bulgur to drain off any excess water and place in a food processor with the onion, fish, turmeric, and coriander. Whizz to form a paste and season.

3 Moisten your hands with water, take small portions of the kibbeh mixture and mould into the shape of an egg. Hollow out a little of each egg with a finger and pack a little of the filling in. Pinch the edges together to seal in the filling and form an egg shape, and then roll them lightly in flour.

4 Heat enough sunflower oil in a heavy-based pan for shallow frying. Fry the kibbeh in batches for 5–6 minutes, until golden brown. Drain on a plate lined with kitchen paper and serve hot with wedges of lemon to squeeze over.

# samak meshwi
### *middle east*

Samak meshwi, or "chargrilled fish" in Arabic, is traditionally enjoyed in the eastern Mediterranean by grilling fish on charcoal, either by placing it on an oiled rack or by threading a kebab stick through it.

**PREP** 35 MINS ❖ **COOK** 6-10 MINS
**SERVES** 4

1 **onion**, finely chopped
2 **garlic cloves**, crushed
1 tsp ground **turmeric**
1 tsp ground **cumin**
1 tsp ground **coriander**
1–2 tbsp **olive oil**, plus extra for brushing
2 good-sized, **firm-fleshed fish**, such as sea bass, sea bream, or trout, gutted, cleaned, and slit open
**salt**
a few sprigs of **thyme**
1 **lime** or **lemon**, cut into wedges, to serve
**flat-leaf parsley**, to garnish

1 Prepare the charcoal grill. For the marinade, place the onion, garlic, and ground spices with the oil in a small bowl and mix well.

2 Cut 2 or 3 slashes into the skin of each fish. Rub the fish inside and out with the spice mixture, sprinkle with salt, and place a few sprigs of thyme inside. Seal the cavity with a wooden or metal skewer. Leave the fish to marinate.

3 Brush a wire rack with oil and place it over the charcoal. Place the fish on the rack and grill for 3–4 minutes, on each side.

4 Slide the grilled fish off the stick and onto a serving dish. Garnish with the parsley, and serve with wedges of lime.

# croûtes à l'ail et aux anchois

*❖ p r o v e n c e ❖*

Anchovies have a strong salty taste, so use them sparingly. They are also plentiful and inexpensive, which make them a popular flavour enhancer. This bold-flavoured fish pairs perfectly with a glass of chilled rosé.

**PREP** 15 MINS ❖ **COOK** 5 MINS ❖ **SERVES** 4

4 thick slices of **rustic bread**
1 **garlic clove**, halved
4 **anchovy fillets**, packed in oil or salt
5 tbsp **olive oil**
½ tsp **red** or **white wine vinegar**
2 tsp finely chopped **flat-leaf parsley**
freshly ground **black pepper**

1 Toast the bread until crisp and golden on both sides. Rub the toast on both sides with the cut sides of the garlic, spearing the garlic on a fork, if you like. Set aside.

2 Drain or rinse the anchovy fillets and pat dry with kitchen paper. In a cup, mash the anchovy fillets, then add the oil and vinegar. Reserve 1 teaspoon of the parsley, and add the rest to the cup. Stir to mix. Season with pepper.

3 Spread the anchovy mixture over one side of each toast. Leave in a warm place, such as the side of the hearth or a low oven, for 2–3 minutes, then sprinkle with the reserved parsley and serve.

# sardines farcies aux épinards

*❖ p r o v e n c e ❖*

It is a sure sign of spring when stuffed sardines start appearing on Provençal menus. Make sure you use small, sustainable fish.

**PREP** 45 MINS ❖ **COOK** 50 MINS ❖ **SERVES** 4

25g (scant 1oz) **unsalted butter**, diced, plus extra softened butter, for greasing
12 fresh **sardines**, about 600g (1lb 5oz) total weight
30g (1oz) mature **Gruyère cheese**, grated
**salt** and freshly ground **black pepper**

**For the spinach stuffing**
750g (1lb 10oz) **young spinach leaves**
**coarse sea salt**
4 tbsp **milk**
25g (scant 1oz) **unsalted butter**
2 **garlic cloves**, crushed
leaves from 3 sprigs of **flat-leaf parsley**, finely chopped
¼ tsp grated **nutmeg**

1 Preheat the oven to 200°C (400°F/Gas 6). Grease a tian or earthenware gratin dish. Clean the sardines under cold running water: cut off the heads with scissors, then open them and remove the innards and the central spine and bones.

2 For the stuffing, rinse the spinach, then place in a non-stick sauté pan and sprinkle with a pinch of coarse salt. Stir over a medium-high heat until wilted. Tip into a colander and leave for 5 minutes, until cool. Squeeze out excess moisture and chop finely.

3 In a pan, bring the milk to a simmer. Season and remove from the heat. Melt the butter in a frying pan over a medium heat. Add the spinach, then add the garlic and parsley and stir well into the spinach. Cook for 1 minute. Beat in the hot milk. Add the nutmeg and adjust the seasoning. Simmer for 5 minutes until it dries a little. Remove from the heat and allow to cool.

4 Open out the sardines flat, skin-side down, placing them with the head end nearest to you. Spread a generous teaspoon of spinach stuffing on each. Roll them up, from head end to tail end. Spread two-thirds of the remaining stuffing in the buttered dish. Arrange the sardines on top and cover with the remaining stuffing. Scatter over the Gruyère and dot with the diced butter. Bake for 15–20 minutes and serve hot.

# sardinas a la plancha

*❖ s p a i n ❖*

Ensure you use sustainable sardines for this delightful Mediterranean dish, where the fish are grilled on the *plancha* – a grill plate that comes as standard on Spanish cookers. You don't need to descale or brush the fish with oil.

**PREP** 15-20 MINS
**COOK** 4-8 MINS ❖ **SERVES** 4

500g (1lb 2oz) fresh **sardines**
1 tbsp **salt**
**lemon quarters**, to serve

1 Gut the sardines – or have the fishmonger do this for you – leaving the heads and scales in place. Gutting is easily done by pushing your index finger through the soft belly and scooping the innards from the cavity. Sprinkle the flanks with salt.

2 Heat a heavy-based metal pan, grill, or barbecue until it is really hot. Grill the sardines fiercely, turning them once, until the skin blisters and turns black. Cook for 2–4 minutes on each side, depending on the thickness of the fish. Serve with quartered lemons and bread.

*how to eat*

Eat the sardines with your fingers, lifting the flesh from the bone from tail to head, leaving a neatly stripped skeleton.

## *essential*
# garlic

Garlic plays many different roles in Mediterranean recipes and has been both a medicinal and a culinary ingredient since the time of the building of the Giza Pyramids.

**Garlic** is extremely versatile – in its mild green infancy, you can add the stalks and bulb to dishes, as with spring onions. Roast young heads with hardly separated cloves alongside lamb as a vegetable. Halve a clove and rub the cut sides on your cooking pot, salad bowl, or toasting breads. Roast or boil unpeeled cloves and squeeze to pop sweet, spicy flesh from the skins. Be more cautious with mature garlic, as pungency increases with age. Take out pungent green shoots before cooking. Only let the flavour dominate if a recipe really requires it, otherwise treat garlic as one of the players in your band of flavourings.

**White garlic** is versatile and popular with cooks all around the Mediterranean.

**Aglio Rosso di Nubia**, red garlic from Nubia, the garlic district of Sicily, has a distinctive taste and pervasive aroma and is used to make pesto sauce for pasta.

**Plaited garlic** looks pretty and keeps well in a cool, airy place.

**Ail Rose de Lautrec** is the best of French pink garlic, with a sweet, aromatic flavour even once the skins have become papery.

# loup de mer en croûte de sel

❖ *provence* ❖

Cracking open the salt crust to reveal a perfectly cooked, moist and tender fish is both a satisfying and exciting moment.

**PREP** 20 MINS ❖ **COOK** 30-40 MINS ❖ **SERVES** 4

1–1.35kg (2¼–3lb) **sea bass**, gutted and scaled

1 **lemon**, thinly sliced

bunch of **herbs**, such as dill, flat-leaf parsley, and coriander, plus 2 tbsp snipped herbs, to garnish

**oil**, for brushing

1.35kg (3lb) **coarse sea salt**

3 **egg whites**

freshly ground **black pepper**

**extra virgin olive oil**, to drizzle

2 **lemons**, each cut into 4 wedges

1 Preheat the oven to 230°C (450°F/Gas 8) for 20 minutes. Rinse the fish in cold water and dry with kitchen paper. Tuck the lemon slices and herbs into the cavity of the fish. Brush one side of the fish with oil.

2 Place the salt, egg whites, and 4 tablespoons water in a large bowl. Mix well, until the salt has the consistency of damp sand. Add more salt if the mixture feels too wet and more water if it is too dry.

3 Line a baking sheet with foil. Use one-third of the salt mixture to form a bed and place the fish, oiled-side down, on top. Brush the top side of the fish with oil and cover with the remaining salt. Crunch up foil into rolls and push them around the salt to keep the fish tucked in.

4 Bake the fish for 30–40 minutes, depending on its size. Remove from the oven and let it stand for 10–15 minutes. Using the blunt side of a knife, tap around the salt crust to loosen it, crack it open, and remove it. Remove the skin, from the tail end to the top. Using an angled spatula, remove the top fillet from the backbone and place on a warmed serving dish. Brush off any salt crust with kitchen paper. Discard the stuffing and backbone and place the bottom fillet on the dish.

5 Scrape off any herbs, skin, and small bones and season with pepper. Drizzle over the oil and scatter over the snipped herbs. Serve with lemon wedges, and some more oil.

# atun escabeche

❖ *spain* ❖

Briefly frying or poaching fish, then marinating it to finish the cooking is a favourite Mediterranean cooking method.

**PREP** 10 MINS, PLUS CHILLING
**COOK** 10-15 MINS **SERVES** 4-6

90ml (3fl oz) **olive oil**

450g (1lb) fresh **boneless tuna** or other fish fillet (see variation below), cut into 1cm (½in) thick slices

1 large mild **onion**, cut into thin rings, rings halved

**salt** and freshly ground **black pepper**

2 **garlic cloves**, crushed

1 tsp **smoked pimentón** (Spanish paprika)

1 scant tsp ground **cumin** or **coriander**

1 tbsp snipped **flat-leaf parsley**

a few sprigs of **thyme**

1 **lemon**, thinly sliced

3 tbsp **white wine vinegar**

1 Heat 1 tablespoon of the oil in a frying pan. Add the tuna slices and sear over a medium heat for 2 minutes on each side, until coloured and a little stiff. Place the slices in a non-metallic dish.

2 Add 2 tablespoons of the oil to the pan, stir in the halved onion rings, season, and cook for 3–5 minutes over a medium heat. Add the garlic, paprika, and cumin. Fry for a further 2 minutes, stirring occasionally. Spoon the contents of the pan over the fish and spread with the back of a spoon to coat evenly. Season again lightly and stir.

3 Scatter over the parsley and thyme. Cover the tuna with the slices of lemon. Mix the remaining oil with the vinegar and pour over the fish. Cover with cling film and refrigerate overnight or for 24 hours. Serve as a starter, chilled, or at room temperature.

## variations

**Escabeche with sea bream, sea bass, or red mullet** Fillets of sea bream, sea bass, or red mullet are also delicious cooked escabeche-style.

**Escabeche with vegetables** Also try the method with vegetables: large spring onions, white parts only, halved, baby carrots, thickly sliced courgettes, baby fennels or button mushrooms.

# tajine bil hout

❖ *Morocco* ❖

In the coastal towns and villages of Morocco, the fish tagines are simple and packed with flavour. For this recipe, you can use any firm-fleshed fish, marinated in the traditional chermoula, and serve it with chunks of crusty bread to mop up all the delicious citrusy juices.

**PREP** 50 MINS, PLUS CHILLING
**COOK** 25-30 MINS ❖ **SERVES** 4

## ingredients

roughly 900g (2lb) **monkfish tail**
6–8 medium **waxy potatoes**
3 tbsp **olive oil**
15g (½oz) **butter**
2–3 **garlic cloves**, finely chopped
12 cracked **green olives**
12 **cherry tomatoes**
salt and freshly ground **black pepper**
small bunch of **coriander**, finely chopped
1–2 **lemons**, cut into wedges

## for the chermoula

1 large **red chilli**
2 **garlic cloves**, roughly chopped
2 tsp **cumin seeds**
1 tsp **coarse salt**
juice of 1 **lemon**
2 tbsp **olive oil**
small bunch of **coriander**, finely chopped

1 **Make the chermoula** marinade. Deseed and roughly chop the chilli. In a mortar and pestle, pound the garlic, chilli, cumin seeds, and salt to form a smooth paste. Beat in the lemon juice and oil, then stir the coriander into the marinade.

2 **Prepare the monkfish tail**. Remove the sinewy part of the fish and then cut it into bite-sized chunks. Place in a bowl, add the chermoula marinade (reserve 1 tablespoon for cooking), and toss gently. Cover and chill in the fridge for 1–2 hours.

3 **Prepare the potatoes**. Bring a pot of water to the boil and add the potatoes. Boil vigorously for 5–6 minutes, until they soften. Drain and refresh under cold running water. Peel and cut them into halves or quarters lengthways.

4 **In a tagine**, heat 2 tablespoons of the oil with the butter, stir in the garlic, and cook for 2–3 minutes, until it begins to colour. Toss in the potatoes, and add the olives and the reserved chermoula. Pour in 125ml (4½fl oz) water, cover, and cook gently for 5–6 minutes. Toss in the tomatoes and season well.

5 **Place the chunks of marinated fish** on top of the potatoes, olives, and tomatoes and drizzle with the remaining oil. Cover and cook gently for 5–6 minutes, until the fish is cooked through. Toss the fish gently into the other ingredients so that all the flavours and colours mingle. Garnish with the coriander and serve the tagine with the lemon wedges to squeeze over.

# triglie di scoglio

### *sicily*

This delicious pan-fried red mullet dish is stuffed with preserved lemons, olives, and parsley. Preserved lemons add a mildly sour flavour to it.

**PREP** 30-35 MINS ❖ **COOK** 30-35 MINS
**SERVES** 4

2 lemons
3 tbsp **coarse salt**
1 **garlic clove**, halved
**sea salt** and freshly ground **black pepper**
30 **black olives**, pitted and roughly chopped
½–1 fresh **red chilli**, deseeded and finely chopped
20 **basil leaves**, roughly chopped
20 **flat-leaf parsley** leaves, roughly chopped
juice of 1 **lemon**
2 tbsp **extra virgin olive oil**
4 fresh **red mullet**, 250–400g (9–14oz) each, gutted, scaled, and cleaned
**light olive oil**, for frying

1 Place the lemons in a small, tight-fitting pan. Cover with water and add the coarse salt. Place a lid or saucer on top of the lemons to keep them submerged. Bring to the boil and simmer for 8–10 minutes until soft. Refresh under cold running water.

2 Cut the lemons in half, remove the flesh and pith, and discard. Using a thin sharp knife, trim the inside of the skin, removing any remaining traces of the pith. Finely chop the lemon skin and set aside.

3 Preheat the oven to 180°C (350°F/Gas 4). Crush the garlic with salt using the back of a knife, until you have a smooth paste. Mix the garlic, olives, chilli, basil, parsley, and preserved lemon in a bowl. Add the lemon juice and extra virgin olive oil, and season.

4 Pat dry the red mullet with kitchen paper. Stuff the cavities with a portion of the olive and lemon mixture. Season the fish inside and out.

5 Heat the light olive oil in a frying pan over a medium-high heat. Pan-fry the mullet for 3 minutes. Turn over and cook on the other side for 2 minutes. Transfer to a baking dish and bake for 5 minutes. Serve with some mixed leaves or braised spinach.

# psari fourni ladolemono

### *greece*

The Greeks like their fish cooked simply, as here, baked in foil with fennel and lemon, and drizzled with good olive oil and lemon juice. Any of the Mediterranean's white-fleshed fish – sea bass, sea bream, or grey mullet can be used.

**PREP** 15 MINS ❖ **COOK** 25-30 MINS, PLUS COOLING ❖ **SERVES** 4

about 1.5kg (3lb 3oz) whole **white-fleshed fish**, cleaned but with head
**salt** and freshly ground **black pepper**
9–10 tbsp **extra virgin olive oil**, plus 1–2 tbsp extra for greasing
½ **lemon**, scrubbed and cut into chunks
handful of **fennel fronds** or **dill**, plus 1 tbsp finely chopped **fennel fronds** or **dill** (optional)
4 tbsp **lemon juice**

1 Wipe the fish inside and out, removing the dark vein that runs along the back of the cavity. Salt it inside and out.

2 Lightly oil a sheet of foil, place the fish on it, and drizzle 1–2 tablespoons of the oil. Tuck the lemon and fennel fronds into the cavity and fold the foil over the fish lengthways, doubling over the top seam to trap the steam. Tuck in the ends.

3 Preheat the oven to 180°C (350°F/Gas 4) and set a roasting tin to heat.

4 Place the fish on the hot tin and bake for 25–30 minutes, depending on the thickness of the fish, until the flesh feels firm when you press it through the foil. Remove from the oven, but do not open the foil. Leave to cool to room temperature.

5 Whisk the oil and lemon juice together with chopped fennel fronds or dill, if using, salt, and pepper. Serve with the fish.

### variation

**Herby ladolemono** You can also prepare this recipe with other aromatic herbs, such as oregano, thyme, parsley, and basil. You can increase the quantity of lemon juice.

# daurade aux tomates

❖ *provence* ❖

Well-flavoured tomatoes make all the difference to this popular sea bream dish. Don't forget to take the cheeks from the fish heads – these are particularly delicious.

**PREP** 10 MINS ❖ **COOK** 25 MINS ❖ **SERVES** 4

4 small **sea bream**, about 340g (12oz) in total, scaled, gutted, and trimmed

1 tbsp **plain flour**

**salt** and freshly ground **black pepper**

5 tbsp **extra virgin olive oil**

1 **onion**, finely chopped

2 **celery sticks**, finely sliced

2 **garlic cloves**, chopped

8 **plum tomatoes**, roughly chopped

5 tbsp **dry white wine**

pinch of **sugar**

2 tbsp chopped **flat-leaf parsley**

1 Preheat the oven to 190°C (375°F/Gas 5). Slash the sea bream 3–4 times on each side. Dust with seasoned flour and arrange in a baking tray.

2 Bake the fish in the oven for 15–20 minutes, or until cooked. The flesh will be white and opaque.

3 Heat the oil in a frying pan, add the onion, celery, and garlic, and cook over a low heat for 2–3 minutes, until softened. Add the tomatoes and wine, and cook for 3–4 minutes, until the juices run. Season and add the sugar. Keep the sauce warm.

4 Slide the fish on to a large, warmed serving dish. Spoon over the tomato sauce and sprinkle with parsley.

### prepare ahead

The tomato sauce can be made 2–3 days in advance. Cover and refrigerate. Bring to room temperature before continuing.

# pesce spada in salmoriglio

❖ *sicily* ❖

Swordfish has long been caught off the coasts of Sicily where it is very popular. Use only sustainable swordfish. Its firm meaty texture makes it perfect for grilling and griddling.

**PREP** 10 MINS, PLUS MARINATING
**COOK** 8 MINS ❖ **SERVES** 4

2 **swordfish steaks**, at least 2.5cm (1in) thick, about 700g (1½ lb) total weight

1 tbsp snipped **herbs**, such as parsley, oregano, or mint, to finish

**For the salmoriglio sauce**

finely grated zest and juice of 1 **lemon**

1 tbsp snipped **flat-leaf parsley**

1–2 **garlic cloves**, crushed

½ tbsp chopped **fresh oregano**, or 1 tsp dried oregano

½ tsp **chilli pepper**

**salt** and freshly ground **black pepper**

6 tbsp **olive oil**

1 For the sauce, place the lemon zest and juice, parsley, garlic, oregano, and chilli pepper in a bowl, mix well, and season. Whisk in the oil and 2 tablespoons of cold water. Brush the steaks with half the sauce and leave to marinate for 5 minutes.

2 Preheat the grill to high, or preheat a griddle pan. Grill or griddle the steaks for 3–4 minutes only on each side, or until just cooked through but still moist in the centre, as swordfish tends to get dry quickly.

3 To serve, cut each steak in half and spoon over the remaining sauce. Season with a little extra pepper, scatter over the snipped herbs, and serve immediately.

### variation

**Tonno alla siciliana** You can substitute the swordfish with tuna steak or salmon.

# mero al romesco

*spain*

Romesco is a classic sauce from Catalonia, Spain, made with tomatoes, garlic, onion, peppers, almonds, and olive oil.

**PREP** 10 MINS ❖ **COOK** 30 MINS ❖ **SERVES** 4-6

3 tbsp **extra virgin olive oil**, plus extra for greasing
1 kg (2¼lb) **halibut fillets**, 2cm (¾in) thick
**salt** and freshly ground **black pepper**
2 **garlic cloves**, finely chopped
75g (2½oz) **almonds**, coarsely chopped
125g (4½oz) **breadcrumbs**
3 tbsp chopped **flat-leaf parsley**

**For the romesco sauce**

350g (12oz) jar **roasted red peppers**, rinsed, patted dry, and coarsely chopped
1 tbsp **sherry vinegar**
¼ tsp **cayenne pepper**
pinch of **smoked pimentón** (Spanish paprika)

1 Preheat the oven to 230°C (450°F/Gas 8). Brush the bottom of an ovenproof dish with oil, add the fish, skin-side down, and season.

2 Heat 2 tablespoons of the oil in a frying pan. Add the garlic, almonds, and breadcrumbs, and fry over a medium heat, stirring, for 6–8 minutes, or until just golden. Do not let the nuts burn. Stir in the parsley, then spoon the mixture over the fish.

3 Bake the fish uncovered for 5 minutes, then loosely cover with foil, and bake for 15 minutes, or until just cooked through. The fish will flake easily when it is ready. Remove from the oven and drizzle 1 tablespoon of oil over the fish.

4 While the fish is cooking, make the romesco sauce. Combine all the ingredients together in a bowl. Serve the fish topped with the sauce.

# merluza a la vizcaina

*spain*

This version of the classic Basque dish uses cod rather than the more traditional hake. The tomatoes together with the wine add the right mix of sweetness and acidity.

**PREP** 10 MINS ❖ **COOK** 30 MINS ❖ **SERVES** 4

2 tbsp **olive oil**
1kg (2¼lb) skinless **cod fillet**, cut into 4 pieces
1 large **onion**, finely sliced
1 **garlic clove**, finely chopped
4 large **plum tomatoes**, skinned, deseeded, and chopped
2 tsp **tomato purée**
1 tsp **sugar**
300ml (10fl oz) hot **fish stock**
120ml (4fl oz) **dry white wine**
2 tbsp chopped **flat-leaf parsley**
**salt** and freshly ground **black pepper**

1 Preheat the oven to 200°C (400°F/Gas 6). Heat the oil in a flameproof casserole large enough to accommodate the cod in one layer. Fry the fish, skin-side down, over a medium-high heat, for 1 minute, or until the skin is crisp. Turn over and cook for 1 more minute. Remove with a slotted spoon and set aside.

2 Add the onion and garlic to the casserole and fry over a medium heat for 4–5 minutes, or until softened, stirring frequently. Add the tomatoes, tomato purée, sugar, stock, and wine, bring to a simmer, and cook, stirring, for 10–12 minutes.

3 Place the fish on top of the sauce and bake for 5 minutes. Remove from the oven, lift out the cod, and keep warm.

4 Place the casserole over a medium-high heat and boil the sauce for 3–4 minutes, until reduced and thickened. Stir in half the parsley and season to taste. Divide the sauce between 4 warm plates and place a piece of fish on top. Serve immediately, sprinkled with the remaining parsley.

**variation**

**Halibut in tomato sauce** Substitute the cod for the same quantity of halibut, and sprinkle the finished dish with basil and dried chilli flakes, instead of the parsley.

# bacalao a la cazuela

*❖ spain ❖*

The salt cod in this hearty dish is braised with vegetables, and made fragrant with the classic Spanish aromas of garlic, bay leaves, and saffron.

**PREP** 20 MINS, PLUS SOAKING
**COOK** 40 MINS ❖ **SERVES** 4

3 tbsp **olive oil**
1 **onion**, finely diced
white parts of 2 **leeks**, finely sliced
3 **garlic cloves**, minced
3 **tomatoes**, peeled, deseeded, and chopped
500g (1lb 2oz) **potatoes**, peeled and diced

salt and freshly ground **black pepper**
2 **bay leaves**
large pinch of **saffron** threads
800g (1¾lb) thick-cut **bacalao** (salt cod), soaked and cut into 4 pieces
120ml (4fl oz) **dry white wine**
2 tbsp chopped **flat-leaf parsley**

1 Heat the oil in a large, shallow, heatproof casserole. Add the onion and leeks, and fry gently, stirring constantly for 5 minutes, or until soft.

2 Add the garlic and tomatoes, and cook for a further 2 minutes, stirring continuously. Add the potatoes, season to taste, and add the bay leaves and saffron.

3 Add the bacalao, skin-side up, on top of the vegetables. Pour in the wine and 250ml (9fl oz) of cold water, then bring to a simmer and cook for 25–30 minutes.

Shake the casserole once or twice every 5 minutes to help release gelatine from the fish to thicken the sauce.

4 Sprinkle over the parsley, and serve straight from the casserole.

**prepare ahead**

Soak the fish for at least 48 hours in enough cold water to cover it, changing the water 2–3 times to remove the saltiness.

# boquerones in vinagre

*spain*

Plentiful throughout the region, anchovies have a short shelflife – the result of their natural oiliness and relatively small size. You can keep them for a few more days by using salt or vinegar or, as here, both. Make this recipe 48 hours ahead.

**PREP** 30 MINS, PLUS MARINATING
**SERVES** 4-6

500g (1lb 2oz) fresh **anchovies**
150ml (5fl oz) **sherry** or **white wine vinegar**
1 tbsp **salt**
2–3 **garlic cloves**, finely sliced
1 tbsp **olive oil,** to drizzle
bunch of **flat-leaf parsley**, chopped, to garnish

1 Rinse the anchovies and drain thoroughly. Press lightly down the body of the fish to loosen the flesh from the bones. Holding the head firmly between finger and thumb, pull down through the belly towards the tail. The spine and ribs should slip through the soft flesh easily, gutting and splitting all in one movement. Nick the spine at the base of the tail, leaving the tail still attached. Repeat until all the fish are gutted and butterflied.

2 Place the vinegar and salt in a bowl with 2 tablespoons of cold water and mix well. Open each fish flat and lay it flesh-side up in a single layer in a shallow dish. Pour the vinegar mixture over the fish, making sure they are well soaked. Sprinkle over the garlic, cover with foil, and leave in the fridge to marinate for 48 hours.

3 To serve, drain the fish, drizzle over the oil, and sprinkle with the parsley. The fish will keep in the fridge for a week.

# rakı soslu barbunya

*turkey*

Once the favourite fish of the Romans, red mullet is one of the most prized fish in the eastern Mediterranean. In this popular Turkish recipe, the fish is doused in rakı, Turkey's national spirit and the preferred drink to accompany mezze and fish.

**PREP** 5 MINS
**COOK** 12 MINS ❖ **SERVES** 4

4 fresh **red mullet**, gutted and cleaned
2–3 tbsp **olive oil**
**salt** and freshly ground **black pepper**
about 150ml (5fl oz) **rakı**
small bunch of **flat-leaf parsley**, finely chopped
1 **lemon**, cut into quarters

1 Preheat the grill. Brush the fish with oil on both sides and season. Line a grill pan with aluminium foil and place the fish on top.

2 Place the grill pan under the grill and cook the fish for 5–6 minutes on each side, allowing the skin to buckle and brown. Remove from the grill and place the fish on a serving dish. Splash the rakı over, set it alight, and wait until the flames die down before serving.

3 To serve, garnish with a sprinkling of parsley and serve each fish with a drizzle of rakı and a wedge of lemon to squeeze over.

# tajine bil kimroun

*❖ Morocco ❖*

This Moroccan prawn tagine, which is also enjoyed in Tunisia, is inspired by the Andalucian flavours just across the water from Tangier. Moroccan dishes are generally cooked in the national cooking vessel, a traditional tagine.

**PREP** 10–15 MINS

**COOK** 25 MINS ❖ **SERVES** 4

4–5 tbsp **olive oil**

20 **king prawns**, heads removed

2 **onions**, finely chopped

2 **garlic cloves**, finely chopped

1–2 tsp **smoked pimentón** (Spanish paprika)

400g can **tomatoes**, drained

small bunch of **coriander**, finely chopped

small bunch of **flat-leaf parsley**, finely chopped

1 tsp **sugar**

**salt** and freshly ground **black pepper**

2 **fennel bulbs**, trimmed and sliced thickly lengthways

1 Heat 2–3 tablespoons of the oil in a tagine. Toss in the prawns and cook for 2–3 minutes, until they turn opaque. Remove the prawns from the pot and set aside. Keep the oil in the pan.

2 Add the onions and garlic to the pot and cook for 3–4 minutes, until they begin to colour. Add the paprika, tomatoes, and half the herbs, then stir in the sugar and season. Cook gently, partially covered, for 10–12 minutes, until the mixture thickens to form a sauce.

3 Meanwhile, steam the fennel for about 5 minutes to soften. Heat the remaining oil in a frying pan and toss in the steamed fennel. Cook gently for 4–5 minutes, until golden. Sprinkle with salt and pepper.

4 Toss the cooked prawns into the tomato sauce. Place the fennel on top, cover, and cook gently for 5 minutes to allow the flavours to mingle. Garnish with the remaining coriander and parsley, and serve from the tagine with rice, couscous, or chunks of fresh, crusty bread.

# garides saganaki

*❖ greece ❖*

The Greeks like dishes with simple titles. Literally translated as "frying-pan prawns", this popular one-pot recipe is traditionally served during the summer.

**PREP** 10 MINS ❖ **COOK** 45 MINS

**SERVES** 4

1 tbsp **olive oil**

1 **onion**, finely chopped

2 **garlic cloves**, crushed or finely chopped

400g can chopped **tomatoes**

2 tbsp **tomato purée**

1 large glass **dry white wine**

½ tsp **sugar**

**salt** and freshly ground **black pepper**

350g (12oz) large cooked, peeled **prawns**

125g (4½oz) **feta cheese**

small handful of **thyme leaves**

1 Heat half the oil in a large frying pan, then add the onion, and cook over a low heat for 8 minutes, or until soft and translucent. Stir through the garlic and cook for a few more seconds, then add the tomatoes, 150ml (5fl oz) cold water, tomato purée, wine, sugar, and a little seasoning. Bring to the boil, then reduce the heat and simmer gently, stirring occasionally, for 20–30 minutes until thick and pulpy.

2 Stir the prawns into the sauce, remove from the heat, and crumble over the feta cheese. Pop under the grill until the cheese melts and turns golden brown, then sprinkle over the thyme leaves. Serve with a crisp salad and fresh crusty bread.

## kreidis kabob
### *middle east*

One of the most popular ways to enjoy the jumbo prawns caught off the coast of Syria, Turkey, Lebanon, Egypt, Tunisia, and Morocco is to thread them onto skewers and grill them over charcoal.

**PREP** 10 MINS, PLUS MARINATING
**COOK** 6 MINS ❖ **SERVES** 4

16 large **prawns**
juice of 2 **lemons**, plus 1 lemon extra, cut into wedges, to serve
4 **garlic cloves**, crushed
1 tsp ground **cumin**
1 tsp **pimentón** (Spanish paprika)
sea salt
8–12 **cherry tomatoes**
1 **green bell pepper**, cut into bite-sized squares
oil, for greasing

1 Shell the prawns down to the tail, leaving a little bit of shell at the end. Remove the veins and discard. Mix together the lemon juice, garlic, cumin, paprika, and a little salt and rub over the prawns. Leave the prawns to marinate for 30 minutes.

2 Meanwhile, prepare the charcoal grill. Thread the prawns onto metal skewers, alternating with the tomatoes and green pepper pieces, until all the ingredients are used up.

3 Place the kebabs on an oiled rack over the glowing coals and cook for 2–3 minutes each side, basting with any of the leftover marinade, until the prawns are tender and the tomatoes and peppers are lightly browned. Serve immediately with lemon wedges.

### variation

**Scallops or lobster kebabs** Instead of prawns, you can prepare shelled scallops or lobster tails in the same way. Peppers and tomatoes are classic kebab ingredients but you can alternate the shellfish with thick pieces of onion, whole garlic cloves, chunks of celery, or lemon wedges, in any combination you like.

## gambas pilpil
### *andalucia*

In this speciality of the tapas bars of Andalucia, freshly caught raw prawns are cooked to order in little earthenware *cazuela* with olive oil, garlic, and tiny dried chillies, and served straight from the stove.

**PREP** 5 MINS ❖ **COOK** 1–2 MINS ❖ **SERVES** 2

150g (5½oz) raw peeled **prawns**
3–4 tbsp **olive oil**
1–2 **garlic cloves**, thickly sliced
4–5 small dried **chillies**, whole but deseeded
sea salt

1 Clean the prawns and devein them, if necessary.

2 Heat the oil in an earthenware *cazuela* or a small frying pan. Add the prawns, garlic, and chillies, sprinkle with a little salt, and fry for 1–2 minutes, until the prawns change colour and become opaque.

3 Serve immediately with cocktail sticks or wooden forks, and plenty of soft-crumbed bread for mopping up the juices.

### cook's tip

If you prefer to use the oven, preheat it to 220°C (425°F/Gas 7) and heat the baking tray before adding the oil and prawns.

# calamares con pimentón piquante

❖ *spain* ❖

This dish of squid in olive oil and paprika is made here with hot pimentón (Spanish paprika), but you could use smoked sweet paprika for a milder version. Serve with other tapas, such as chorizo and olives.

**PREP** 5 MINS ❖ **COOK** 5 MINS ❖ **SERVES** 4

450g (1lb) **squid**, cleaned
2 tbsp **olive oil**
2 **garlic cloves**, finely chopped
**salt**
2 tsp hot **pimentón** or ground **chilli**
1 tbsp fresh **lemon juice**
**lemon wedges**, to serve

1 Slice the squid "tube" into rings, then cut each tentacle in half.

2 In a frying pan, heat the oil over a medium heat, add the garlic, and fry for 1 minute, stirring, then increase the heat and add the squid. Fry for 3 minutes, stirring frequently.

3 Season to taste, then add the paprika and lemon juice. Transfer to small serving plates and serve immediately with lemon wedges to squeeze over.

# calamares en su tinta

❖ *spain* ❖

A Basque speciality, this delicious way of preparing both varieties of inkfish – cuttlefish and squid – is popular all over Spain. The ink is splendidly black, but has a delicate flavour, which makes the effort of collecting it worthwhile.

**PREP** 20 MINS ❖ **COOK** 30-35 MINS ❖ **SERVES** 4

750g (1lb 10oz) **squid** or **cuttlefish**, whole and unprepared
4–5 tbsp **olive oil**
2 medium **onions**, sliced into half moons
2 **garlic cloves**, chopped
500g (1lb 2oz) skinned, chopped **tomatoes** (fresh or canned)
1 tbsp **fresh breadcrumbs**
3 tbsp **flat-leaf parsley**
**salt** and freshly ground **black pepper**

1 Rinse the squid or cuttlefish thoroughly and take out the bones. Remove the tentacles and innards from the body and remove the silvery ink sacks from among the innards. Break them into a small sieve placed over a bowl to reserve the inky liquid. One or two sacks are enough to turn the sauce midnight black.

2 Remove and discard the beaks, eyes, and soft innards. Chop the tentacles and rest of the body into small pieces and use them to stuff the tubes.

3 Heat the oil in a large pan. Add the onions and garlic, and fry gently, until they soften. Add the tomatoes and bring to the boil. Reduce the heat and simmer for 4–5 minutes to thicken the sauce.

4 Add the squid tubes, spooning the sauce over the top. Bring to the boil for a moment, reduce the heat, cover loosely with a lid, and cook gently for 20–25 minutes, or until the tubes are perfectly tender. Add a little boiling water if necessary so the juices don't dry out.

5 Meanwhile, mash the reserved ink with the breadcrumbs and parsley. Remove the tubes from the pan and stir the ink mixture into the sauce. Return the tubes to the pan and reheat gently without allowing the sauce to boil, or the ink will turn grainy. Season to taste.

# kalamarakia yemista

❖ *greece* ❖

Squid stuffed with rice and almonds, and flavoured with parsley and dill, are cooked gently in wine sharpened with lemon juice in this fisherman's dish.

**PREP** 20 MINS ❖ **COOK** 1¼ HRS ❖ **SERVES** 4-6

1kg (2¼lb) medium-sized **squid**, cleaned (with tentacles)

### For the stuffing

4–5 tbsp **olive oil**, plus extra to drizzle
1 medium **onion**, finely chopped
50g (1¾oz) **round-grain rice**
50g (1¾oz) chopped blanched **almonds**
150ml (5fl oz) **white wine**
2 tbsp chopped **flat-leaf parsley**
1 tbsp chopped **dill**, plus extra to garnish
**salt** and freshly ground **black pepper**

1 Rinse the squid well, scrape off the fine veil that covers the body and tube, and trim off the wings. Reserve the tubes and chop the tentacles, bodies, and wings.

2 For the stuffing, heat the oil in a medium frying pan and fry the onion with the rice until the grains turn opaque. Add the squid, almonds, and half the wine, and boil to evaporate the alcohol. Reduce the heat, add a splash of cold water, and simmer uncovered for about 10 minutes, until the rice has absorbed all the liquid. Stir in the herbs and season.

3 Place a teaspoon of the stuffing into each of the tubes, closing the opening with a cocktail stick. Do not overfill as the rice still needs room to expand. Place the stuffed squid in a pan, add the remaining wine and enough water to cover three-fourths of the caps. Bring to the boil, reduce the heat, cover, and simmer gently for 20–30 minutes, until the squid is perfectly tender. Garnish with pepper, dill, and a drizzle of oil. Serve warm or at room temperature. Do not reheat.

### cook's tip

To clean the squid, push your finger into the cap and pull out the body and tentacles, including the soft innards and clear plastic bone. Rinse the cap and reserve. Turn the body inside out and remove the dark stomach cavity. Discard the innards, eyes, and the sharp little beak. Scrape the tentacles to remove the little toenails.

# praires farcies

*✦ provence ✦*

Clams filled with a flavoursome herb butter make a wonderful appetizer. You can also use mussels or blanched portabello mushrooms.

**PREP** 1 HR, PLUS CHILLING  ❖  **COOK** 30 MINS
**SERVES** 4-6

1 kg (2¼lb) fresh clean **clams**
sea salt and freshly ground **black pepper**
3 tbsp **toasted breadcrumbs**

### For the herb butter
3 tbsp **baby spinach leaves**
3 tbsp **rocket leaves**
1 tbsp chopped **chervil** or **tarragon**
1 tbsp chopped **chives**
1 tbsp chopped **flat-leaf parsley**
1 tbsp chopped **shallot**
1–2 **garlic cloves**, smashed
2 **anchovy fillets** preserved in oil or brine, drained and chopped
1 tsp **drained capers**
100g (3½ oz) soft **unsalted butter**
2–3 tbsp **olive oil**
1 tbsp **lemon juice**
sea salt and freshly ground **black pepper**

1 Scrub the clams with a stiff brush under cold running water. Soak in salted water for 30 minutes, stirring occasionally. Drain, rinse, and repeat once more.

2 Place the clams in a heavy-based pan. Add 250ml (9fl oz) cold water, bring to the boil, cover, reduce the heat, and cook for 5–7 minutes, stirring several times, until the clams open. Drain and leave until cool. Discard any unopened clams. Remove the clams from their shells with a sharp knife. Select half of the halved shells and put 2 clams in each. Discard remaining shells.

3 For the herb butter, rinse the spinach and rocket, then pat dry. Whizz the leaves, herbs, shallot, garlic, anchovies, capers, and butter in a food processor. Add the oil and lemon juice, and whizz again. Season, place on cling film, and roll into a sausage. Refrigerate for 2–3 hours until firm.

4 Preheat the oven to 200°C (400°F/Gas 6). Place the herb butter in a bowl and beat in the breadcrumbs. Using a teaspoon, fill the shells with the mixture, making sure you cover the clams generously. Place the shells, stuffed-side up, in a baking dish. Bake for 8–10 minutes until sizzling. Leave for 2–3 minutes before serving.

# midye dolması

*✦ turkey ✦*

This classic Turkish dish of steamed mussels stuffed with rice, pine nuts, and currants is an Ottoman favourite in Istanbul and Izmir.

**PREP** 40 MINS  ❖  **COOK** 20 MINS  ❖  **SERVES** 4-6

3–4 tbsp **olive oil**
2–3 **shallots**, or 1 **red onion**, finely chopped
2 tbsp **pine nuts**
2 tbsp **currants**, soaked in warm water for 5 minutes, then drained
2 tbsp ground **cinnamon**
1 tsp **allspice**
1–2 tsp **sugar**
1–2 tsp **tomato paste**
120g (4¼oz) **short-grain rice**, or **pudding rice**, well rinsed and drained
**salt** and freshly ground **black pepper**
small bunch of **flat-leaf parsley**, finely chopped, plus a few sprigs to garnish

small bunch of **mint leaves**, finely chopped
small bunch of **dill fronds**, finely chopped
12–16 large, fresh **mussels**, cleaned and kept in a bowl of cold water
1–2 **lemons**, cut into thin wedges, to serve

1 Heat the oil in a pan, stir in the shallots, and cook until soft. Add the pine nuts and currants, and stir for 1–2 minutes, until the nuts just colour and the currants plump up.

2 Add the spices, sugar, and tomato paste. Stir in the rice, then pour in enough hot water to just cover, and bring to the boil. Season, reduce the heat, and simmer for 10 minutes, until all the water has been absorbed. Cool and toss in the herbs.

3 Using a knife, prise open the mussels. Stuff a spoonful of rice into them, then close and pack into a steamer kept in a deep pan. Lay damp greaseproof paper over the mussels and cover with a plate weighed down with kitchen weight. Cover the steamer and bring to the boil. Reduce the heat and steam for 15–20 minutes. When cool, garnish with parsley and serve with lemon wedges.

# paella

## *spain*

This dish from Valencia, on Spain's east coast, has become a global classic. Feel free to adjust the meat and seafood ingredients to suit your personal preferences. What matters is using top-quality short- or medium-grain rice and cooking it carefully.

**PREP** 20 MINS ❖ **COOK** 1 HR ❖ **SERVES** 4-6

### ingredients

3 tbsp **olive oil**

400g (14oz) skinless, boneless **chicken thighs**, cut into bite-sized pieces

**salt** and freshly ground **black pepper**

150g (5½oz) **chorizo**, sliced

1 large **onion**, diced

1 large **red pepper**, deseeded and sliced

400g (14oz) **paella rice** or other short-grain rice

3 **garlic cloves**, finely chopped

2 large pinches of **saffron threads**, soaked in 100ml (3½fl oz) hot water for 10 minutes

400g can chopped **tomatoes**

125g (4½oz) **French beans**, cut into 2cm (¾in) slices

300g (10oz) **small mussels**, scrubbed and debearded (discard any that do not open)

300g (10oz) raw, unpeeled **king prawns**, deveined and legs removed

1–2 tbsp chopped **flat-leaf parsley**

1 **Heat the oil** in a wide heavy-based frying pan over a medium heat, add the chicken and seasoning, and cook for 10–12 minutes until browned all over. Remove and set aside on a large plate lined with a double layer of kitchen paper.

2 **Cook the chorizo** for 1–2 minutes on each side until browned. Remove and set aside. Add the onion and red pepper to the pan and cook for 5–7 minutes until soft. Add the rice and stir, so all the grains are coated, and cook for 2–3 minutes.

3 **Stir in 900ml (1½ pints)** water, then the garlic, saffron with its soaking liquid, and plenty of seasoning. Push the chicken pieces down into the rice.

**4** **Place the chorizo slices** in the pan, followed by the tomatoes and beans, and bring to the boil. Simmer on a low heat, uncovered, for about 30 minutes until all the liquid has evaporated and the rice is al dente. Do not stir or the rice will become sticky.

**5** **Add the seafood** for the last 15 minutes, cover, and cook until the mussels open and the prawns turn pink. Remove from the heat and discard any unopened mussels. Cover with a kitchen towel and leave for 5 minutes. Garnish and serve.

# grand aïoli

*❖ p r o v e n c e ❖*

This dish is a favourite in Provence
and makes a great centrepiece for
a cold summer buffet lunch.

**PREP** 30-35 MINS, PLUS OVERNIGHT CHILLING
**COOK** 20 MINS ❖ **SERVES** 4-6

450–500g (1lb–1lb 2oz) fresh **cod fillet**
**coarse sea salt** and freshly ground
  **black pepper**
1 **bay leaf**
sprig of **thyme**
1 tsp **fennel seeds**
300g (10oz) baby **new potatoes**, scrubbed
6–8 young **carrots**, scraped
225g (8oz) baby **green beans**, tops removed
2 baby **fennels**, trimmed and
  quartered lengthways
6–8 baby **courgettes**, tops removed
12 baby **cherry tomatoes**
6 shelled **hard-boiled eggs**

### For the aïoli sauce
4 **garlic cloves**, crushed
**salt** and freshly ground **black pepper**
2 small or medium **egg yolks**
200ml (7fl oz) **olive oil**
2 tsp **lemon juice**

1 Rub the cod with 1–2 handfuls of salt.
Wrap in foil, place in a plastic bag, and
refrigerate overnight, or for up to 24 hours.
Rinse thoroughly in cold water and pat dry.

2 Place the fish in a sauté pan, cover with
cold water, add the bay leaf, thyme, and
fennel seeds, and season with pepper. Bring
to the boil over a medium heat. Remove
from the heat when bubbling. Cover and let
stand for 5–7 minutes, until just beginning
to flake and barely cooked through.

3 Drain and trim away any skin, bones,
and membranes. Cut into 6 even-sized
pieces. Place the potatoes in a pan with
lightly salted water, bring to the boil, and
cook for 5 minutes. Add the carrots and
cook for 10–12 minutes, until just tender.
Drain, refresh under cold running water,
and drain again.

4 In a separate pan, place the beans and
fennels in lightly salted water and bring
to the boil. Add the courgettes and cook for
5–8 minutes until just tender. Drain, refresh
and drain again.

5 For the sauce, pound the garlic with a
little salt in a mortar and pestle. Leave
to stand for 1 minute. Transfer to a bowl,
add the egg yolks, and whisk until thick and
creamy. Leave for 2 minutes. Add the oil, a
few drops at a time, and whisk well until
thick. Season to taste and stir in the lemon
juice. Cover with cling film and refrigerate.

6 Arrange the vegetables and cod on a
platter. Tuck in the tomatoes and hard-
boiled eggs. Season with a little pepper and
serve with the sauce.

# zarzuela

*❖ s p a i n ❖*

This sumptuous Catalan fish stew
makes a splendid one-course dish
for a lunch or supper party.

**PREP** 20 MINS ❖ **COOK** 50 MINS ❖ **SERVES** 6

6 tbsp **olive oil**
3 x 100g (3½oz) **monkfish fillets**, halved
1 large mild **onion**, finely chopped
900g (2lb) ripe **tomatoes**, deseeded,
  chopped or halved
2 x 400g can chopped **tomatoes**
3 **garlic cloves**, crushed
3–4 tbsp **brandy**
4 tbsp ground **almonds**
1 tsp dried **thyme**
1 tsp **saffron threads** (or a generous pinch
  of ground saffron)
1 tsp **smoked pimentón** (Spanish paprika)
**salt** and freshly ground **black pepper**
200ml (7fl oz) hot **fish stock**
4 tbsp dry **white wine**
juice of ½ **lemon**
450g (1lb) **mussels**, well scrubbed
6 uncooked shelled **jumbo prawns**
200g (7oz) **squid rings**, defrosted if frozen
12 small **scallops**
2 tbsp chopped **flat-leaf parsley**

1 Heat 3 tablespoons oil in a sauté pan over
a medium heat. Add the monkfish, cook
for 3 minutes, turn over, and cook for 3 more
minutes. Lift out and reserve. Heat the rest of
the oil in the pan, add the onion, and fry for
5 minutes, until soft. Add the tomatoes,
garlic, and brandy, and cook for 5 minutes.

2 Stir in the almonds, thyme, saffron, and
paprika. Simmer for 5–8 minutes, until
most of the juice has evaporated. Return
the fish to the pan and coat well with the
mixture. Season, cover, and take off the heat.

3 Bring the stock, wine, 4 tablespoons water,
and the lemon juice to the boil in a pan.
Add the mussels, reduce the heat, cover, and
cook for 5 minutes, stirring, until the mussels
open. Lift out and place in a colander.

4 Add the prawns to the stock, simmer, add
the squid and scallops, and simmer for
3–5 minutes. Open the mussels and discard
the shells and any unopened mussels. Return
the pan to a medium heat. Add the prawns,
squid, scallops, and stock. Stir, add the
mussels, and cook for 3–5 minutes. Adjust
the seasoning, scatter over parsley and serve.

# soupe de poissons

### *provence*

Full of Mediterranean flavours, *soupe de poissons* really needs no accompaniment, except perhaps some toasted crusty bread.

**PREP** 20 MINS ❖ **COOK** 1 HR ❖ **SERVES** 6

5 tbsp olive oil
4 medium onions, chopped
2 leeks, chopped
1.5–2kg (3lb 3oz–4½lb) mixed fish and seafood
4 pieces dried fennel stalks, 5cm (2in) long
4 medium, ripe tomatoes, quartered
9 garlic cloves, crushed
5 sprigs of flat-leaf parsley
3 bay leaves
15cm (6in) strip dried orange peel
1 tbsp tomato purée
salt and freshly ground black pepper
pinch of saffron strands

1 Put the oil in a large saucepan. Add the onions and leeks, and cook over a medium heat until just golden. Gut the larger fish. Rinse the fish and seafood. Add to the pan and stir, then add the fennel, tomatoes, garlic, parsley, bay leaves, orange peel, and tomato purée. Stir and cook for 8–10 minutes, until the fish is just beginning to flake. Pour in 2.5 litres (4½ pints) hot water and season. Reduce the heat and simmer for 20 minutes.

2 Remove from the heat. Leave to cool, stir and mash down the soft fish pieces with the back of a large spoon. Remove the fennel, orange peel, and bay leaves. Pulse to a rough purée in a food processor. Push the soup through a very fine sieve into a pan and simmer over a medium heat.

3 Soften the saffron in a ladleful of the soup, then stir into the pan. Season and ladle the soup into warm bowls.

### cook's tip

Be sure to use a good variety of fresh fish. Enhance the colour with a saffron infusion.

### variation

**Soupe de poissons with spaghetti** Add pieces of spaghetti towards the end of cooking. Chop 60g (2oz) dry spaghetti into 2cm (¾in) pieces and throw into the soup after sieving. Simmer for 10 minutes, then add the saffron.

# bouillabaisse

### *provence*

Once a rough and ready stew made by throwing the fish left unused on the quayside at the end of the day into a bubbling pot, *bouillabaise* is now a celebrated dish along the French Riviera.

**PREP** 30 MINS, PLUS STANDING
**COOK** 30 MINS ❖ **SERVES** 6

1.25kg (2¾lb) mixed white fish, cleaned and boned – heads, bones, and tails reserved
2 sprigs of thyme
2 sprigs of rosemary
2 sprigs of flat-leaf parsley
grated zest of 1 lemon
6 crushed black peppercorns
1 large pinch of saffron strands
3 garlic cloves, crushed
6 tbsp olive oil
1 onion, thinly sliced
1 leek, thinly sliced
1 fennel bulb with fronds, thinly sliced
400g can chopped tomatoes
120ml (4fl oz) dry white wine
6 raw jumbo prawns, shelled
200g (7oz) cooked seafood medley, such as mussels, squids, and shrimps
1 tbsp Pernod or other aniseed-flavoured liqueur or brandy (optional)
salt and freshly ground black pepper

**For the rouille sauce**
1 small hot chilli, seeded and chopped
2 garlic cloves, crushed
1 egg yolk
small pinch of saffron strands
about 200ml (7fl oz) extra virgin olive oil

1 Rinse the fish inside and out, drain well, and pat dry. Cut into 5cm (2in) pieces. Place the heads, bones, and tails in a pan, add enough boiling water to cover well, then add the thyme, rosemary, parsley, lemon zest, and peppercorns. Simmer for 15 minutes.

2 For the rouille sauce, combine the chilli, garlic, egg yolk, and saffron, using a blender, food processor, or mortar and pestle. Once the mixture is smooth, leave to infuse for at least 5 minutes. Gradually trickle in the oil, working it in a little at a time until you have a very thick, smooth sauce. Season to taste.

3 Put the saffron in a cup, add 2 tablespoons of the stock, the garlic, and 3 tablespoons of the oil. Mix well and pour over the pieces of fish. Leave to stand. Heat the remaining oil in a saucepan, add the onion, leek, and fennel, and cook, stirring for 5–7 minutes. Add the tomatoes, and stir for 2 minutes.

4 Pour the stock through a sieve into the pan. Mash down the flavourings to extract as much as possible and pour in the wine. Bring to a simmer and cook for 20–30 minutes, stirring frequently, until mushy, mellow, and fragrant.

5 Add the fish, placing the most delicate fish on top, and leave to bubble for 5 minutes. Shake the pot from time to time to prevent the mixture from sticking to the base. Do not stir or the fish pieces will disintegrate.

6 Add the prawns and return to the boil for 5 minutes, until the fish is flaky and the prawns are cooked. Stir in the seafood medley, Pernod, if using, and return to the boil. Add a little more water, if necessary, so the fish remains covered.

7 Taste and adjust the seasoning. Ladle the broth into a soup tureen. Divide the fish, seafood, and vegetables between 6 deep plates. Serve immediately with croutons (see p267), rouille sauce, and boiled floury potatoes, if you like.

### cook's tip

You can replace the heads, bones, and tails with a good fish stock concentrate.

# meat and poultry

# albóndigas

❖ *spain* ❖

These little veal and pork meatballs can also
be served as tapas. Try them with
plain white rice or crusty bread.

**PREP** 20 MINS ❖ **COOK** 1 HR ❖ **MAKES** 48

750g (1lb 10oz) **minced veal**
250g (9oz) **minced pork**
2 **garlic cloves**, finely chopped
115g (4oz) **flat-leaf parsley**, finely chopped,
     plus 2 tbsp chopped **flat-leaf parsley**,
     to garnish
**salt** and freshly ground **black pepper**
½ tsp ground **nutmeg**
5 tbsp dry **breadcrumbs**
100ml (3½fl oz) **milk**
2 tbsp **light olive oil**
3 **onions**, finely chopped
1 tbsp **plain flour**, plus extra for dusting
400ml (14fl oz) **red** or **white wine**
2 large **eggs**, beaten
250ml (9fl oz) **sunflower** or **groundnut oil**,
     for frying

1 Place the veal, pork, garlic, and parsley
in a bowl and mix well. Season with
pepper and nutmeg, and set aside.

2 Place the breadcrumbs in another bowl,
pour in the milk, and set aside to soak.

3 Heat the olive oil in a casserole over
a medium heat, and cook the onions,
stirring, for 4–5 minutes, or until softened.
Sprinkle in the flour and cook for 1 more
minute. Pour in the wine and season to taste.
Bring to a simmer, then reduce the heat
and cook for 15 minutes, or until the sauce
is reduced. Press the sauce through a sieve
and return to the casserole, over a low heat.

4 Squeeze the excess milk from the
breadcrumbs and add the crumbs to
the meat with the eggs and 3 tablespoons
of the sauce. Mix thoroughly, then roll the
mixture into golf ball-sized balls and dust
each with a little flour.

5 Heat the sunflower or groundnut oil in
a large frying pan. Fry the meatballs in
batches, turning frequently, for 5 minutes,
or until evenly browned. Remove from the
pan, drain on kitchen paper, and transfer
to the casserole.

6 Poach the meatballs gently in the sauce
for 20 minutes, or until they are no longer
pink when cut in half. Pour over the sauce,
garnish with parsley, and serve warm.

# saltimbocca alla romana

❖ *italy* ❖

A luxuriously simple Roman dish that is quick to
prepare – as its name, "jump-in-the-mouth",
suggests. Pork, chicken, or turkey escalopes
can replace the veal. Beef escalopes will take
a little longer to cook.

**PREP** 20 MINS ❖ **COOK** 8-10 MINS ❖ **SERVES** 4

500g (1lb 2oz) **veal escalopes**
100g (3½oz) **prosciutto**, finely sliced
about a dozen **sage leaves**
3 tbsp **plain flour**, for dusting
**salt** and freshly **ground pepper**
100g (3½oz) **butter**
1 glass of **marsala** or any other **sweet wine**
4 tbsp diced **sourdough bread**

1 Place each escalope between two sheets
of greaseproof paper or cling film and
flatten with a heavy rolling pin, if not already
done. Divide, if large, into 2–3 pieces. Divide
the prosciutto into similar-sized pieces. Top
each escalope with prosciutto and a sage
leaf and reserve the remaining sage leaves.
Roll up the escalopes to form neat bolsters
and dust with seasoned flour.

2 Heat half the butter in a large non-stick
frying pan and add the bolsters. Fry
gently on all sides until lightly browned.
Add the wine, boil until all the alcohol
has evaporated, then add a glass of cold
water and bring to the boil again. Reduce
the heat, cover the pan, and leave to
simmer for about 8–10 minutes, until the
sauce is well-reduced and the escalopes are
cooked right through.

3 Meanwhile, heat the rest of the butter in
a small frying pan. Drop in the reserved
sage leaves and fry until transparent – do
not let them brown. Remove and reserve.
Reheat the pan and fry the bread until
golden on all sides.

4 Serve the escalopes in the sauce with
the buttery croutons and sage leaves.

**variation**

**Bocconcini** *Bocconcini*, or "little mouthfuls",
are prepared by replacing the sage leaves in
the middle of the roll with a finger of cheese
– fontina, Gruyère, or Emmental – and
finishing them in a little tomato sauce
rather than wine.

# vitello tonnato

### *italy*

This dish of veal smothered in a tuna mayonnaise and finished with capers is a party dish found throughout Italy and sold ready-prepared in trattorias. It is best made a day ahead and served with a salad of bitter leaves.

**PREP** 30 MINS, PLUS COOLING AND CHILLING
**COOK** 1–1½ HRS ❖ **SERVES** 4-6

1kg (2¼lb) boned **leg** of **veal**, rolled and tied
1 **bay leaf**
1 small **onion**, diced
½ tsp **black peppercorns**
**salt** and freshly ground **black pepper**
sprig of **thyme**

4 tbsp **salt-preserved capers**, well rinsed, to garnish
**lemon** quarters, to serve

### For the tuna mayonnaise
2 **egg yolks**
150ml (5fl oz) light **olive oil**
125g (4½ oz) canned **tuna**, drained
3–4 canned **anchovy fillets**, finely chopped
1 tbsp **lemon juice**

1 Preheat the oven to 180°C (350°F/Gas 4). In a casserole, add the veal with the bay leaf, onion, peppercorns, 1 tablespoon of salt, thyme, and a cup of cold water. Cover tightly with a lid and roast in the oven for 1–1½ hours, or until perfectly tender.

2 Remove the casserole from the oven and leave the veal to cool in its juices. Remove and reserve the meat.

Remove the fat from the juices in the pan and add 250ml (9fl oz) cold water to make stock. Boil lightly.

3 For the tuna mayonnaise, whizz the egg yolks in a food processor and gradually work in the oil until thick. With the motor running, add the tuna, anchovies, and lemon juice and blitz until smooth. Add the veal broth to the mayonnaise and blitz again until you get the consistency of double cream. Season to taste.

4 Slice the meat and arrange on a serving dish. Pour the tuna mayonnaise over the meat. Cover with cling film and refrigerate for 1–2 hours or overnight. Scatter over the capers and serve with quartered lemons.

# spezzatino di manzo alla toscana

### ❖ *tuscany* ❖

Italian cuisine at its simple best. Chianti is the wine of Tuscany, but you can use any good-quality, full-bodied red wine for this peppery beef dish.

**PREP** 35–40 MINS, PLUS MARINATING
**COOK** 2–2½ HRS ❖ **SERVES** 6

5–6 sprigs of **sage**

**salt** and freshly ground **black pepper**

300ml (10fl oz) **olive oil**

1.4kg (3lb) **braising steak**, diced into 5cm (2in) cubes

125g (4½oz) **pancetta lardons**

1 large **onion**, diced

6 **garlic cloves**

400g (14oz) can chopped **tomatoes**

2 **bay leaves**

250ml (9fl oz) hot **beef stock**, plus extra if required

500ml (16fl oz) **red wine**

500g (1lb 2oz) loaf **crusty Italian peasant-style bread**, such as fettunta, to serve

1 Chop the sage leaves from 2 sprigs. Mix 1 tablespoon pepper with all but 3 tablespoons oil. Pour one-quarter of the mix over the chopped sage and coat the beef in it. Cover with cling film and refrigerate, stirring occasionally, for 8–12 hours.

2 Chop the remaining sage. Transfer the meat to a plate and pat dry. Heat 1½ tablespoons of oil in a pan over a high heat. Brown half the meat and set aside. Add the rest of the oil to the pan and brown the rest of the beef. Reduce the heat to medium, add the pancetta, and cook for 2–3 minutes.

3 Add the onion and cook, stirring, until soft. Add the beef, 5 finely chopped garlic cloves, tomatoes, bay leaves, sage, 1 tablespoon pepper, stock, and wine. Bring to the boil, stirring occasionally. Cover, reduce the heat, and simmer for 1¾–2 hours, until tender, stirring. Add more stock or water if needed. Discard the bay leaves and taste for seasoning. If the sauce is thin, increase the heat and boil.

4 Preheat the oven to 190°C (375°F/Gas 5). Cut the bread into 1cm (½in) slices and place on a baking sheet. Brush with the sage oil and season. Bake for 7–10 minutes and toast both sides. Cut the reserved garlic clove in half and rub over each slice. Transfer to a wire rack. Spoon the beef into a warmed dish and serve with the toasted bread.

# daube

### ❖ *provence* ❖

This famous beef stew of Provence is perfect for a winter dinner party. It is easy to prepare and requires no last-minute work, but you need to start a day or two ahead to give the powerful aromatic flavours time to develop.

**PREP** 15 MINS, PLUS OVERNIGHT MARINATING
**COOK** 2½–3½ HRS ❖ **SERVES** 4

1.5kg (3lb 3oz) lean stewing **steak**

2 **garlic cloves**, crushed

1 large **white onion**, chopped

1 **banana shallot**, chopped

3 **bay leaves**

1 **carrot**, chopped

1 small **fennel bulb**, chopped

7cm (3in) strip of dried **orange peel**

10 black **peppercorns**

2 sprigs of **thyme** or **oregano**

2 sprigs of **flat-leaf parsley**

750ml (1⅓ pints) **red wine**

2 tbsp **olive oil**

100g (3½oz) **lardons** or diced **pancetta**

**salt** and freshly ground **black pepper**

1 To marinate the beef, cut the steak into 5cm (2in) chunks and place in a bowl. Add the garlic, onion, shallot, bay leaves, carrot, fennel, orange peel, peppercorns, thyme, and parsley. Pour in the wine, stir well, cover, and refrigerate overnight.

2 Remove the beef from the marinade and wipe well with kitchen paper. Strain the marinade through a sieve into a bowl. Reserve both the ingredients and marinade.

3 Pour the oil into a large flameproof pan, add the lardons, and stir over a medium heat for 2–3 minutes, until sizzling. Add the beef, increase the heat a little, and cook for 10 minutes, until brown on all sides.

4 Tip in the drained marinade ingredients. Cook and stir for 5 minutes, then pour in the marinade. Add a little boiling water – just enough to cover the ingredients – and bring to the boil.

5 Reduce the heat to low. Cover and cook for 2½–3 hours, until very tender. After 2 hours, stir and remove the parsley, thyme, and bay leaves. Taste and adjust the seasoning. Simmer, uncovered, for 15 minutes and serve hot. If you prefer a deeper flavour, leave until cold, then remove and discard the surface fat, and reheat, covered, over a low heat.

# lahma meshwi
### ❖ *north africa* ❖

Chermoula is a classic North African marinade for fish and shellfish, but it also pairs well with grilled meats, as here. In Morocco, it is used liberally in tagines and couscous dishes.

**PREP** 15 MINS, PLUS MARINATING
**COOK** 15 MINS ❖ **SERVES** 6

12 **lamb cutlets**, trimmed
4 ripe **plum tomatoes**, chopped
**salt** and freshly ground **black pepper**
1 tbsp **balsamic vinegar**
1 tbsp **olive oil**
small bunch of **mint leaves**, chopped, to garnish
**coriander leaves**, chopped, to garnish

### For the marinade
2–3 **garlic cloves**, chopped
1 **red chilli**, deseeded and chopped
1 tsp **coarse salt**
small bunch of **coriander**, chopped
small bunch of **flat-leaf parsley**, chopped
2 tsp ground **cumin**
1 tsp **paprika**
4–5 tbsp **olive oil**
juice of 1 **lemon**

1 For the marinade, place the garlic, red chilli, and coarse salt in a mortar and pestle and pound, until they form a paste. Add the coriander and parsley, and pound to a coarse paste. Add the cumin and paprika, then pour in the oil and lemon juice. Mix well.

2 Place the cutlets in a dish. Rub the marinade over the lamb, and marinate for 30 minutes.

3 Season the tomatoes, drizzle with the olive oil, the balsamic vinegar, coriander, and mint. Set aside.

4 Preheat the grill on its highest setting. Remove the cutlets from the marinade and grill for 5 minutes on each side, or until cooked through and crisp. Serve the lamb with the tomato salad on the side.

*how to serve*
Chermoula can be used as a condiment with grilled meat and poultry or it can be drizzled over salads and soups.

# riñones al jerez

*❖ spain ❖*

Veal kidneys, tender and pale, are cooked in sherry, which takes its name from Jerez, the sherry makers' town. Chicken livers can be cooked in the same way – they are nicest when still pink, so take care not to overcook them.

**PREP** 15 MINS, PLUS SOAKING
**COOK** 15-20 MINUTES ❖ **SERVES** 4-6

1 **veal** or **beef kidney**, skinned and cored
1 tbsp **sherry vinegar**
2 tbsp **plain flour**
**salt** and freshly ground **black pepper**
4 tbsp **olive oil**
4 **garlic cloves**, thinly sliced
2 tbsp chopped **flat-leaf parsley**
1 glass of **dry sherry**, such as oloroso or fino
1–2 **bay leaves**

1 Thinly slice the kidney and soak in cold water with the vinegar for 1–2 hours to remove any taste of ammonia. Drain and pat dry. Dust the slices lightly through the seasoned flour and set aside.

2 Heat the oil in a large non-stick frying pan and fry the garlic for 1–2 minutes, until soft. Add the kidney pieces and fry until brown, then stir in the parsley and sherry, and boil until the alcohol has evaporated.

3 Add a glass of cold water and the bay leaves, boil again, cover with a lid, reduce the heat, and simmer gently for 10–15 minutes, topping up with more water if necessary, until the kidneys are tender and the juices reduced to an oily, well-flavoured sauce. Taste and adjust the seasoning, if necessary.

### variation

**Lamb or pork kidneys with sherry** You can prepare lamb or pork kidneys in the same way. Chicken livers are also good with a sherry sauce – they are nicest when still pink, so take care not to overcook them.

# kofta meshweya

*❖ middle east ❖*

These tender minced lamb kebabs with a hint of Middle Eastern spices are wonderful dipped in a mild yogurt sauce.

**PREP** 15 MINS, PLUS CHILLING
**COOK** 8-10 MINS ❖ **MAKES** 16

1 slice of **white bread**, crusts removed and torn into small pieces
3 tbsp **milk**
450g (1lb) **minced lamb**
8 sprigs of **coriander**, leaves finely chopped
8 sprigs of **flat-leaf parsley**, leaves finely chopped
1 tbsp ground **cumin**
1 **garlic clove**, crushed
½ tsp **salt**
½ tsp freshly ground **black pepper**
**vegetable oil**, for brushing

**For the sauce**
115g (4oz) **cucumber**, deseeded and diced
300g (10oz) **plain yogurt**

1 Place 16 wooden skewers in hot water and leave to soak. Soak the bread in the milk for 5 minutes.

2 Place the minced lamb, coriander, parsley, cumin, garlic, salt, and pepper in a large bowl. Squeeze the milk from the bread and add the bread to the bowl. Mix thoroughly with your hands. Discard the remaining milk.

3 With wet hands, roll 2 tablespoons of the mixture into round balls, then repeat with the remaining mixture to make 16 koftas. Carefully skewer each kofta with a wooden skewer.

4 Meanwhile, preheat the grill to its highest setting. Line the grill pan with foil and lightly brush the grill rack with vegetable oil. Position the rack about 10cm (4in) from the heat.

5 Place the koftas on the rack and grill, turning frequently, for 8 minutes for slightly pink, or 10 minutes for well done. Mix the cucumber and yogurt with salt to taste and serve alongside the koftas.

# warak malfouf
### *lebanon*

This dish of tender cabbage leaves, with pervasive gentle aromas of lemon and mint, is Lebanese home cooking at its best. These mezze favourites can be served hot or cold with yogurt and pitta bread. Choose a round cabbage with few crinkled leaves as these may be difficult to roll.

**PREP** 35 MINS ❖ **COOK** 1½ HRS

**SERVES** 4 AS A MAIN COURSE, 6-8 AS MEZZE

## ingredients

1 large or 2 smaller **green cabbages**, about 1.5kg (3lb 3oz) in total weight

**sea salt** and freshly ground **black pepper**

light **vegetable, beef, or chicken stock**, made from a good concentrate (optional)

6-8 tbsp **olive oil**

500g (1lb 2oz) minced **braising steak**

1 large mild **onion**, finely chopped

3 **garlic cloves**, crushed

1 tsp **cinnamon**

1 tsp **allspice**

3 tbsp dried **mint**

150g (5oz) **medium-grain rice**, washed and drained

finely grated zest and juice of 2 **unwaxed lemons**

2 large **tomatoes**, thinly sliced

1 **Core the cabbage**. Steam over, or boil in, lightly salted simmering water until the leaves are tender. Place in a colander and drain. Leave until cool enough to handle. Reserve the cooking liquid. You will need about 600ml (1 pint) liquid. Top up with stock or water, if needed.

2 **Heat 1½ tablespoons oil** in a hot frying pan, and fry the beef until browned. Transfer to a plate lined with kitchen paper. Add 1 tablespoon oil to the pan and stir in the onion. Reduce the heat, add 1 teaspoon garlic, spices, and 1 tablespoon mint, and stir for 2 minutes. Add the rice and cook, stirring, until the onion is soft and the rice translucent. Tip into a bowl, add the beef, and season.

3 **Lightly oil a deep sauté pan**. Sprinkle over half the lemon zest, and half the remaining mint and garlic. Cover with the tomato. Separate the cabbage leaves. Cut the larger leaves in half. Cut out the thick central white ribs. Chop the ribs and any small leaves and spread over the tomatoes.

4 **Place a heaped tablespoon** of the beef and rice mix in the middle of each leaf. Roll up from the cut end, fold in the sides, and roll into a cigar shape. Place the rolls side by side in the pan. The rolls should not be tightly packed. Repeat in layers until all the rolls are in the pan. Add the remaining garlic, half the lemon juice, the remaining zest, and half the remaining oil.

5 **Place a plate** over the rolls. Hold it down with one hand. Pour in the cooking liquid until it comes up to the plate. Cover the pan with a lid, and bring to the boil over a medium heat. Remove the lid and simmer over a low heat for at least 40 minutes. Remove the plate, scatter over the remaining mint, lemon juice, and oil, and simmer for 5 more minutes. Serve warm.

# lamb tagine with green peas and preserved lemons

❖ *Morocco* ❖

This lovely dish benefits from being made well in advance to allow the flavours to develop. The lemon zest adds a mellow citrus flavour and a splash of colour.

**PREP** 15 MINS, PLUS MARINATING
**COOK** 1 HR 20 MINS ❖ **SERVES** 6

1 tsp chopped **flat-leaf parsley**, plus extra to garnish

1 tbsp chopped **coriander**, plus extra to garnish

1kg (2¼lb) **leg of lamb**, cut into slices

2 **onions**, finely chopped

3 **garlic cloves**, chopped

1 tsp grated **fresh root ginger**

9 tbsp **olive oil**

600ml (1 pint) hot **meat stock**

2 **preserved lemons**, cut into quarters, pulp removed and discarded, zest thinly sliced

**salt** and freshly ground **black pepper**

450g (1lb) **frozen peas**

1 **lemon**, zest peeled into long, thin strips or cut into wedges, to garnish

1 Combine the parsley, coriander, lamb, onions, garlic, ginger, and olive oil in a large dish and leave to marinate overnight, covered with cling film, in the fridge.

2 Remove the lamb, reserving the marinade and setting it aside. In a hot frying pan, brown the lamb evenly, then transfer to a large flameproof casserole, pour over the reserved marinade, add the stock, and bring to the boil. Reduce the heat and simmer, covered, for 1 hour.

3 Add the preserved lemons to the pan and simmer for another 30 minutes, or until the meat is very tender.

4 Adjust the seasoning, if necessary, then add the peas and simmer for a further 5 minutes. Serve while still hot with chopped parsley and coriander sprinkled over, and garnish with strips of lemon zest.

# kibbeh samiyeh

❖ *middle east* ❖

Kibbeh are everyday dumplings, or patties, made with bulgur and minced meat or chicken, fish, or cooked vegetables.

**PREP** 20 MINS ❖ **COOK** 45 MINS ❖ **SERVES** 4–6

2 tbsp **olive oil**, plus extra for greasing

115g (4oz) fine **bulgur**, rinsed and drained

450g (1lb) lean **lamb**, finely minced

1 **onion**, grated

2 tsp ground **cinnamon**

1 tsp ground **cumin**

1 tsp ground **allspice**

**salt** and freshly ground **black pepper**

## For the topping

2 tbsp **olive oil**

2 **onions**, sliced

2–3 tbsp **pine nuts**

1 tsp ground **cinnamon**

1 tbsp **pomegranate molasses**

small bunch of **flat-leaf parsley**, finely chopped

1 Preheat the oven to 180°C (350°F/Gas 4). Grease a 25 x 17cm (10 x 7in) ovenproof dish. Tip the bulgur into a bowl and pour just enough boiling water to cover it. Place a clean kitchen towel over the top and leave to steam for 10 minutes, until the bulgur has absorbed all the water.

2 In a bowl, pound the lamb with the onion and spices. Season and knead well. Squeeze the bulgur with your hands to get rid of any excess water and add to the bowl. Knead the mixture well and pound it by lifting in the air and slapping into the bottom of the bowl, until pasty and slightly sticky.

3 Tip the mixture into the greased dish and spread evenly. Flatten the top with your knuckles and spread the oil over the surface. Using a sharp knife, cut into wedges or diamond shapes and pop into the oven for 30 minutes, until browned.

4 For the topping, heat the oil in a frying pan and stir in the onions until just brown. Add the pine nuts, stir until golden, then add the cinnamon and pomegranate molasses. Season.

5 When the kibbeh is ready, spread the onion mix over the top and return to the oven for 5 minutes. Lift the portions onto a serving dish and top with the parsley. Serve with a salad of beans or crunchy vegetables.

# pinchitos moruños

✤ *andalucia* ✤

"Little Moorish thorns" is the Spanish name for these tender all-meat kebabs spiced with cumin and coriander. They are a popular street food at festivals in Andalucia, cooked to order on a little charcoal brazier.

**PREP** 10 MINS, PLUS MARINATING
**COOK** 8-10 MINS ✤ **SERVES** 4-6

750g (1lb 10oz) **lamb**, **beef**, or **pork**, trimmed and diced into bite-sized pieces
2–3 tbsp **olive oil**
1 tbsp **cumin seeds**
1 tbsp crushed **coriander seeds**
1 tbsp dried **thyme**
1 tsp **turmeric** or powdered **saffron**
**salt**

1 Place the meat pieces in a bowl and work in the rest of the ingredients, except the salt. Set aside for 1–2 hours for the flavours to infuse, or leave overnight in the fridge.

2 Preheat the grill or barbecue to its highest temperature. Thread the meat onto fine metal skewers – if using bamboo skewers, soak them in water before using.

3 Grill over a high heat, turning the skewers frequently, until the meat is well browned but still juicy. Season lightly with salt and serve with crusty bread.

*how to eat*
In Spain, the skewers are served with a hunk of pitta or Lebanese flatbread on the end to help you pull the meat off without burning your fingers.

# tajine bil mishmish

✤ *morocco* ✤

Dried apricots and orange juice, along with cumin, coriander, ginger, and thyme, give this dish the distinct flavour of Moroccan cuisine.

**PREP** 10 MINS, PLUS MARINATING
**COOK** 1½ HRS ✤ **SERVES** 4

1 **onion**, thinly sliced
1 tsp ground **coriander**
1 tsp ground **cumin**
1 tsp ground **ginger**
1 tsp dried **thyme**
2 tbsp **sunflower oil** or **peanut oil**
900g (2lb) **boneless lamb**, such as shoulder or chump steaks, cut into 2.5cm (1in) cubes
2 tbsp **plain flour**
300ml (10fl oz) **orange juice**
600ml (1 pint) hot **chicken stock**
115g (4oz) ready-to-eat dried **apricots**
200g (7oz) quick-cook **couscous**
**salt** and freshly ground **black pepper**
**mint leaves**, to garnish (optional)

1 Place the onion, coriander, cumin, ginger, thyme, and 1 tablespoon of the oil in a large non-metallic bowl, then mix in the lamb. Cover and marinate for at least 3 hours or overnight in the fridge.

2 Preheat the oven to 160°C (325°F/Gas 3). Place the flour in a small bowl and stir in the orange juice until smooth. Set aside.

3 Heat the remaining oil in a flameproof casserole over a high heat. Add the lamb mixture and fry, stirring frequently, for 5 minutes, or until browned.

4 Stir the flour mixture into the casserole with the stock. Bring to the boil, stirring, then remove the casserole from the heat, cover, and place in the oven for 1 hour.

5 Remove from the oven. Stir in the apricots, cover, and return to the oven. Cook for a further 20 minutes, or until the lamb is tender.

6 Place the couscous with a little salt in a large heatproof bowl and pour over boiling water to a depth of 2.5cm (1in). Cover with a folded kitchen towel and leave to stand for 10 minutes, or until the grains are tender. Fluff with a fork and keep warm. When the lamb is tender, taste and adjust the seasoning. Sprinkle with mint leaves, if you like, and serve with the hot couscous.

# stifado apo arni

*greece*

Roasting lamb is popular during Easter in Greece. Slow cooking makes the meat very succulent and tender.

**PREP** 10 MINS, PLUS MARINATING
**COOK** 4½–5 HRS ❖ **SERVES** 4

1.35kg (3lb) **leg of lamb**
2 tbsp **olive oil**
3 **garlic cloves**, crushed
1 tsp ground **cinnamon**
1 tsp dried **thyme**
1 tsp dried **oregano** or **marjoram**
juice of 1 **lemon**
**salt** and freshly ground **black pepper**
1 **onion**, sliced into rings
2 **carrots**, halved lengthways
2 tbsp chopped **flat-leaf parsley**

1 Preheat the oven to 150°C (300°F/Gas 2). Place the lamb in a roasting tin. In a small bowl, mix the oil, garlic, cinnamon, and herbs, and brush over the lamb. Sprinkle with the lemon juice and season to taste.

2 Half-fill the tin with water, add the onion and carrots. Cook for 3 hours, basting every 30 minutes and topping up with more water if necessary.

3 Cover with foil and cook for a further 1½–2 hours, or until the meat comes away from the bone.

4 Remove from the oven and leave to rest for 20 minutes. Arrange the lamb on a platter, scatter the parsley over, and serve.

# souvlakia

*greece*

The Greek kebab differs from the Turkish kebab in that the meat is not marinated or spiced and the flavouring comes from herbs, olive oil, and lemon. The higher the proportion of meat to vegetables, the more the dish is prized.

**PREP** 20 MINS ❖ **COOK** 8-10 MINS
**SERVES** 4-6

500g (1lb 2oz) **lean pork**, trimmed and cut into bite-sized cubes
4–6 **shallots** or small **onions**, skinned and halved
1 **green pepper**, deseeded and cut into chunks
1–2 firm **beef tomatoes**, cut into chunks
**salt** and freshly ground **black pepper**
2–3 tbsp dried **oregano**
**lemon juice**, for drizzling
**olive oil**, for drizzling
1 **lemon**, cut into quarters, to serve

1 Preheat the grill or barbecue to its highest temperature.

2 Thread the meat onto 4–6 long metal skewers with any fat facing outwards, alternating with the vegetables. Pack the pieces tightly to allow for shrinkage. Dust with salt, pepper, and oregano, and finish with a squeeze of lemon and a few drops of oil.

3 Grill the kebabs, turning them as they cook, until the fat crisps and the vegetables blister black at the edges. Serve straight from the grill with the lemon quarters.

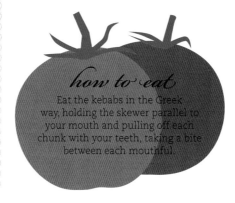

*how to eat*

Eat the kebabs in the Greek way, holding the skewer parallel to your mouth and pulling off each chunk with your teeth, taking a bite between each mouthful.

# moussaka

*greece*

The Greeks like to serve this classic dish in squares cut from a large baking tray. Try baking this version in individual gratin or pie dishes.

**PREP** 30 MINS, PLUS STANDING
**COOK** 1 HR 30 MINS ❖ **SERVES** 4

2 large **aubergines**, cut into 5mm (¼in) slices
**salt** and freshly ground **black pepper**
5 tbsp **olive oil**
1 large **onion**, chopped
450g (1lb) lean **lamb mince**
100ml (3½fl oz) **red wine**
400g can chopped **tomatoes**
1 tsp **sugar**
100ml (3½fl oz) hot **lamb stock**
2 tsp dried **oregano**
450g (1lb) **potatoes**, peeled and cut into 5mm (¼in) slices
4 tbsp grated **Parmesan cheese**
4 tbsp dried **breadcrumbs**

**For the topping**
200g (7oz) **Greek yogurt**, strained
3 large **eggs**
1 tbsp **cornflour**
115g (4oz) **curd cheese**
60g (2oz) **feta cheese**, crumbled

1 Sprinkle the aubergine slices with salt and set aside for 30 minutes. Rinse well under cold running water, drain, and pat dry.

2 Heat 2 tablespoons of the oil in a deep-sided frying pan, add the onion, and cook over a low heat, stirring often, until soft. Increase the heat, add the mince, and fry until just brown. Add the wine, boil for 1–2 minutes, then add the tomatoes, sugar, stock, and 1 teaspoon oregano. Season and simmer for 30 minutes, until the sauce is thick.

3 Brush the aubergine slices with the remaining oil and grill in batches until softened on both sides. Boil the potato slices in water until just tender. Drain.

4 For the topping, whisk the yogurt, eggs, and cornflour until smooth, then whisk in the curd and feta.

5 Preheat the oven to 180°C (350°F/Gas 4). Layer the aubergine with the meat mixture into 4 baking dishes. Arrange the potato slices on top in an overlapping layer. Spread the topping over, scatter with the Parmesan, breadcrumbs, and the remaining oregano. Bake for 45 minutes, or until golden brown.

# roz bi lahma

### *middle east*

Fragrant and full of colour, this pilaf has many layers of flavour. Swap in different dried fruits and nuts for variety. Dates and apricots are often used in Turkish dishes, as are almonds.

**PREP** 15 MINS   ❖   **COOK** 1 HR   ❖   **SERVES** 4-6

2 tbsp **olive oil**, plus extra for drizzling

675g (1½ lb) **leg of lamb**, cut into bite-sized pieces

1 **onion**, finely chopped

**salt** and freshly ground **black pepper**

3 **garlic cloves**, finely chopped

1 **green chilli**, deseeded and finely sliced

1 tsp dried **mint**

1 tsp ground **cinnamon**

60g (2oz) **golden** or regular **sultanas**

350g (12oz) easy-cook **basmati rice**

900ml (1½ pints) hot **lamb stock**

60g (2oz) **hazelnuts**, toasted and roughly chopped

small handful of **dill**, finely chopped

100g (3½oz) **pomegranate seeds** (about 1 pomegranate)

75g (2½oz) **feta cheese**, crumbled (optional)

1 Heat the oil in a large flameproof casserole over a medium-high heat, add the lamb (in batches, if necessary), and cook for 6–8 minutes, until browned on all sides. Remove and set aside.

2 Add the onion to the casserole and cook over a medium heat for 3–4 minutes, until soft. Season, stir in the garlic, chilli, mint, and cinnamon, and cook for another 2 minutes, then stir in the sultanas.

3 Stir through the rice so that all the grains are coated well and the juices soaked up. Return the lamb to the casserole, pour over the stock, and reduce to a simmer. Partially cover and cook for 30–40 minutes, topping up with a little more hot stock if it begins to dry out. Taste

and season, then stir through the hazelnuts and dill, and scatter with the pomegranate seeds. Top with the feta, if using, and serve with warm pitta bread and a lightly dressed crisp green salad.

### *how to prepare*

To retrieve the seeds, cut a pomegranate into quarters and squeeze over a bowl, easing out the seeds with a sharp knife. Pick out and discard the pieces of white membrane.

# keftedes tiganites

*❖ greece ❖*

You can also serve these bite-sized meatballs spiced with aniseed and cinnamon as a mezze with a glass of chilled ouzo.

**PREP** 20 MINS ❖ **COOK** 25 MINS ❖ **MAKES** 30

500g (1lb) **minced lamb, beef, or pork**
150g (5½oz) fresh **breadcrumbs**
1 medium **onion**, grated
1 large **egg**, beaten
**salt** and freshly ground **black pepper**
plain **flour**, for dusting
**olive oil**, for frying

1 Work the meat with the breadcrumbs, onion, and egg. Season and mix well until you have a firm, smooth paste – you may need to add more breadcrumbs. With damp hands, form the paste into walnut-sized balls and dust them through a plateful of seasoned flour.

2 In a large non-stick frying pan, heat the oil to a depth of 1cm (½in) and slip in the meatballs in batches. Fry over a medium heat until brown all over. Reduce the heat, cover loosely with a lid, and cook gently until firm and tender, for about 20–25 minutes.

**cook's tip**

To serve as a main course with rice or macaroni, finish the meatballs in a red wine sauce. To prepare, when the meatballs are nearly done, pour out all but 1 tablespoon of the oil, add 2 glasses of red wine and 1 glass of cold water, a cinnamon stick, 1 teaspoon fennel seeds, and a spoonful of tomato paste. Bring to the boil and shake the pan to distribute the sauce and simmer for another 10 minutes.

# köfte kebab

*❖ turkey ❖*

These spicy lamb kebabs are studded with flecks of green from the parsley and coriander. They are served with a white bean and tomato salad.

**PREP** 45-50 MINS, PLUS MARINATING
**COOK** 4-5 HRS ❖ **SERVES** 4-6

2 **garlic cloves**, halved
**salt** and freshly ground **black pepper**
a little **olive oil**
1 **onion**, finely chopped
2 tsp ground **cumin**
2 tsp **paprika**
1 tsp **cayenne pepper**
500g (1lb 2oz) **lamb mince**
handful of **flat-leaf parsley leaves**, roughly chopped
handful of **coriander leaves**, roughly chopped
100g (3½oz) unsalted **pistachios**, roughly chopped

### For the salad

300g (10oz) **dried cannellini beans**
2 **garlic cloves**, left whole
½ bunch of **flat-leaf parsley**, leaves picked and chopped (stalks reserved)
3 tbsp **extra virgin olive oil**
3 tbsp **red wine vinegar**
1 tsp ground **cumin**
2 ripe **tomatoes**, cut into 1cm (½in) cubes

1 For the salad, soak the beans overnight in cold water. Drain and rinse under cold running water, then tip in a heavy-based pan and cover with cold water. Add the garlic, parsley stalks, and a splash of oil. Bring to the boil, reduce the heat, and simmer for 1 hour 20 minutes to 1 hour 40 minutes, until the beans are soft but with a bit of bite. Drain off the liquid. Add the vinegar, remaining oil, and cumin, and stir through. Season well. Leave for about 20 minutes. Add the tomatoes and parsley leaves just before serving.

2 For the kebabs, soak 4–6 bamboo skewers in cold water for at least 30 minutes. Crush the garlic with a little salt to make a paste.

3 Heat a little oil in a heavy-based pan over a medium-high heat. Fry the onion for 4 minutes, until soft. Add the garlic paste, cumin, paprika, and cayenne, and fry for 2–3 minutes, until aromatic. Remove from the heat, transfer to a bowl, and leave to cool for 5 minutes. Add the mince, parsley, coriander, and pistachios. Season well.

4 Mould the lamb mixture onto one end of each skewer, making a cylinder of meat around roughly half its length. Heat a little oil in a heavy pan over a medium-high heat. Fry the kebabs in batches until golden brown all over. Drain on kitchen paper and serve with the salad.

# terbiyeli köfte

❖ *turkey* ❖

In this Turkish recipe, tiny meatballs are cooked in stock thickened with a traditional mix of egg and lemon, which gives the dish a slightly tart flavour but keeps it light and creamy.

**PREP** 25 MINS, PLUS MARINATING
**COOK** 35 MINS ❖ **SERVES** 4-6

450g (1lb) finely minced **lean lamb**

1 tbsp medium-grain or long-grain **rice**, washed and drained

small bunch of **dill**, finely chopped

bunch of **flat-leaf parsley**, finely chopped, plus extra to garnish

**sea salt** and freshly ground **black pepper**

1 litre (1¾ pints) **hot stock** (optional)

2 medium-sized **carrots**, peeled and diced

2 medium-sized **potatoes**, peeled and diced

2 **egg yolks**

juice of 2 **lemons**

1 tbsp strained **yogurt**

1 tsp dried **mint**

1 Place the lamb in a bowl with the rice, dill, and parsley, and season well. Knead the mixture together for about 5 minutes and slap it down into the base of the bowl to release the air. Take small portions of the mixture into the palm of your hand and mould into very tight cherry-sized balls.

2 Pour 1 litre (1¾ pints) hot water or stock into a heavy-based pan and bring it to the boil. Add the carrots and cook for 2–3 minutes, then add the meatballs. Reduce the heat, cover the pan, and simmer for 10–15 minutes. Add the potatoes and simmer, uncovered, for a further 10 minutes.

3 In a bowl, beat the egg yolks with the lemon juice, yogurt, and mint. Spoon a little of the cooking liquid into the mixture, then tip it all into the pan, stirring continuously, and gently heat it through. Be careful not to bring the sauce to the boil as it will curdle.

4 Check the seasoning and spoon the meatballs with the sauce into shallow bowls. Garnish with parsley and serve with a rice pilaf or chunks of crusty bread.

# arni sto fourno

❖ *greece* ❖

Olives, feta, and thyme are all synonymous with Greek cuisine. Here they are combined with a succulent leg of lamb stuffed with red peppers and served with roasted potatoes.

**PREP** 30 MINS ❖ **COOK** 2¼-2¾ HRS
**SERVES** 4-6

1 **leg of lamb**, boned and butterflied (about 1.8kg/4lb after boning), or a boneless shoulder

**salt** and freshly ground **black pepper**

2 tbsp **olive oil**

1 tbsp dried **oregano**

2 **red peppers**, deseeded and finely chopped

60g (2oz) **pitted black olives**, finely chopped

175g (6oz) **feta cheese**, finely chopped

3 **red onions**, roughly chopped

4–6 **tomatoes**, roughly chopped

450ml (15fl oz) **red wine**

a few sprigs of **thyme**

1 Preheat the oven to 160°C (325°F/Gas 3). Lay out the lamb flat and season well. Rub both sides all over with the oil and oregano. Cover one side of the lamb with the red peppers, then the olives, followed by the feta. Starting from one end, roll up the lamb, tucking in any loose pieces to neaten it. Tie it up with butcher's string, so it is secure.

2 Heat a large flameproof casserole over a medium heat, add the lamb, and cook for 4–6 minutes on each side, until it begins to colour. Add the onions and tomatoes to the pan, and cook for a further minute, then pour in the wine. Bring to the boil, then reduce to a simmer and add some seasoning and the thyme. Cover and bake in the oven for 2–2½ hours, or until cooked. Check occasionally and top up with a little hot water, if it seems dry.

3 Remove from the oven, cover the meat loosely with foil, and leave to rest for 15 minutes. Remove the string and cut into slices. Serve with some of the sauce, together with baby spinach and potatoes roasted in olive oil with rosemary.

# rojões de porco

*portugal*

Floury potatoes are a perfect match for rich pork loin in this comforting meal. Make it a day ahead as the flavours improve with reheating.

**PREP** 15 MINS ❖ **COOK** 2½ HRS ❖ **SERVES** 6

5 tbsp **olive oil**

1.5–1.8kg (3lb 3oz–4lb) **pork loin**, boned and rolled, rind removed

3 mild **onions**, thinly sliced

3 **garlic cloves**, crushed

2 tsp smoked **paprika**

1 tsp rubbed **sage**

1 tsp **dried thyme** or 2 tsp **fresh thyme leaves**

1 tbsp **tomato paste**

**salt** and freshly ground **black pepper**

675g (1½lb) large **floury potatoes**, peeled and quartered

300ml (10floz) **dry white wine**, plus extra if required

3 **bay leaves**

2 tbsp snipped **flat-leaf parsley**, to finish.

1 Heat half the oil in a large, heavy-based flameproof casserole. Add the meat and fry until brown all over. Lift out and set aside on a plate. Add 1 tablespoon of the oil in the pot, spread the onions, and sweat over a medium heat for 6–8 minutes, until tender and golden brown. Stir in the garlic.

2 In a bowl, mix together the paprika, sage, thyme, tomato paste, and the remaining oil. Season, then coat the meat with the mixture, patting it in well. Return the meat to the pot and cook, covered, for 10 minutes, then turn over and cook for a further 10 minutes.

3 Meanwhile, preheat the oven to 180°C (350°F/Gas 4). In a pan of lightly salted water, boil the potatoes for 10–15 minutes, until half-cooked, then drain. Surround the meat with the potatoes. Pour over the wine, tuck in the bay leaves, season, and simmer.

4 Cover the pot tightly and transfer to the oven. Roast for 1½ hours, or until very tender. You might need to add a splash of wine at the end. Remove from the oven and leave with the lid on for about 20 minutes. Adjust the seasoning, remove the bay leaves, scatter over the parsley, and serve immediately.

# fabada

*spain*

A simple Spanish spicy sausage and bacon stew is ideal comfort food, and this time-saving version uses canned beans.

**PREP** 5 MINS ❖ **COOK** 40 MINS ❖ **SERVES** 4

250g (9oz) **morcilla** (Spanish black pudding)

250g (9oz) **chorizo sausage**

250g (9oz) thick-cut **tocino**, **pancetta**, or **streaky bacon rashers**,

1 tbsp **olive oil**

2 x 400g can **white beans**, drained

pinch of **saffron powder**

1 **bay leaf**

1 Cut the morcilla, chorizo, and bacon into large chunks. Heat the oil in a large pan, add the sausages and bacon, and fry, stirring, over a medium-low heat for 2 minutes.

2 Stir in the beans, saffron, bay leaf, and about 500ml (16fl oz) of cold water to cover. Bring to the boil, reduce the heat, cover, and simmer for 30 minutes. Serve hot.

**variation**

**Dried bean stew** Soak 500g (1lb 2oz) dried white beans overnight in a large saucepan. Drain the beans and add fresh water to cover. Boil rapidly for 10 minutes, then skim off any froth, reduce the heat, cover, and simmer, stirring occasionally, for 2–3 hours, or until the beans are tender. Check the water level occasionally to make sure the beans are just covered.

# *essential*
# spices

Until the discovery of the New World at the end of the 15th century, the Mediterranean was very involved in the spice trade, which greatly influenced the region's history.

**Spices were once** worth their weight in gold. Roman soldiers' salaries were paid in salt and their rent in peppercorns. Battles were fought to control the trade, and spices became demonized, but over the centuries countries bordering the Mediterranean became familiar with them. They learnt to cultivate spices when possible, and to integrate combinations of flavours into dishes. Local preferences vary – in Provence, Northern Spain, and Italy, spices are used with a very light touch. The heat level rises somewhat in Southern Spain, Sicily, the Maghreb, and the Eastern Mediterranean, but there are very few hot chilli dishes on menus. The pestle and mortar is best for grinding and blending spices, and always fry them long enough to release their essential oils and carrying flavours.

**Coriander seeds** and ground coriander have a sweet, spicy taste, with a hint of aniseed. It is very popular in the eastern and southern Mediterranean.

**Sumac** has a pleasant sour, mildly astringent flavour and is a favourite in Syria, Lebanon, and the Middle East.

**Saffron** is the dried stigmas of the saffron crocus, which came to Spain with the Arabs. It releases a heady aroma, sweetly pungent bitterness, and an orange colour. Buy red strands rather than powder and beware of imitations.

**Ras el hanout** means "head of the shop" in Arabic. Recipes vary, but it is a secret blend of the best spices available. It is popular in Morocco and North Africa.

**Cinnamon sticks** and ground cinnamon add sweetness to Middle Eastern rice dishes, savoury foods, and desserts.

**Zahtar** is a peppery, woody herb like thyme or oregano. It is also a condiment made from the dried herb, mixed with sesame seeds and sumac. Good for use in baking and popular in the Eastern Mediterranean.

**Caraway seeds** add a strong distinctive flavour to baking, cabbage, and cheese.

**Cumin seeds** and ground cumin have a warm aroma and flavour North African dishes.

**Turmeric** is much used in the Eastern Mediterranean for its colour and bitter, earthy, peppery flavour. It also has medicinal properties.

**Harissa paste**, a hot mix of chilli and spices, comes from Tunisia and is a staple in North Africa.

**Cardamom pods** with their sticky black seeds came to the Mediterranean from the east. The third most expensive spice after saffron and vanilla, it is used ground to flavour Arabic coffee and desserts.

**Ginger** is very spicy when ground, less so freshly grated. It is much loved in Morocco and the Middle East.

ame seeds have a high oil tent with a nutty flavour, ich is more pronounced en roasted.

**Paprika** came from the New World through Spain where it is a staple condiment. It is also used in the eastern Mediterranean.

# cocido madrileño

*❖ s p a i n ❖*

A classic Spanish one-pot meal, this is a fabulously warming dish for a bitterly cold night. There are a lot of different meats here, but make sure the chorizo and morcilla you choose are of good quality.

**PREP** 25 MINS ❖ **COOK** 2¾ HRS ❖ **SERVES** 6-8

4 tbsp **olive oil**

4 small **onions**, quartered

2 **garlic cloves**, sliced

4 thick slices of **belly pork**, about 500g (1lb 2oz) in total

4 **chicken thighs**, about 300g (10oz) in total

250g (9oz) **beef braising steak**, cut into 4 slices

175g (6oz) **tocino** or **smoked streaky bacon**, cut into 4 pieces

4 small **pork spare ribs**, 150g (5½oz) in total

100ml (3½fl oz) **white wine**

175g (6oz) **chorizo**, cut into 4 pieces

175g (6oz) **morcilla**, **boudin noir**, or **Schwarzwurst**

1 small **ham bone**

1 **bay leaf**

**salt** and freshly ground **black pepper**

8 small **waxy potatoes**, peeled

4 **carrots**, peeled and halved lengthways

400g can **chickpeas**, drained

1 **savoy** or **green cabbage heart**, quartered

3 tbsp chopped **flat-leaf parsley**, to garnish

1 Heat 1 tablespoon of the oil in a large saucepan. Add the onions and garlic, and fry for 10 minutes, stirring occasionally. Heat the remaining oil in a frying pan and fry the pork, chicken, beef, tocino, and spare ribs in batches until lightly browned all over, then transfer to the saucepan with the onions.

2 Pour the wine into the frying pan, reduce by half, then pour into the saucepan. Add the chorizo, morcilla, ham bone, and bay leaf to the saucepan, season to taste, then pour in enough cold water to cover.

3 Bring to the boil, reduce the heat, cover, and simmer for about 1½ hours. Add the potatoes and carrots, and cook for a further 30 minutes. Add the chickpeas and cabbage, and cook for another 15 minutes.

4 To serve, remove the bay leaf and ham bone, and divide the meat and vegetables between warmed plates. Add a few spoonfuls of the hot broth and sprinkle with parsley.

# cassoulet

*❖ l a n g u e d o c ❖*

This great Languedocian winter dish takes its name from the pot it is traditionally cooked in, the rounded earthenware *cassole*.

**PREP** 20 MINS ❖ **COOK** 1 HR, PLUS STANDING
**SERVES** 6

700–900g can **goose** or **duck confit**

1 large **white onion**, finely chopped

225g (8oz) **cooked ham** or **gammon**, cut into chunky pieces

1 large **carrot**, thickly sliced

6 **garlic cloves**, crushed

500ml (16fl oz) hot **chicken stock**

4 tbsp **brandy**

3 **tomatoes**, chopped

3 **bay leaves**

4 sprigs of **thyme**

freshly ground **black pepper**

6 **Toulouse** or other **spicy sausages** (luganega, Cumberland, merguez, or chorizo)

800g can small **white haricot beans**

100g (3½oz) **white breadcrumbs** made from toasted day-old bread

a few sprigs of **flat-leaf parsley**

1 Lift the meat out of the can. Discard the fatty skin and separate the meat into chunks. Discard the bones. Reserve the fat.

2 In a heavy-based pan, cook the onion in 2 tablespoons of fat, stirring, until soft. Stir in the confit meat, ham, carrot, and garlic. Cook, stirring, for 2–3 minutes. Tip in the stock, brandy, tomatoes, bay leaves, and thyme. Season with pepper. Stir, cover, and simmer over a low heat for 30 minutes, stirring 2–3 times.

3 Meanwhile, grill or pan-fry the sausages until cooked through. If frying, drain with kitchen paper. Cut each into 2–3 pieces.

4 Drain the beans and spread in the bottom of a casserole pot, ladle over the stew, and discard the bay leaves and thyme. Top with the remaining beans. Add a little hot water if it looks dry. Place the sausages in the beans. Cover and keep in a cool place for at least 2 hours or up to 24 hours.

5 Preheat the oven to 200°C (400°F/Gas 6). Spoon the breadcrumbs over the cassoulet and scatter over the parsley. Drizzle over some of the remaining fat. Cover with a lid or a double layer of foil and bake for 20 minutes. Then remove the lid or foil and brown for 15–20 minutes. Serve hot.

## tagine djaj bil mishmish

❖ *Morocco* ❖

The dried fruit and warm spices in this dish are the unmistakable flavours of the Middle East. It is best enjoyed with couscous, and may be cooked in advance and refrigerated until ready to be served.

**PREP** 15 MINS ❖ **COOK** 35–40 MINS ❖ **SERVES** 4

2 tbsp **sunflower oil**

1 **onion**, finely chopped

1 **garlic clove**, finely chopped

1 tsp ground **ginger**

1 tsp ground **cumin**

1 tsp **turmeric**

pinch of ground **cinnamon**

pinch of dried **chilli flakes** (optional)

1 tbsp **tomato purée**

600ml (1 pint) hot **chicken stock**

4 tbsp fresh **orange juice**

250g (9oz) mixed **dried fruit**, such as apricots and raisins

**salt** and freshly ground **black pepper**

675g (1½lb) **skinless, boneless chicken breasts and thighs**, cut into large chunks

2 tbsp chopped **coriander**, to garnish

1 Heat the oil in a large flameproof casserole over a medium heat. Add the onion, garlic, ground spices, and chilli flakes, if using, and fry, stirring, for 5 minutes, or until the onions have softened. Stir in the tomato purée and stock and bring to the boil, stirring.

2 Add the orange juice and dried fruit. Season to taste. Reduce the heat, partially cover, and simmer for 15 minutes, or until the fruit are soft and the juices have reduced slightly.

3 Add the chicken, cover, and simmer for a further 20 minutes, or until the chicken is tender and the juices run clear. Adjust the seasoning, garnish with coriander, and serve hot with herbed rice.

## ferakh maamer

❖ *Morocco* ❖

This festive dish is packed with powerful aromas and infuses bland poussins with flavour. You can also use pigeons or a large chicken instead.

**PREP** 15 MINS ❖ **COOK** 1¼ HRS ❖ **SERVES** 4

400g (14oz) ready-to-cook **couscous**

**salt** and freshly ground **black pepper**

4 ready-to-cook **poussins**

400ml (14fl oz) hot light **chicken stock**

pinch of **saffron strands**

1 tbsp snipped **mint leaves**

1 tbsp snipped **coriander leaves**

2 tsp **lemon juice**

### For the stuffing

4 tbsp **olive oil**

1½ tbsp **runny honey**

3 tbsp **pine nuts**

3 tbsp **raisins**

2 **spring onions**, white (and green) parts only, finely chopped

1–2 **garlic cloves**, crushed

½–1 scant tsp **harissa paste**

½ tsp ground **cinnamon**

1 tsp ground **cumin**

½ tsp ground **ginger**

1 tsp dried **mint**

1 tsp dried **coriander**

1 Cook the couscous according to the packet instructions. For the stuffing, mix all the ingredients in a bowl. Add half the cooked couscous, season, and toss well.

2 Lightly salt the cavity of each poussin, then spoon in the stuffing. Stir the unused stuffing into the remaining couscous.

3 In a deep, ovenproof sauté pan, heat the stock over a medium heat and add the saffron. Simmer, add the poussins, cover, reduce the heat, and cook for 20 minutes.

4 Preheat the oven to 220°C (425°F/Gas 7). Remove the lid and transfer the pan to the oven. Bake for 15–20 minutes. Remove most of the liquid. Cover and return to the turned off oven for 10 minutes.

5 Reheat the couscous in a pan and add 2–3 tablespoons of the cooking liquid. Season and stir in half the fresh herbs. Bring the remaining cooking liquid to the boil in a pan. Stir in the lemon juice. Season. Place the poussins on a platter and surround with the couscous. Drizzle over the cooking liquid, scatter over the remaining herbs, and serve.

# a taste of
# MOROCCO

Varied and seductive, Moroccan cuisine reflects the country's history. First came the Berbers with couscous, tagines, and harira soup, then the nomadic Bedouins using dates, milk, and pungent salty smen made from fermented butter. The Arabs brought nuts, dried fruits, and spices. Dried ginger, cumin, and turmeric is a ubiquitous Moroccan spice combination. Saffron and cinnamon are favourites, while cardamom is used for creamy desserts. The Moors from Andalucia introduced olives and olive oil, almonds and oranges, herbs, plums and peaches, and the method of enhancing savoury dishes with fruit. Morocco eagerly adopted the flavours that came in from the New World – sweet and hot peppers, tomatoes, potatoes, and squashes.

**Dates** are a staple food, best grown in southern Morocco. They are essential during the month of Ramadan, when they accompany harira as the breaker of the day's fast.

Camels have been largely replaced by wheels in the cities of Morocco but you still see them everywhere in the South.

Koutoubia Mosque in Marrakech looms tall, red and beautiful behind the palm trees in the Medina quarter of the city near the famous Jma el Fna square.

**Almonds** feature in dozens of sweet recipes as well as in many tagines and savoury dishes. Sweet almond paste is a favourite pastry filling.

**Ginger** was one of the earliest Oriental spices to be adopted into Moroccan cooking and it remains a favourite, fresh or dried.

Porte de la Marine in the harbour of the lovely resort of Essaouira.

A street market exhibits colourful, extravagant displays of dried herbs, cinnamon sticks, dried chilli peppers, dried roses, tiny containers of khol, and small tagine pots.

**Preserved lemons** are an essential ingredient, adding a unique, slightly pungent touch to many dishes.

**Couscous** is steamed over stock and combined with vegetables, fish, meat, and dried fruit. Traditionally, Friday is couscous day in Morocco to celebrate the day of prayer.

**Argan oil** is extracted from the nut of the fruit of the argan tree. It can be mixed with almond paste and honey to make amlou spread.

# An informal dinner in Morocco

Meals at home are often served on low tables, with dishes designed to stretch a little if needed for the occasional last-minute guest. A family supper might start with a dish of olives, aubergine and tomato zahlouk mopped up with plenty of kesra or strips of toasted pitta bread. There will be a big bowl of kesksou to accompany little lamb cutlets and piquant chermoula. A refreshing orange salad with pomegranate, pistachio, mint, and a little rosewater rounds off the dinner.

**Zahlouk**
page 12

**Kesksou**
page 122

**Kesra**
page 259

**Salade d'oranges à la marocaine**
page 278

**Mint tea**

**Lahma meshwi**
page 162

# pollo al ajillo

*andalucia*

The Andalucian way of cooking chicken is to chop it up into small pieces and fry it gently in olive oil and plenty of garlic until the skin crisps and browns and the meat falls off the bones.

**PREP** 20 MINS, PLUS SOAKING
**COOK** 30-40 MINS ❖ **SERVES** 4-6

1 **chicken**, about 1.4kg (3lb 2oz) in weight
2 tbsp **plain flour**
**salt** and freshly ground **black pepper**
4–5 tbsp **olive oil**
8–10 **garlic cloves**, soaked to soften the skin
1 glass of **dry sherry** or **white wine**
1–2 **bay leaves**

1 Using a heavy knife to tap through the bones, joint the chicken into 16 bite-sized pieces, including the back. Place the pieces into a plastic food bag with the flour seasoned with salt and pepper. Shake to coat.

2 Heat the oil in a medium frying pan. Add the chicken and garlic, and turn the pieces in the hot oil until the skin begins to brown.

3 Add the sherry and bay leaves, and boil gently for 1 minute. Reduce the heat, cover loosely with a lid, and cook gently on a low heat for 20–30 minutes, until the meat is perfectly tender and the chicken is deliciously crisp and sauced with a little garlicky oil. Remove the bay leaves and serve.

# pollo ripieno con olive, cipolla e rosmarino

*sicily*

The olives, garlic, and chilli combine beautifully in this dish and stimulate all the taste buds. For a lighter meal, cut each baby chicken in half before serving.

**PREP** 15 MINS ❖ **COOK** 1 HR ❖ **SERVES** 4

4 **onions**, finely sliced
100g (3½oz) **black olives**, pitted and roughly chopped
5 sprigs of **rosemary**, leaves chopped
4 **garlic cloves**, halved
2 small dried **red chillies**, crushed
2 tbsp **olive oil**, plus extra for browning
juice of 1 **lemon**
**salt** and freshly ground **black pepper**
4 **poussins** or **baby chickens**, about 500g (1lb 2oz) each

1 Preheat the oven 200°C (400°F/Gas 6). Place the onions in a bowl. Mix the olives and rosemary together, and add to the onions. Finely chop the garlic with the dried chilli. Add to the onion mixture with the oil and lemon juice. Mix well and season. Stuff each chicken with a generous amount of the stuffing.

2 Heat a little oil in a heavy-based ovenproof pan over a medium-high heat. Season the outside of the chickens. Brown the chickens all over in the pan.

3 When browned, transfer the whole pan to the oven and roast for 30–35 minutes, until the meat is tender, basting regularly with all the roasting juices. (If cooking a larger chicken, allow a longer cooking time – usually 1 hour to 1 hour 20 minutes.) To check, insert the point of a small knife by the bone; if the juices run clear, the chicken is cooked.

4 Serve the roasted chickens with roast potatoes wedges and a fresh salad of bitter and peppery leaves.

*how to serve*

Serve the chicken with fat chips, fried in olive oil until crisp, and a salad of cos lettuce and mild raw onion.

# djaj meshwi
*lebanon*

This flavoursome marinated chicken recipe can also be cooked on the barbecue. Served with a pleasantly pungent Lebanese garlic sauce called *toum*, this dish is a garlic lover's delight.

**PREP** 15 MINS, PLUS MARINATING AND RESTING
**COOK** 35 MINS
**SERVES** 4 AS A MAIN COURSE, 8 AS MEZZE

8 bone-in **chicken thighs**, trimmed and wiped
1–2 tbsp snipped **fresh herbs**, such as coriander, mint, and parsley, to garnish
**lemon wedges**, to serve

### For the marinade
5 tbsp **olive oil**
1 tbsp **Greek-style yogurt**
juice and finely grated zest of 1 small **lemon**
½ tsp **sumac**
½ tsp **cinnamon**
1 tsp dried **thyme**
1 tsp dried **mint**
1 tsp ground **coriander**
**salt** and freshly ground **black pepper**

### For the garlic sauce
3–4 **garlic cloves**, crushed
3 tsp **lemon juice**
3 tbsp **vegetable oil**
5 tbsp **olive oil**

1 Using a sharp knife, make deep cuts in the chicken. For the marinade, mix all the ingredients and season to taste. Place the chicken in a plastic food bag. Spoon in the marinade mixture. Seal the bag and massage until the chicken is well coated. Refrigerate for at least 3 hours, or overnight.

2 Preheat the grill to medium-hot. Preheat the oven to 180°C (350°F/Gas 4). For the sauce, place the garlic, a pinch of salt, 2 teaspoons of the lemon juice, vegetable oil, and olive oil in a deep jar. Using a hand-held blender, whizz for 1–2 minutes, until the ingredients start to thicken. Whizz in the rest of the lemon juice and 1 tablespoon cold water. Adjust the seasoning.

3 Remove the chicken from the bag and shake off the excess marinade. Season with salt. Grill for 12 minutes on each side, or until the juices run clear. Place in a baking dish, cover with foil, and bake for 10 minutes. Turn off the oven and leave the dish in for 10 minutes. Scatter over the fresh herbs and serve with lemon wedges and the garlic sauce.

# tajine djaj bi zaytoun wal hamid
*morocco*

This lovely spiced chicken tagine is a good supper party dish. It will remain hot after cooking for up to 30 minutes, tightly covered in a warm place, ready to release its appealing aromas when the lid comes off.

**PREP** 10 MINS ❖ **COOK** 1 HR ❖ **SERVES** 4

3 tbsp **olive oil**
1 large **white onion**, thinly sliced
2–3 **garlic cloves**, crushed
1 scant tbsp ground **ginger**
good pinch of **saffron strands**
1 tsp dried **mint**
1 tsp ground **coriander**
1 scant tsp ground **cinnamon**
½ tsp **harissa paste** (optional)
1 large or 2 small **preserved lemons** (see p38), finely chopped
4 tbsp chopped **coriander leaves**
6 **chicken thighs**, bone in
1 tbsp **raisins**
**salt** and freshly ground **black pepper**
3 tbsp **green or violet olives**
1 tbsp slivered **almonds**

1 In a flameproof tagine or a heavy-based pan with a lid, heat the oil over a medium heat, then add the onion, and cook until soft. Stir in the garlic, ginger, saffron, mint, ground coriander, cinnamon, harissa, if using, lemons, and half the coriander leaves.

2 Place the chicken in the pan. Scatter over the raisins and season lightly. Add a glass of cold water, cover tightly, and simmer for about 35–40 minutes.

3 Remove the lid, scatter over the olives, cover again, and cook for a further 10 minutes. Adjust the seasoning, scatter over the almonds and the remaining coriander leaves, and serve hot.

# quaglie marinate con salsa di capperi

*❖ sicily ❖*

This dish of quails with caper sauce is great served on a bed of herbed couscous or a pilaf of rice or pearl barley. You can replace the quails with small spatchcock poussins.

**PREP** 15 MINS, PLUS SOAKING AND RESTING
**COOK** 15 MINS ❖ **SERVES** 4

2 **quails**
2 **garlic cloves**, finely chopped
1 small dried **red chilli**, finely crushed
**salt** and freshly ground **black pepper**
finely grated zest and juice of 1 **lemon**
1 tbsp finely chopped **marjoram**, **thyme**, or **oregano leaves**
1 tbsp **red wine vinegar**
1 tbsp **runny honey**
1 glass **white wine**
2 tbsp **pine nuts** or blanched **almonds**, dry-roasted until pale golden
2 tbsp roughly chopped **flat-leaf parsley**

**For the caper sauce**
1 **preserved lemon** (see p38), chopped
1 tbsp salted **capers**, rinsed, drained, squeezed dry, and chopped
2 tbsp chopped **marjoram** or **basil leaves**
1 tbsp **red wine vinegar**
3 tbsp **extra virgin olive oil**

1 Soak 4 bamboo skewers in cold water for 30 minutes. Turn the quails onto their front. Cut around the triangular piece of the backbone and remove with the wishbone attached. Use the side of a knife to flatten the bird. Insert a skewer through a wing, then through the leg. Repeat on the other side.

2 In a bowl, work the garlic, chilli, and a pinch of salt to make a paste. Mix with the lemon zest and juice, herbs, vinegar, honey, and wine. Add the quails and season with pepper. Refrigerate for 2 hours.

3 For the caper sauce, mix the ingredients and season. Preheat the oven to 220°C (425°F/Gas 7). Remove the quails from the marinade, season, and grill, skin-side down, for 3–4 minutes until brown. Turn over, place on a hot griddle pan, and roast for 5 minutes.

4 Cook the remaining marinade in a pan until reduced by half and pour over the birds. Serve with the sauce and a scattering of pine nuts and parsley.

# pato amb peras

*❖ spain ❖*

A party dish in Catalonia, this classic combination of rich duck meat and tart pear will also work well with goose.

**PREP** 30 MINS, PLUS RESTING
**COOK** 1 HR 50 MINS ❖ **SERVES** 4

1 **duck** (1.5–2kg/3lb 3oz–4½lb in weight)
3 **garlic cloves**
1 **bay leaf**
**salt** and freshly ground **black pepper**
6 small firm **pears**
1 short **cinnamon stick**
2–3 curls of **orange zest**
300ml (10fl oz) **red wine**
1 tbsp **plain flour**
30g (1oz) **raisins**
6 tbsp **sugar**

1 Preheat the oven to 180°C (350°F/Gas 4). Wipe the bird inside and out with a damp cloth and prick the skin all over without piercing the meat.

2 Tuck the garlic and bay leaf into the cavity and place the duck, breast-side down, on a rack over a baking tin half-filled with hot water. Roast for 1½ hours, turning it after 30 minutes. If it browns too quickly, cover with foil and reduce the heat. Check and top with boiling water. Discard the water, but reserve the duck drippings as they accumulate on the surface of the water.

3 Peel the pears, leaving the stalks in place, and arrange them stalk-up in a single layer in a pan. Add the cinnamon, orange zest, and enough wine to cover half the fruit. Bring to the boil, reduce the heat, cover, and simmer for 10 minutes, until the lower half is deep red but still firm. Remove the pears and set aside, reserving the poaching liquid.

4 Remove the duck from the oven and let it rest for 10 minutes. Meanwhile, melt a tablespoon of the reserved duck drippings in a small pan, sprinkle with the flour, and cook gently until the mixture turns sandy. Strain the poaching liquid into the pan, add the raisins, and boil gently to reduce. Season.

5 Joint the duck. Melt the sugar with the water in a pan and boil gently until it caramelizes. As soon as it turns nut-brown, remove from the heat and pour a little over each pear. Serve the duck joints with the sauce and the pears.

# pizzas, pies, and tarts

# coca d'espinacs
### ❖ *spain* ❖

This Valencian version of the Neapolitan pizza is given a juicy topping of greens finished with a Middle Eastern sprinkling of pine nuts, raisins, and olive oil.

**PREP** 10 MINS, PLUS RISING AND PROVING
**COOK** 20 MINS ❖ **SERVES** 2

100g (3¹/₂oz) strong **bread flour**
**salt**
25g (scant 1oz) **fresh yeast** or 1 tsp **dried yeast**
1 tbsp **olive oil**, plus extra for greasing

## For the topping
about 500g (1lb 2oz) **spinach leaves**, rinsed
1–2 **garlic cloves**, slivered
1 tbsp **pine nuts**, toasted
1 tbsp **raisins** or **sultanas**
**olive oil**, for drizzling

1 Sift the flour with a little salt into a warm bowl. Dissolve the yeast in 4 tablespoons warm water, sprinkle with a little flour, and leave for about 15 minutes to froth.

2 Make a well in the flour, then pour in the oil and the yeast mixture. Draw the flour into the liquid and knead the dough into a smooth ball. Place the dough in a bowl, cover with cling film or wipe with an oiled palm, and leave in a warm place for 1–2 hours, until doubled in size.

3 Preheat the oven to 220°C (425°F/Gas 7). Wash the spinach, drain all but a little water and cook it sprinkled with a little salt in a lidded pan. As soon as the leaves start to wilt, remove from the heat, squeeze dry, and chop roughly. Set aside.

4 Knead the dough well to distribute the air bubbles and cut in half, then pat or roll each piece into a round about 1cm (¹/₂in) thick. Transfer to a lightly oiled baking tray, top with the spinach, sprinkle with garlic, pine nuts, and raisins, drizzle with a little olive oil, and leave for 10 minutes to prove.

5 Bake for 15–20 minutes, until the crust is puffy and blistered at the edges.

### cook's tip

In its simplest and most traditional form, the *coca* is a flatbread, much like the Middle Eastern pitta, finished with a drizzle of olive oil and salt. Slices of Serrano ham, cheese, chorizo, and fried green peppers are served on the side.

# pizza fiorentina
### ❖ *italy* ❖

You can make the dough for this eye-catching pizza a day ahead, if you like. Store in the fridge and knead lightly before using.

**PREP** 20 MINS, PLUS RISING ❖ **COOK** 20 MINS
**SERVES** 4

500g (1lb 2oz) **strong white plain flour**, plus extra for dusting
2 x 7g sachet **fast-action dried yeast**
**salt** and freshly ground **black pepper**
2 tbsp **olive oil**, plus extra for greasing

## For the topping
350g (12oz) **passata**
225g (8oz) **spinach**, cooked, drained, and chopped
¼ tsp freshly grated **nutmeg**
1 tsp **thyme** leaves
175g (6oz) **mozzarella cheese**, sliced
4 **eggs**
4 tbsp grated **Parmesan cheese**

1 Put the flour in a mixing bowl, then stir in the yeast and ½ tablespoon salt. Add the oil and 350ml (12fl oz) tepid water, then mix to make a dough. Knead on a floured surface for 10 minutes, or until smooth.

2 Roll the dough into a ball and place in a lightly oiled bowl. Cover loosely with oiled cling film. Leave in a warm place until the dough has doubled in size.

3 Preheat the oven to 200°C (400°F/Gas 6). Divide the dough into 4 pieces and roll out into 23cm (9in) rounds. Lift out onto greased baking trays and spread with passata, leaving a 2.5cm (1in) border.

4 Spread the spinach on top in an even layer and sprinkle with nutmeg and thyme. Lay on the mozzarella slices and crack an egg on each. Sprinkle with the Parmesan cheese. Bake for 20 minutes, or until the edges are crisp. Season to taste with pepper, and serve immediately.

# pizza napolitana
### ❖ *italy* ❖

This daddy of all pizzas is made with a flip of bread dough scrounged from the day's baking, rolled thinly and topped with a slick of tomato and olive oil, a shred of basil, and melting mozzarella.

**PREP** 10 MINS, PLUS RISING
**COOK** 50 MINS ❖ **SERVES** 4

500g (1lb 2oz) "00" or strong white bread flour, plus extra for dusting
1 tbsp dried yeast
salt
1 tbsp semolina (optional), plus extra for dusting
2 tbsp olive oil, plus extra for greasing
4–5 sage leaves, roughly torn

## For the topping
2–3 tbsp olive oil, plus extra to drizzle
2 garlic cloves, chopped
2 x 400g cans plum tomatoes
1 tbsp tomato paste
pinch of chilli flakes or peperoncini
100g (3½oz) fresh mozzarella, drained and thinly sliced
handful of basil leaves, torn

1 Sift the flour into a warm bowl with the yeast, 1 teaspoon of salt, and the semolina (if using). Work in 300ml (10fl oz) of warm water and the oil, and knead to make a smooth, elastic dough. Form into a ball, place in the bowl, cover with a damp kitchen towel, and set in a warm place for 1–2 hours to rise.

2 For the topping, heat the oil in a pan, add the garlic and fry gently until soft, then add the tomatoes and tomato paste. Season with salt and add the chilli flakes. Mash thoroughly and simmer for 15–20 minutes, stirring, until reduced to a thick sauce. Check the seasoning and set aside to cool.

3 Preheat the oven to 230°C (450°F/Gas 8). On a board dusted with flour and a little semolina, roll out the dough to a thickness of a pound coin, or cut into 4 pieces, work each into a ball, and roll out to make pizzas.

4 Grease a baking sheet and dust with semolina. Transfer the pizzas to the sheet and leave for 10–15 minutes. Make a little edge to hold in the filling. Spread with the tomato sauce, top with mozzarella, finish with a sprinkle of basil, and drizzle with a little oil. Bake for 12–15 minutes, until the edges are crisp and blistered brown.

# pizzette al formaggio e fichi
### ❖ *italy* ❖

These individual pizzas are topped with blue cheese and finished with a classic partnership of figs and parma ham.

**PREP** 40 MINS, PLUS RISING
**COOK** 50-65 MINS ❖ **SERVES** 4

## For the dough
500g (1lb 2oz) strong white plain flour, plus extra for dusting
2 x 7g sachets fast-action dried yeast
½ tsp salt
2 tbsp olive oil, plus extra for greasing

## For the topping
4 tbsp extra virgin olive oil
140g (5oz) Gorgonzola cheese, rind removed, crumbled
12 slices of Parma ham, torn into strips
4 fresh figs, peeled and each cut into 8 wedges
2 tomatoes, deseeded and diced
115g (4oz) wild rocket leaves
freshly ground black pepper

1 Place the flour in a bowl and stir in the yeast and salt. Add the oil and 350ml (12fl oz) lukewarm water, then mix to form a dough. Knead on a floured surface for 10 minutes, or until smooth. Roll the dough into a ball and place in a lightly oiled bowl. Cover loosely with oiled cling film. Leave in a warm place until the dough has doubled in size.

2 Preheat the oven to 200°C (400°F/Gas 6). Transfer the dough to a lightly floured surface, knead lightly, divide into 4 and roll out to 23cm (9in) round pizza bases.

3 Place the pizza bases on greased baking trays. Brush with half the oil and scatter over the cheese. Bake in the oven for 20 minutes, or until the bases are crisp and turn golden. Remove from the oven.

4 Arrange the ham, figs, and tomatoes on top, and return to the oven for 8 minutes, or until the toppings are just warmed and the bases are golden brown. Scatter over the rocket, season with plenty of black pepper, and serve immediately, drizzled with the remaining oil.

# lahma bi ajeen
### ❖ *middle east* ❖

These traditional Arab pizzas, popular in Egypt, Jordan, Lebanon, Syria, and Turkey (*lahmacun*), are commonly eaten as a street snack.

**PREP** 3-4 HRS ❖ **COOK** 20 MINS ❖ **SERVES** 2-4

1 scant tsp dried yeast
½ tsp sugar
350g (12oz) strong white flour, plus extra for dusting
½ tsp salt
a few drops of sunflower oil

## For the topping
1 tbsp olive oil
knob of butter
1 onion, finely chopped
2 garlic cloves, finely chopped
225g (8oz) finely minced lean lamb
2 tbsp tomato paste
1 tbsp sugar
1–2 tsp dried red chilli, finely chopped
1 tsp dried mint
salt and freshly ground black pepper
1–2 tsp sumac
bunch of flat-leaf parsley, roughly chopped
1 lemon, cut into wedges

1 Place the yeast and sugar in a bowl with 75ml (2½fl oz) lukewarm water. Set aside for about 15 minutes, until it froths.

2 Sift the flour and salt into a bowl. Make a well, add the yeast mix and 200–250ml (7–9fl oz) lukewarm water, and knead on a floured surface into a pliable dough until smooth. Drip the sunflower oil into the base of the bowl and roll the dough into it. Cover with cling film and leave in a warm place for 1 hour, until doubled in size.

3 For the topping, heat the olive oil and butter in a heavy-based pan. Stir in the onion and garlic until soft. Leave to cool. Place the lamb in a bowl and add the tomato paste, sugar, chilli, mint, and the onion and garlic mixture. Season and knead the mixture. Cover and set aside.

4 Preheat the oven to 220°C (425°F/Gas 7). Grease 2 baking sheets and place in the oven. Knock back the dough and knead on a floured surface. Divide into 4 parts and roll into thin, flat circles. Place on the baking sheets, spread over a thin layer of the meat, and bake for 15–20 minutes, until the meat is cooked. Sprinkle with sumac and parsley, and serve with lemon wedges to squeeze over.

# spanakopita

❖ *greece* ❖

Crisp, buttery filo pastry with a soft filling of spinach and feta provides the perfect summer lunch. You can prepare this with your favourite buttery shortcrust or puff-pastry, home-made or ready-prepared.

**PREP** 35 MINS ❖ **COOK** 1¼ HRS ❖ **SERVES** 4

## ingredients

900g (2lb) spinach
small bunch of dill or fennel fronds
small bunch of flat-leaf parsley
6–8 spring onions
1–2 garlic cloves
2 tbsp olive oil
4 eggs
225g (8oz) feta cheese
freshly ground black pepper

## for the pastry

150g (5½oz) butter, melted
250g (9oz) filo pastry (about 14 sheets, 40 x 30cm/16 x 12in)

1 **Prepare the filling**. Rinse and shred the spinach with the dill and parsley. Finely chop the onions and garlic.

2 **Place a medium saucepan** over a low heat, add the oil and wait until a faint blue haze rises. Stir in the onion and garlic and fry, stirring, for 2–3 minutes, until soft but not browned. Add the spinach and toss over the heat until the leaves wilt. Boil, drain, and remove from the heat. Leave to cool, then chop finely.

3 **Crack the eggs** into a bowl, beat well, crumble in the feta cheese, and season with pepper. Beat in the spinach and herbs.

**4** **Prepare the base.** Brush a 23 x 30cm (9 x 12in) rectangular baking tin with butter. Line the tin with a double layer of filo, letting it flop over the top. Brush with butter and top with another double layer. Repeat until two-thirds of the filo is used up. Preheat the oven to 160°C (325°F/Gas 3).

**5** **Spread the filling** evenly over the base. Top with a double layer of filo and brush with butter. Repeat until all the filo is used up. Fold over the flaps from the side, crumpling them a little. Trickle with any remaining butter and sprinkle with a few drops of cold water. Bake in the centre of the oven for 1 hour, or until the pastry is crisp and golden brown all over. Cut into squares and serve warm.

# pissaladière

*⋄ provence ⋄*

This classic onion and olive tart is Provence's version of a pizza. Use meltingly tender onions and well-drained, good-quality anchovies.

**PREP** 40 MINS, PLUS RESTING
**COOK** 1¼ HRS ⋄ **SERVES** 8

125g (4½oz) **unsalted butter**, plus extra for greasing
250g (9oz) **plain flour**, plus extra for dusting
½ tsp **salt**
2 tbsp **caster sugar**
1 **egg yolk**

### For the filling

4 tbsp **olive oil**, plus a little extra to finish
1.25kg (2¾lb) large **mild onions**, thinly sliced
4 fresh **sage leaves**, snipped
3 **garlic cloves**, crushed
**salt** and freshly ground **black pepper**
12 **anchovy fillets** in oil, drained
about 20 small **black olives**
a few sprigs of **thyme**

1 In a small bowl, beat the butter until soft and creamy. Sift the flour onto a work surface and make a well. Add the salt, sugar, and 3 tablespoons cold water, and mix. Add the yolk and butter. Work the ingredients together to make a soft dough. Flatten it with your palm against the work surface, then gather together and flatten again. Form into a ball and wrap in a cloth dusted with flour. Leave for 2 hours or overnight.

2 Grease a 30cm (12in) loose-bottomed tart tin. On a floured surface, roll out the dough thinly. Lift onto the tin and press in lightly without stretching. Prick a few times with a fork. Cover and keep in a cool place.

3 Heat the oil in a pan. Add the onions and sage, cover, and sweat for 15 minutes on a low heat, stirring occasionally, until soft but not brown. Add the garlic, season, stir, cover, and cook on a low heat, stirring, for 45 minutes, until the onions are really soft.

4 Preheat the oven to 200°C (400°F/Gas 6). Line the tin with greaseproof paper and fill with dried beans. Bake for 15–20 minutes, until crisp and cooked. Cool, then remove the beans and paper. Leave the oven on.

5 Spread the onions in the pastry case. Arrange the anchovies on top and dot with olives. Sprinkle with oil, bake for 15 minutes, and serve. Scatter over some more sage or thyme just before serving.

# focaccia di ricotta

*⋄ italy ⋄*

These light, herby flatbreads are the fast food of Liguria. Sold hot from the bakestone in specialist bakeries in much the same way as pizza in the rest of Italy, they are a satisfying snack.

**PREP** 15 MINS, PLUS RISING AND PROVING
**COOK** 25 MINS ⋄ **SERVES** 4-8

750g (1lb 10oz) **"00"** or strong **bread flour**
1 tsp **salt**
7g sachet **dried yeast** or 25g (scant 1oz) **fresh yeast**
100ml (3½fl oz) **extra virgin olive oil**, plus extra for drizzling
about 100g (3½oz) fresh **ricotta cheese**
**semolina**, for dusting
a dozen **sage leaves**, torn or shredded
**coarse salt**

1 Mix the flour with the salt and yeast. If using fresh yeast, rub in as for shortcrust pastry. Add the olive oil and about 300ml (10fl oz) warm water, draw the liquid into the flour gradually, and mix to a slightly wet, soft dough. Form into a smooth ball and place in a bowl. Cover the top of the bowl loosely with cling film and set in a warm place for 1 hour, or until the dough is light, spongy, and doubled in volume.

2 Meanwhile, set the ricotta to drain in a sieve. Oil 2–3 baking sheets and sprinkle lightly with semolina, tipping off the excess.

3 On a semolina-dusted board, knead the dough to distribute the air bubbles and work in the ricotta and half the sage leaves. Cut the dough in half and work each piece into a ball, transfer to the baking sheets, and pat out to the thickness of your little finger. Dust with a little more semolina, cover loosely with a clean kitchen towel, and leave to prove for 30–40 minutes, until puffed.

4 Preheat the oven to 220°C (425°F/Gas 7). Punch the surface of the dough with stiff fingers to make dimples, trickle a little oil into the dips, scatter with salt and the reserved sage leaves. Sprinkle with a little warm water.

5 Bake for 20–25 minutes, until well-risen and browned. Trickle a little more oil over the hot focaccia and serve.

# musakhan

*⋄ middle east ⋄*

This Palestinian peasant dish is popular in Syria, Jordan, and Egypt. Traditionally, it is prepared on a thick bread base and is served on its own, but this is the street version, which can be served as a tasty snack.

**PREP** 10-15 MINS ⋄ **COOK** 25 MINS
**SERVES** 4

2 tbsp **olive oil**, plus extra for greasing
knob of **butter**
2 **onions**, sliced
2–3 **garlic cloves**, crushed
2–3 skinless **chicken breasts**, cut into thin strips
2 tsp **sumac**
1 tsp ground **cinnamon**
1 tsp **allspice**
juice of 1 **lemon**
**salt** and freshly ground **black pepper**
4 **pitta breads**, halved to form 8 pockets
small bunch of **flat-leaf parsley**, roughly chopped
6–8 tbsp strained **yogurt**

1 Preheat the oven to 180°C (350°F/Gas 4). Heat the oil and butter in a large, heavy-based frying pan and stir in the onions. When the onions begin to soften, stir in the garlic and fry for 4–5 minutes, until the onions turn golden brown.

2 Toss in the chicken and sumac and cook for 2–3 minutes. Add the cinnamon, allspice, and lemon juice, and cook until the chicken is tender and cooked through but still juicy. Season to taste.

3 Fill the pitta pockets with the hot chicken mixture and place on a lightly greased baking sheet. Transfer to the oven and toast for about 10 minutes. Spoon a little parsley into each pocket, top with a dollop of yogurt, and serve hot.

*how to serve*
Serve these chicken snacks with a selection of pickles, finely sliced fresh chillies, finely sliced red onions, harissa paste, or garlic-flavoured yogurt.

# yogurt

The original healthy food, yogurt is an essential part of breakfast in the Eastern Mediterranean and a favourite multi-tasking ingredient.

**Greek yogurt**, like other strained yogurts, has a thick, creamy texture and a higher fat content than plain yogurt.

**Quite where and how** yogurt came into being is uncertain but it came to the Mediterranean from the East. Pliny the Elder commented that "barbarous nations" managed to "thicken milk into a substance with an agreeable acidity". With its pleasant, mildly sour flavour and its clean smooth texture, yogurt is versatile nutritious food. With honey, it is a marriage made in culinary heaven, and it's equally at home with salt, pepper, and spice.

**Ayran**, a chilled, frothy Turkish drink, is made by whizzing half yogurt and half milk with a pinch of salt – both refreshing and energizing.

**Natural yogurt** can be made from ewe's milk, goat's milk, cow's milk, or a mixture of milks.

**Labna**, a Middle Eastern strained yogurt, is very creamy and is served with a drizzle of olive oil, sometimes with herbs and chopped nuts.

# bstilla bil djaj

❖ *Morocco* ❖

Traditionally prepared for festive occasions, this savoury saffron pie, with an unusual dusting of icing sugar and cinnamon, is a Moroccan classic.

**PREP** 45 MINS  ❖  **COOK** 40 MINS  ❖  **SERVES** 4-6

pinch of **saffron fronds**
2–3 tbsp **olive oil**
100g (3½oz) **butter**, plus extra for brushing
3 **onions**, halved and finely sliced
2 **garlic cloves**, finely chopped
2 tbsp **toasted almonds**, chopped
1–2 tsp ground **cinnamon**, plus 2 tsp extra for dusting
1 tsp ground **ginger**
1 tsp ground **coriander**

½ tsp ground **cloves**
250g (9oz) skinless **chicken fillets**, cut into bite-sized pieces
1 tbsp **runny honey**
bunch of **flat-leaf parsley**, finely chopped
large bunch of **coriander**, finely chopped
**salt** and freshly ground **black pepper**
7–8 sheets of **filo pastry**
1 **egg yolk**, beaten with a little water, to glaze
1–2 tbsp **icing sugar**, for dusting

1 Preheat the oven to 190°C (375°F/Gas 5). In a heavy-based pan, roast the saffron over a low heat for 1–2 minutes. Powder in a mortar while still hot. Dissolve in 100ml (3½oz) water. Set aside.

2 In a heavy-based pan, heat the oil with a little butter. Fry the onions over a medium heat for 4–5 minutes, until soft. Stir in the garlic, almonds, and spices. Toss in the chicken for 1–2 minutes, coat in the

mixture, then add the honey and saffron water. Cook for 4–5 minutes, until there is little liquid left. Toss in the herbs, season, and set aside to cool.

3 Melt the remaining butter. Separate the filo sheets and cover with a damp cloth. Grease a round, ovenproof dish and cover with a sheet of filo, letting the sides hang over the edge. Brush with some butter and place another sheet on top. Repeat to add 2 more layers.

4 Spread the chicken and onion mixture on top of the pastry and fold over the edges. Cover with the rest of the sheets, brushing each with butter. Tuck the hanging edges under the pie. Brush the egg wash over the top of the pastry. Bake for 25 minutes, until crisp and golden. Dust with icing sugar and make a lattice pattern with the cinnamon. Serve hot.

# *essential*
# pomegranates

Legend has it that this ancient fruit was stored on
Noah's Ark for its well-hidden, sweetly tart red seeds.

**Don't let** the pomegranate's tough exterior put you off.
Take a sharp knife, slice off the top and the base, cut into
quarters or wedges, and squeeze to realease the endless
jewel-like seeds into a bowl, using a teaspoon to scrape
them off. Discard the bitter white membranes. The brilliant
seeds are packed with vitamin C and are very versatile
– use them in pilafs, salads, baking, and desserts. You can
even whizz them in a blender, and push through a fine
sieve to make your own juice.

**Pomegranate syrup**,
sometimes called
molasses, is boiled
down from the juice
of tart pomegranates.
Use like good balsamic
vinegar for dressings
and sauces, or as a
glaze.

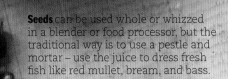

**Seeds** can be used whole or whizzed
in a blender or food processor, but the
traditional way is to use a pestle and
mortar – use the juice to dress fresh
fish like red mullet, bream, and bass.

# shish barak
### *middle east*

Similar to the *mantı* of Turkey, these meat dumplings are popular in Lebanon and Syria. They are often prepared using a traditional dough, but you can also use filo pastry.

**PREP** 40 MINS  •  **COOK** 30 MINS  •  **SERVES** 4-6

6 sheets of **filo pastry**, each cut into half
2 tbsp **butter**, plus extra for greasing
1kg (2¼lb) thick, creamy **yogurt**
2 **garlic cloves**, crushed
**salt** and freshly ground **black pepper**
1 tbsp **olive oil**
1 tsp **dried mint**

### For the filling
2 tbsp **olive oil**
2 **onions**, finely chopped
1 **red chilli**, deseeded and finely chopped
2 tbsp **pine nuts**
2 tsp dried **oregano**
2 tsp ground **cinnamon**
1 tsp **allspice**
1 tsp **pimentón** (Spanish paprika)
450g (1lb) minced **lean lamb**
1 tbsp **pomegranate syrup**

1 For the filling, heat the oil in a heavy-based pan and stir in the onions and chilli, until just brown. Stir in the pine nuts for 1 minute, until they begin to colour, then add the oregano, cinnamon, allspice, and paprika. Toss in the minced lamb and fry for 2–3 minutes, until it is cooked. Season and stir in the pomegranate syrup. Turn off the heat and leave to cool.

2 Preheat the oven to 200°C (400°F/Gas 6). Place the rectangular filo sheets in a stack on a clean surface.

3 In a small pan, melt the butter, then brush the top sheet with a little butter. Spoon some of the filling in a line along one of the long edges, leaving about 1cm (½in) gap at either end. Roll up the sheet into a long finger, tucking in the edges as you go, then shape into a tight coil. Repeat with the remaining sheets and filling. Place the coils on a lightly greased baking tray. Bake for 25 minutes, until lightly golden and crisp.

4 Beat the yogurt with the garlic and season. Arrange the dumplings on a serving dish, spoon over some yogurt, drizzle over the oil, and sprinkle over the mint. Serve with the rest of the yogurt and chunks of crusty bread.

# fatayer bi jibn wal qarat
### *middle east*

Popular Middle Eastern snacks, these crisp filo pastries are filled with a sweet and spiced mixture. Serve as a light snack or canapé.

**PREP** 20 MINS, PLUS COOLING
**COOK** 30 MINS  •  **MAKES** 24

100g (3½oz) **pumpkin** or **squash**, peeled and deseeded
25g (scant 1oz) **raisins**, chopped
100g (3½oz) **feta cheese**, finely crumbled
freshly ground **black pepper**
½ tsp ground **cinnamon**
6 sheets of **filo pastry**, 40 x 30cm (16 x 12in), thawed if frozen
50g (1¾oz) **butter**, melted, plus extra for greasing
**flour**, for dusting

1 Finely dice the pumpkin and place in a small saucepan. Pour in enough water to just cover, bring to the boil, cover, and simmer gently for 5 minutes, or until tender. Drain well and allow to cool.

2 Preheat the oven to 180°C (350°F/Gas 4). Mix the pumpkin with the raisins and feta. Season with pepper and add the cinnamon. Set aside.

3 Lay the filo sheets on top of each other and cut into 4 long strips, about 7.5cm (3in) wide. Stack the strips on top of each other and cover with damp kitchen towel.

4 Taking 1 strip of pastry at a time, brush with butter, and place a heaped teaspoon of the pumpkin mixture 2.5cm (1in) from one end. Fold over the end of the strip of pastry to cover the filling.

5 Fold a corner of the pastry over diagonally to form a triangular pocket of filled pastry. Working upwards, keep folding diagonally, from one side to the other, to retain the triangular shape, until all the pastry is folded, making sure any gaps in the pastry are pressed closed.

6 On a lightly floured work surface, keep the triangles in a pile, covered with a damp kitchen towel to stop them drying out, while preparing the other pastries.

7 Transfer the triangles to a greased baking tray. Brush with the remaining butter and bake for 20–25 minutes, or until crisp and golden. Serve warm.

**variation**

**Cheese and potato pastries** Replace the pumpkin with finely diced potato or sweet potato.

# hortapitta
### ❖ *greece* ❖

Peppery spring leaves and creamy curd cheese are the perfect match for the crisp buttery layers of filo pastry in this savoury Greek pie.

**PREP** 15 MINS ❖ **COOK** 1 HR ❖ **SERVES** 4

about 150g (5½oz) **melted butter**
300g packet **filo pastry**

## For the filling
about 750g (1lb 10oz) **spring leaves**,
 such as spinach, chicory, or dandelion
2–3 **spring onions**, finely chopped
generous handful of **fennel fronds**
 or **dill**, chopped
**salt** and freshly ground **black pepper**
1 tbsp **lemon juice**
250g (9oz) **soft white cheese**
2 **eggs**

1 Brush a baking tray with a little melted butter and layer in two-thirds of the filo sheets, leaving a generous edge overlapping the top and brushing with butter between each double layer. Take care to keep the filo pastry covered with cling film or a kitchen towel while you work so it does not dry out.

2 Pick over and remove any thick stalks from the spring leaves. Rinse, leaving them damp, and place in a pan with the spring onions and fennel fronds. Salt lightly, cover, and cook over a high heat for 2–3 minutes, until the leaves wilt. Allow to cool a little in a colander, then squeeze out as much moisture as possible. Chop finely, sprinkle with the lemon juice, and set aside.

3 Preheat the oven to 180°C (350°F/Gas 4). In a bowl, beat the cheese with the eggs, season, and beat in the greens. Spread the mixture evenly into the prepared pie base. Top with the remaining filo, brushing with butter between each double layer. Fold over the flaps and crumple the top a little with the final layer of filo. Drizzle over the remaining melted butter.

4 Bake for 40–50 minutes, until crisp and golden. Leave to cool to room temperature. Serve with a salad of chunky onions, tomatoes, black olives, and cos lettuce dressed with lemon juice, olive oil, and salt. Trickle with the remaining butter.

# tepsi böreği
### ❖ *turkey* ❖

Crisp pastry encases a delicious mix of spinach, feta, and pine nuts in this classic Middle Eastern dish. Serve with a crisp salad or seasonal vegetables.

**PREP** 30 MINS, PLUS COOLING AND STANDING
**COOK** 1 HR ❖ **SERVES** 6

900g (2lb) **spinach**
100g (3½oz) **butter**, plus extra
 for greasing
1 tsp ground **cumin**
1 tsp ground **coriander**
1 tsp ground **cinnamon**
2 **red onions**, finely chopped
60g (2oz) **dried apricots**, chopped
60g (2oz) **pine nuts**, toasted
6 sheets of **filo pastry**, 40 x 30cm
 (16 x 12in), thawed if frozen
**salt** and freshly ground **black pepper**
300g (10oz) **feta cheese**, crumbled
**flat-leaf parsley**, to garnish
**lemon zest**, to garnish

1 Rinse the spinach, shake off the excess water, and pack into a large pan. Cover and cook over a medium heat, turning occasionally, for 8–10 minutes, until just wilted. Drain well through a sieve, pressing the spinach against the sides to remove as much water as possible. Set aside to cool.

2 Meanwhile, melt 25g (scant 1oz) butter and fry the spices with the onions over a low heat, stirring occasionally, for 7–8 minutes, or until soft but not browned. Stir in the apricots and pine nuts, then set aside. Preheat the oven to 200°C (400°F/Gas 6). Grease and line a 20cm (8in) springform tin.

3 For the pie, melt the remaining butter. Brush the tin with the melted butter and cover the base with a sheet of pastry, leaving the edges overhanging, and brush with butter. Continue with 5 more sheets, brushing each with butter.

4 Blot the spinach with kitchen paper, then chop finely. Stir into the onion mixture and season. Pile half into the pastry case and spread evenly. Sprinkle over the cheese, then cover with the remaining spinach mixture. Fold the overhanging pastry over the spinach, piece by piece, brushing with butter. Brush the top with any remaining butter and place the tin on a baking tray.

5 Bake for 35–40 minutes, or until crisp and golden. Let stand for 10 minutes before carefully releasing from the tin. Serve hot or warm, cut into wedges, and garnished with parsley and strips of lemon zest.

# a taste of ANDALUCIA

The flavours of Andalucia reflect its heritage as a part of Catholic Spain, which belonged to the Islamic world during eight centuries of Moorish occupation. The Arabs left behind irrigation, new ingredients, and their own cooking style. The cinnamon, saffron, cumin, coriander, apricots, artichokes, carob, aubergines, oranges, and rice they introduced are cornerstones of dishes today, as is the use of dried fruits and honey in savoury dishes and almonds in desserts. In the Andalucian fusion of cookery traditions, egg-yolk desserts originated in Jerez, where the whites were used to clarify sherry and the yolks given to convents, to be turned into custard cakes by the nuns. Andalucia is the only part of Spain with a coast facing the Atlantic Ocean. Sevilla became a gateway to the Mediterranean for ships laden with treasures from the New World.

**Habas frescas**, young broad beans, are prepared like green beans and eaten whole. Older, they are podded, shelled, and dried for winter.

**Noras** are plum-sized red peppers, popular dried. Tear up and soak in boiling water to soften.

**Churros** are Spain's doughnuts and favourite snack. Dipped in hot chocolate they make an excellent breakfast.

CHURRERIA

SEGUI

**Mariscos** are boiled shellfish. Morsel-sized food, they make perfect tapas: clams, cockles, sea snails, razor clams, and prawns are all popular.

**Green globe artichokes**, with their succulent fleshy leaves and bottoms and meaty flavour, grow well in the Andalucian climate.

**Green olives** include large, fat sevillanos and small, golden manzanillas. Cracked and flavoured, pitted and stuffed – no tapas table should be without them.

Orange trees blossoming or bearing fruit are a joy to the eyes all over Andalucia.

**Membrillo** is a dense sugary quince paste, a delicious sweet-salt combination served sliced with cheese as tapas.

**Hot or mild chorizo sausage** is made from black pigs fed on acorns and chestnuts in Jabugo near Sevilla.

**Green asparagus** is a much-loved seasonal ingredient – the younger, the better.

Many tapas bars specialize in pork products, starring a prince of cured hams, jamón ibérico from Jabugo. It is a favourite served cut in short curls with a long thin knife, often with thinly sliced chorizo.

# An Andalucian feast of tapas

The table groans with a casual assortment of small dishes, glasses, bread, stuffed green olives, wooden toothpicks, and paper napkins. It's a free for all, as people help themselves to long slivers of sweet salt Serrano ham, bite-sized diced nutty manchego, marinated anchovies, and cubes of broad bean tortilla. There are garlicky chicken drumsticks, chickpeas with spinach, stewed mushrooms, roast potatoes, and salted roasted almonds.

**Bolillos**

**Boquerones in vinagre**
page 142

**Pollo al ajillo**
page 184

**Champiñones al ajillo**
page 252

**Stuffed green olives**

**Tortilla de habas**
page 80

**Almendras tostadas**
page 38

**Tostadas de garbanzos con espinacas**
page 243

# sıgarı böreği
## ❖ *turkey* ❖

These cheese pastries from Turkey are traditionally made in cigar shapes and triangles. Serve them as part of a mezze spread.

**PREP** 25 MINS ❖ **COOK** 10-12 MINS
**MAKES** 20

200g (7oz) **feta cheese**, finely crumbled
1 **egg**, beaten
pinch of ground **nutmeg**
big bunch of **flat-leaf parsley**, **mint**, and **dill**, finely chopped
freshly ground **black pepper**
8 sheets of **filo pastry**, 40 x 30cm (16 x 12in), thawed if frozen
60g (2oz) **butter**, melted
**flour**, for dusting

1 Preheat the oven to 180°C (350°F/Gas 4). Place the cheese in a bowl, whisk in the egg, then add the nutmeg, parsley, mint, and dill. Season to taste with pepper.

2 Lay the filo sheets on top of each other and cut into 3 long strips, 10cm (4in) wide.

3 Taking one strip of pastry at a time, brush with butter and place 1 heaped teaspoon of the cheese mixture at one end. Roll up the pastry, like a cigar, folding the ends in about one-third of the way down to encase the filling completely, then continue to roll. Make sure the ends are tightly sealed.

4 Lightly dust the work surface with flour and keep the rolled pastries in a pile, covered with a damp cloth, while preparing the remainder.

5 Place the pastries in a single layer on a large greased baking tray. Brush with the remaining butter and bake for 10-12 minutes, or until crisp and golden. Best served hot or slightly warm.

### prepare ahead

The pastries can be prepared up to 24 hours before baking.

### variation

**Spinach boreks** In step 1, fry 2 chopped spring onions in 1 tablespoon of olive oil. Stir in 150g (5½oz) baby spinach leaves, and fry until wilted. Drain, cool, then chop finely. Mix with 1 tablespoon of chopped dill and 75g (2½oz) crumbled feta cheese.

# panzerotti
## ❖ *italy* ❖

Little pasties stuffed with a savoury paste of olives and onions are popular at party time in the south-western region of Puglia.

**PREP** 15 MINS, PLUS RISING ❖ **COOK** 20 MINS
**SERVES** 6-8

500g (1lb 2oz) strong **white bread flour**, plus extra for dusting
1 tsp **salt**
1 tsp **dried yeast**
1 tsp **sugar**
2 tbsp **olive oil**

### For the filling

2-3 tbsp **olive oil**
500g (1lb 2oz) **mild onions**, finely sliced
100g (3½oz) **green olives**, pitted and chopped
2-3 **anchovy fillets**, chopped
1 tbsp grated **Parmesan cheese**
¼ tsp **chilli flakes** or **pepperoncini**
1 x 400g can **plum tomatoes**, chopped

1 Sift the flour with the salt into a large warm bowl. Heat about 600ml (1 pint) water. In a bowl, mix the yeast with a little of the warm water and the sugar and leave to froth. Make a well in the flour, then add the oil and the yeast mixture. Stir and work in enough water to make a soft, slightly wet dough. Knead thoroughly until smooth and no longer sticky. Form the dough into a ball, place into a bowl, cover with cling film, and leave to rise in a warm place for 1 hour, until doubled in size.

2 For the filling, heat the oil in a frying pan, add the onions, and cook gently, until soft but not browned. Stir in the rest of the ingredients, bring to the boil, and reduce to a thick sauce. Set aside to cool.

3 Preheat the oven to 190°C (375°F/Gas 5). Break off walnut-sized pieces of the dough and, on a well-floured board, roll out each into a thin round the size of a coffee saucer. Place a teaspoonful of the filling in the centre of each round, wet the rim with water, and fold over to enclose the filling, pressing the edges together to seal. Transfer to an oiled baking sheet and bake for 15 minutes, until puffed and brown. Serve hot.

### cook's tips

You can also deep-fry the panzerotti. Heat enough oil to submerge them, wait until the oil shimmers, slip in a few at a time, and fry until puffed and golden.

# empanadillas de atún

*❖ s p a i n ❖*

These savoury Spanish pastries make very versatile snacks. You can replace the tuna with cooked chicken or chorizo, and make bite-sized versions to serve as tapas.

**PREP** 45 MINS, PLUS CHILLING
**COOK** 40-50 MINS ❖ **MAKES** 24

450g (1lb) **plain flour**, plus extra
  for dusting
**salt** and freshly ground **black pepper**
85g (3oz) **butter**, diced
2 **eggs**, beaten, plus extra to glaze

### For the filling
1 tbsp **olive oil**, plus extra for greasing
1 **onion**, finely chopped
120g can chopped **tomatoes**, drained
2 tsp **tomato purée**
140g can **tuna**, drained
2 tbsp finely chopped **flat-leaf parsley**

1 For the pastry, sift the flour into a large mixing bowl together with ½ teaspoon of salt. Add the butter and rub in with your fingertips until the mixture resembles fine breadcrumbs. Add the eggs with 4–6 tablespoons cold water and combine to form a dough. Cover with cling film and chill for 30 minutes.

2 For the filling, heat the oil in a frying pan, add the onion, and fry over a medium heat, stirring often, for 5–8 minutes, or until translucent. Add the tomatoes, tomato purée, tuna, and parsley, and season to taste. Reduce the heat and simmer for 10–12 minutes, stirring occasionally.

3 Preheat the oven to 190°C (375°F/Gas 5). Roll out the pastry to a thickness of 3mm (⅛in). Cut out 24 rounds with a 9cm (3½in) round pastry cutter. Place 1 teaspoon of the filling in the centre of each round, then brush the edges with water, fold over, and pinch together.

4 Place the empanadas on an oiled baking tray and brush with egg wash. Bake for 25–30 minutes, or until golden brown. Serve warm.

# empanada gallega

✤ *spain* ✤

A speciality of Galicia in northwest Spain, this satisfying pie is baked daily in bakeries and sold to hungry workers at midday.

**PREP** 10 MINS ❖ **COOK** 1¼ HRS ❖ **SERVES** 2

275g (9½oz) **self-raising flour**, plus extra for dusting

½ tsp **salt**

2 tbsp **white wine** or **dry cider**

150ml (5fl oz) **milk** or **water**

4 tbsp **olive oil** or **soft lard**, plus extra for greasing

1 **egg yolk**, beaten with a little water, to glaze

## For the filling

5–6 tbsp **olive oil**

1 large **onion**, finely sliced

1–2 **garlic cloves**, chopped

350g (12oz) **pork shoulder**, diced

2 tbsp diced **Serrano ham** or **lean bacon**

2 large **potatoes**, peeled and diced

2 **red peppers**, deseeded and diced

1 tsp dried **thyme**

**salt** and freshly ground **black pepper**

1 glass **white wine** or **cider**

1 For the filling, heat the oil in a large frying pan and gently cook the onion and garlic for 5–10 minutes, until soft. Add the meats and cook for a further 10 minutes, then add the potatoes, peppers, and thyme. Season and simmer for 15–20 minutes until the juices have evaporated and the mixture begins to fry. Add the wine and bring to the boil on a high heat. Then reduce the heat to low and cook for a further 10 minutes, until the potatoes have softened but are still a little firm, and the juices have nearly all evaporated. Remove from the heat and leave to cool.

2 For the pastry, sift the flour with the salt in a bowl and make a well in the middle. In a small pan, heat the wine, milk, and oil on a low heat until warm to the touch. Pour the liquid into the well in the flour. Working fast, draw in the dry ingredients and knead

until you have a smooth, elastic dough. Add a little more flour, if necessary. Lightly dust a board and rolling pin with flour, and roll out the dough into a rectangle, about 25 x 20cm (10 x 8in). Cut the rectangle across the short side into 2 pieces, one measuring 20 x 10cm (8 x 4in) and the other 20 x 15cm (8 x 6in).

3 Preheat the oven to 200°C (400°F/Gas 6). Transfer the larger piece to a greased baking tray and spread the filling all over, leaving a margin of about 2.5cm (1in). Place the smaller piece on top of the filling, then bring up the sides of the larger pastry to meet the lid. Using your forefinger and thumb, pinch the two edges to seal. Take care not to leave any gaps – spoon out some of the filling, if necessary. Make a small hole in the top to let out the steam, and brush with egg wash.

4 Bake for 10–15 minutes, until the pastry is set but still pale. Turn down the heat to 180°C (350°F/Gas 4) and bake for a further 30–40 minutes, until the filling is heated right through and the pastry is golden brown. Serve hot or cool.

# vegetables, herbs, and salads

## salade de fenouil à la pêche et au jambon cru

*♦ provence ♦*

This pretty fennel and peach salad from the French Riviera makes a refreshing starter on a hot summer's day.

**PREP** 15-20 MINS ❖ **SERVES** 4

2 small **fennel bulbs**, trimmed at the base and very thinly sliced

juice and finely grated zest of ½ **lemon**

1 tbsp **extra virgin olive oil**

**salt** and freshly ground **black pepper**

2 ripe **peaches** or **nectarines**, halved, cored, and sliced

1 tbsp chopped **flat-leaf parsley**

½ tbsp chopped **mint leaves**

1 slice of **cured ham** (about 5mm–1cm/ ¼in–½in thick), such as prosciutto crudo, Serrano, or Bayonne ham, diced

1 In a shallow bowl, toss the fennel with the lemon juice and zest, oil, and a little salt. Add the peaches or nectarines, sprinkle over half the herbs, and season with pepper. Toss lightly.

2 Arrange on a serving platter. Scatter over the ham and the remaining herbs. Serve immediately.

### cook's tip

You can also use a mandolin or the thin slicing disk of a food processor to slice the fennel. There is no need to peel the peaches, but if you prefer, poach them in boiling water for 2–3 minutes, then drain and peel.

### variations

**Fennel salad with peaches and pine nuts** Replace the cured ham with 3 tablespoons of pine nuts toasted in a small, non-stick frying pan until brown.

**Fennel salad with watermelon** Replace the peaches and cured ham with 225g (8oz) seedless watermelon, rind removed, cut into 2.5cm (1in) cubes, and 2 heaped tablespoons of shredded feta or goat's cheese.

## insalata di arance alla siciliana

*♦ sicily ♦*

Refreshing orange salads are popular in the southern Mediterranean and are served alongside stews and grilled meat or fish.

**PREP** 15-20 MINS ❖ **SERVES** 4

1 small-medium **red onion**, thinly sliced

2 ripe **oranges**

8–10 **black olives**

juice and finely grated zest of ½ **lemon**

2 tbsp **fruity olive oil**

**salt** and freshly ground **black pepper**

a few leaves of **wild rocket** (optional)

1 Place the onion in a bowl of cold water. Using a sharp knife, remove the peel and pith from the oranges, and slice thinly.

2 Place the oranges in a shallow serving dish. Drain the onion slices, place on a double layer of kitchen paper, and pat dry. Arrange the slices on the oranges. Scatter the olives on top.

3 In a small cup, combine the lemon juice and zest and the oil. Season to taste and drizzle over the salad. If you like, scatter over the rocket. Leave to stand for 5 minutes before serving.

### variation

**Moroccan orange salad with onion and olives** To make the Moroccan version of this salad, add a teaspoon of cumin seeds and a pinch of pimentón (Spanish paprika), and finish with chopped coriander leaves.

# çoban salatası

### ✧ *turkey* ✧

Variations of this Turkish "shepherd's salad" are popular throughout the Middle East, particularly in Syria and Lebanon. Simple and refreshing, it is often served as part of a mezze spread or to accompany grilled meat and poultry.

**PREP** 20 MINS ❖ **SERVES** 4, AS A MEZZE DISH

2 large **tomatoes**
1 small **cucumber**
1 **red onion**
1 **green pepper**, or 2 long, **green**
   **Turkish peppers**
big bunch of **flat-leaf parsley**,
   coarsely chopped
1–2 tbsp **olive oil**
juice of 1 **lemon**
**salt** and freshly ground **black pepper**

1 Bring a small pan of water to the boil on a high heat and blanch the tomatoes for 2–3 seconds. Drain under cold running water and peel off the skins. Place on a wooden board, cut in half, and remove the seeds. Chop the flesh into bite-sized pieces and place in a bowl.

2 Peel the cucumber, cut into quarters lengthways, and chop into bite-sized chunks. Sprinkle with salt and leave to drain for 5 minutes.

3 Meanwhile, halve the onion lengthways, then cut in half again crossways. Following the grain, cut into bite-sized pieces and add to the bowl. Halve the pepper and remove the stalk, seeds, and pith. Cut into bite-sized pieces and add to the bowl.

4 Rinse and drain the cucumber and add to the bowl along with the parsley. Pour in the oil and lemon juice, season, and toss well just before serving.

### variation

**Gypsy salad** This traditional Turkish salad can also be made by omitting the cucumber and adding 1–2 chopped fresh chillies and about 200g (7oz) crumbled feta cheese.

# insalata di pomodori e mozzarella con cipolla rossa

### ✧ *italy* ✧

Versatile and easy to prepare, this simple salad of tomatoes, red onion, and mozzarella bursts with vibrant colours and delicious Italian flavours.

**PREP** 10 MINS ❖ **SERVES** 4

8 ripe **plum tomatoes**, sliced
6 **cherry tomatoes**, halved
1 small **red onion**, peeled and sliced
handful of **basil leaves**, torn
**extra virgin olive oil**, to drizzle
**salt** and freshly ground **black pepper**
2 handfuls of **wild rocket leaves**
**balsamic vinegar**, to drizzle
2 balls of **mozzarella**, torn

1 Place the tomatoes, onion, and half of the basil leaves in a bowl. Drizzle over plenty of olive oil, season well, and toss through.

2 Arrange the rocket leaves on a serving platter and drizzle over a little oil and some balsamic vinegar. Season and spoon over the tomato and basil mixture. Add the torn mozzarella. Scatter over the remaining basil leaves, and drizzle again with a little oil and balsamic vinegar. Serve immediately.

### cook's tips

It is worth investing in an aged balsamic from Modena for its deliciously concentrated sweetness and spiciness to combine with a leafy extra virgin Tuscan olive oil.

To make red onions taste less bitter, soak them in cold water for 30 minutes after slicing. Drain well and pat dry with kitchen paper before using.

# salade niçoise

*✴ provence ✴*

This salad is a simple feast based on salad leaves, fresh spring onions, tomatoes, olives, olive oil, and anchovies. Flaked tuna and hard-boiled eggs are optional but desirable.

**PREP** 30 MINS ❖ **SERVES** 4

1 large or 2 small **Batavia lettuces**
4 just-ripe **tomatoes**
4 **eggs**, hard-boiled
3 large **spring onions**
8 **anchovy fillets** packed in oil
½ small **red pepper**
200g (7oz) cooked **green beans**
2 tbsp small **black olives**
150g (5½oz) **canned tuna** in oil, drained and flaked
2 tsp **lemon juice**

**For the dressing**
6 tbsp **extra virgin olive oil**
1 **garlic clove**, crushed
5 **basil leaves**, finely chopped
1 tbsp **red or white wine vinegar**
**salt** and freshly ground **black pepper**

1 For the dressing, place all the ingredients in a cup and whisk well, then set aside for the flavours to mellow.

2 Separate the lettuce leaves. Rinse, drain, and dry in a salad spinner. Tear the leaves into bite-sized pieces. Halve the tomatoes, then cut each half into 2–3 wedges. Peel the eggs and quarter lengthways. Chop both the white and green parts of the spring onions. Drain the anchovy fillets well on kitchen paper, then cut in half lengthways. Remove the seeds from the red pepper, then cut into very fine strips.

3 Place some lettuce leaves in a (round or oval) shallow dish, add a layer of tomato, and scatter in some green beans, red pepper, and spring onion pieces. Repeat the layering until you have used up all these ingredients.

4 Whisk the dressing again. Taste and adjust the seasoning. Spoon over the salad and toss gently.

5 Tuck in the hard-boiled eggs, scatter over the olives, and distribute the anchovies and tuna flakes over the salad. Season with black pepper and sprinkle with the lemon juice. Serve immediately.

**cook's tip**

Avoid adding cooked potatoes, rice, or sweetcorn to your niçoise – they do not really fit into the mixture of fresh vegetables that makes up the original dish.

# shlada al falfla hamra al khizzou

*morocco*

The juicy oranges contrast with the crisp carrot and crunchy sesame seeds, adding wonderful textures to this simple yet delicious salad. Serve with grilled or roasted meats.

**PREP** 15 MINS ❖ **COOK** 1 HR ❖ **SERVES** 4-6

3 tbsp **sesame seeds**

3–4 generous handfuls of **rocket** or lettuce leaves

500g (1lb 2oz) **carrots**, peeled and grated

2 **oranges**, peeled, pith removed, and flesh cut into segments

**salt** and freshly ground **black pepper**

juice of 1 **lemon**

30 fresh **flat-leaf parsley** leaves, roughly chopped

### For the paprika dressing

1 tsp runny **honey**

¼ tsp **salt**

½ tsp **pimentón** (Spanish paprika)

1 tsp **mustard**

60ml (2fl oz) **extra virgin olive oil**

1 tbsp **red wine vinegar**

freshly ground **black pepper**

1 Dry-fry the sesame seeds over a medium-high heat for 2–3 minutes, taking care not to scorch them. Remove from the heat.

2 Arrange the rocket or lettuce in a bowl with the carrots and orange segments. Season. Squeeze the lemon juice over the top and scatter with the parsley.

3 Place all the ingredients for the dressing in a glass jar with a secure-fitting lid, add 1 tablespoon water, and shake to combine thoroughly. Pour over the top of the carrot salad and garnish with the toasted sesame seeds.

# tabbouleh

*middle east*

This healthy Lebanese and Syrian speciality of parsley, mint, tomatoes, and bulgur is refreshing all year round and makes a great accompaniment to fish.

**PREP** 20 MINS, PLUS STANDING ❖ **SERVES** 4

115g (4oz) **bulgur wheat**

juice of 2 **lemons**

75ml (2½fl oz) **extra virgin olive oil**

freshly ground **black pepper**

225g (8oz) **flat-leaf parsley**, coarse stalks removed

75g (2½oz) **mint leaves**, coarse stalks removed

4 **spring onions**, finely chopped

2 large **tomatoes**, deseeded and diced

1 head of **Little Gem lettuce**

1 Place the bulgur wheat in a large bowl. Pour over enough cold water to cover, and leave to stand for 15 minutes, or until the wheat has absorbed all the water and the grains have swollen.

2 Add the lemon juice and oil to the wheat, season to taste with pepper, and stir to mix.

3 Just before serving, finely chop the parsley and mint. Mix the herbs and spring onions into the wheat.

4 Arrange the lettuce leaves on a serving plate, spoon the salad into the leaves, and top with the tomatoes.

variation

**Fruit tabbouleh** Replace the chopped tomatoes with 2–3 tablespoons of pomegranate seeds or plump, juicy raisins, and the same quantity of toasted pine nuts.

# insalata tricolore

*italy*

Green, white, and red are the colours of the Italian flag, and are echoed in this tempting dish, which is a treat for the eyes and taste buds.

**PREP** 15 MINS ❖ **COOK** 5 MINS ❖ **SERVES** 4

200g (7oz) small **plum tomatoes**
**salt** and freshly ground **black pepper**
2 **garlic cloves**, peeled and thinly sliced
2 **spring onions**, trimmed and
    finely chopped
60ml (2fl oz) **extra virgin olive oil**
2 tbsp **balsamic vinegar**, plus extra
    to drizzle
2 tbsp **small capers**, drained and rinsed
150g (5½oz) small **buffalo mozzarella balls**,
    torn in half
handful of **basil leaves**, roughly chopped
2 ripe **Hass avocados**

1 Preheat the grill on its highest setting. Place the tomatoes in a single layer on a baking tray, season to taste, and sprinkle the garlic and spring onions over the top. Drizzle with the oil.

2 Place the baking tray under the grill for 4–5 minutes, or until the tomatoes just begin to soften and the garlic turns golden brown.

3 Place the hot tomatoes, garlic, spring onions, and cooking juices in a bowl. Add the vinegar, capers, mozzarella, and basil. Toss gently and set aside.

4 Peel, stone, and quarter the avocados. Place 2 avocado quarters on each plate.

5 Spoon the tomato mixture over the avocado quarters and drizzle with balsamic vinegar. Serve immediately.

# horiatiki salata

*greece*

This ever-popular Greek salad is a wonderful summer dish that is ideal for a buffet or served alongside barbecued meats.

**PREP** 20 MINS ❖ **SERVES** 4-6

600g (1lb 5oz) ripe **large** or **beef tomatoes**
½ **cucumber**
200g (7oz) **feta cheese**, drained and
    cut into small cubes
100g (3½oz) **black olives**
juice of ½ **lemon**
handful of **Greek basil** or **basil**
3–4 tbsp **extra virgin olive oil**
**salt** and freshly ground **black pepper**

1 Cut the tomatoes into chunks. Peel away some of the cucumber skin, quarter the cucumber lengthways, and remove the seeds, then cut into chunks. Put both the tomatoes and cucumber into a large bowl.

2 Add the feta and olives to the tomatoes and cucumber. Squeeze the lemon juice over the salad and toss.

3 Transfer to a serving platter and sprinkle with the basil, drizzle with the oil, then season to taste.

**cook's tip**

Greek basil has a much smaller leaf than other varieties and a strong flavour, ideal for this summer salad. Alternatively, use the more readily available basil, torn into small pieces.

**prepare ahead**

The salad can be made and dressed 1–2 hours in advance; add the basil, to serve.

# *essential*
# lemons and oranges

Lemons come at the very top of the cook's list of kitchen essentials.
Oranges, their sweet cousins, aren't far behind.

**First recorded** in Southern Italy 2000 years ago, and seriously cultivated in Liguria as early as the 15th century, lemons are a magic all-rounder. They marinate and tenderize meats, dress salads, and liven up heavy soups and stews with their finely grated zest. A few drops of lemon juice is all you need to bring out the flavour of fresh fish or seafood. And their lovely acidity rescues desserts from cloying sweetness. Oranges also have a lot to offer: the fragrance of blossoms and essential oils; the flavour of dried peel in slow cooked dishes; juice, as good freshly squeezed as reduced into syrup; and an ability to boil up with sugar into a long-lasting preserve.

**Navel oranges** are good for juicing, eating, and cooking.

**Valencia oran**
(see bottom
are easy to
and have a
pleasing, sh
sweetness.

**Eureka lemons** grow easily and in abundance, producing fruit and flowers all year round.

**Sorrento lemons**, native to Italy, are rich in aromatic oils and are used for making limoncello liqueur.

**Candied lemon peel** is made by boiling peel slowly in syrup, draining on a rack, and then drying in a low-heat oven.

**Preserved lemons** add a unique flavour to Moroccan tagines. Take care to rinse them well before using.

**Bitter oranges** are unpleasant to eat but their sourness, thick skin, and numerous seeds make them great for marmalade.

# light and lemony patlıcan salatası

## ❖ *turkey* ❖

Aubergines soak up olive oil like sponges. Poaching them in aromatic stock and finishing off with lemon zest keeps the oil content down and the flavours light and vibrant.

**PREP** 1¼ HRS ❖ **COOK** 10 MINS
**SERVES** 4-6

500g (1lb 2oz) ripe **aubergines**, diced into 2.5cm (1in) cubes
**salt** and freshly ground **black pepper**
1.2 litre (2 pints) hot **vegetable** or **chicken stock**
finely grated zest and juice of ½ **lemon**
1 **garlic clove**, crushed
1–2 tbsp snipped **basil** and/or **mint**
2–3 tbsp **olive oil**

1 Place the aubergine cubes in a large bowl, cover with cold water, and add 1–2 tablespoons of the salt. Stir to dissolve the salt and leave for 1 hour. Drain, rinse, and drain again.

2 Bring the stock to the boil in a saucepan. Add the aubergines, reduce the heat to a simmer, and cook for about 10 minutes, until they are just cooked but still retain their shape. Drain well and place in a shallow bowl.

3 Place the lemon zest and juice, and garlic in a bowl and mix well. Drizzle the mixture over the aubergines and scatter over the fresh herbs. Drizzle over the oil, toss lightly, and adjust the seasoning. Leave to stand for at least 10 minutes before serving.

# pantzaria salata me skordalia

## ❖ *greece* ❖

This salad of young beetroot with its leaves is served with *skordalia*, a garlic dip. The Greeks enjoy the dip with salt-cod fritters and steamed mussels, or as an accompaniment to pitta bread.

**PREP** 20 MINS ❖ **COOK** 45-55 MINS
**SERVES** 4-6

6–8 young **beetroots** with leaves
**salt** and freshly ground **black pepper**
1 **lemon**, plus extra lemon quarters, to serve

### For the garlic dip
2 large **potatoes**, scrubbed
6–8 **garlic cloves**
1 tsp **salt**
about 150ml (5fl oz) **extra virgin olive oil**
2–3 tbsp **wine vinegar** or **lemon juice**

1 Rinse the beetroots and trim off the leaves, leaving 2.5cm (1in) of the stalk still attached to the base. Reserve the leaves – if they have wilted a little, place the stems in water to revive.

2 In a pan of boiling salted water, cook the beetroots for 20–30 minutes, or until tender. When the beetroots are cool enough to handle, peel off the skins, slice, or cut into cubes, and reserve.

3 Shred the beetroot leaves and their stems. In a pan of boiling salted water, cook them for 5–6 minutes until the stalks are tender. Transfer to a colander and drain thoroughly, squeezing to extract all the water. Fluff with a fork and dress with a squeeze of lemon.

4 For the garlic dip, boil the potatoes in a pan of salted water until tender, then drain. (Chop the potatoes into cubes before boiling to reduce the cooking time, if you prefer.) When cool enough to handle, remove the skin. While still warm, push the potatoes through a potato ricer, or mash them thoroughly until smooth.

5 Pound the garlic with the salt in a mortar and pestle or process in a food processor, and work in the oil. Gradually beat the garlicky oil into the hot mashed potatoes, adding vinegar as the mixture forms an emulsion. Continue until you have a thick smooth purée. Season to taste. Serve the beetroot and its leaves in separate heaps, with a bowl of garlic dip on the side, pitta wedges, and lemon quarters for squeezing.

# patlıcan salatası

*❖ turkey ❖*

In this recipe from Istanbul, the trick is not to overcook the aubergines. Add the tomato, herbs, and lemon at the last minute for a fresh, zesty touch.

**PREP** 1 HR ❖ **COOK** 30-40 MINS
**SERVES** 4-6

500g (1lb 2oz) ripe **aubergines**, cut into 2.5cm (1in) cubes
**sea salt** and freshly ground **black pepper**
3–4 tbsp **olive oil**
1 **red onion**, finely chopped
1–2 **garlic cloves**, crushed
2–3 **bay leaves**, crushed

1 large **tomato**, blanched, peeled, and diced
1 tbsp snipped **flat-leaf parsley**
1 tbsp snipped **basil** and/or **coriander** and/or **mint**
finely grated zest of ½ **unwaxed lemon**

1 Place the aubergines in a large bowl, cover with some cold water, add 1–2 tablespoons of the salt, and stir to dissolve. Leave for 1 hour, then drain, rinse, and pat dry with kitchen paper.

2 Heat 1–2 tablespoons of the oil in a heavy-based saucepan over a low heat. Add the aubergines, onion, garlic, and bay leaves, then season to taste and stir well to mix. Cover and cook on a low heat, stirring frequently, for 30–40 minutes, until the aubergines are just cooked but still retain their shape.

3 Remove the bay leaves. Stir in the tomato, parsley, and the remaining oil. Cook, stirring, for 10 minutes until the tomato has wilted. Remove from the heat and stir in the rest of the herbs and the lemon zest. Adjust the seasoning and serve warm or at room temperature.

## zeytinyağlı enginar
❖ *turkey* ❖

A popular seasonal dish in Turkey and Lebanon, the artichokes are cooked in olive oil with broad beans and almonds. They can also be cooked by themselves and served with a lemon wedge.

**PREP** 40 MINS ❖ **COOK** 30 MINS ❖ **SERVES** 4

175g (6oz) freshly shelled **broad beans**
4 **globe artichokes**, trimmed to their bottoms
125ml (4½fl oz) **olive oil**
juice of 1 **lemon**
2 tsp **granulated sugar**
**salt**
90g (3oz) blanched **almonds**
small bunch of **dill**, finely chopped
1 **tomato**, skinned, deseeded, and cut into strips

1 Place the beans in a large saucepan of water and bring to the boil. Reduce the heat and simmer for 15–20 minutes, until tender. Drain and refresh under cold running water. Remove the skins and set aside.

2 Place the artichoke bottoms in a shallow heavy-based saucepan. In a small bowl, mix together the oil, lemon juice, and 50ml (1¾fl oz) water, and pour over the artichokes. Cover and poach gently for 20 minutes. Add the sugar, salt, beans, and almonds, and continue to poach for 10 more minutes, until the artichokes are tender. Toss in half the dill and turn off the heat. Cool.

3 Lift the artichokes out of the pan and place hollow-side up on a serving dish. Spoon the bean and almond mixture into the middle of the artichokes and around them. Drizzle some of the cooking liquid over, garnish with the rest of the dill and the tomato, and serve at room temperature.

*how to prepare*
To prepare artichokes, pull off the outer leaves and cut off the stalks. Remove the purple chokes, leaves, any hard bits, and the fibres. Rub the bottoms with lemon juice and salt.

## melanzane e zucchine grigliate
❖ *italy* ❖

Best served at room temperature so the garlic-vinegar dressing can infuse the vegetables, this duo of aubergines and courgettes works well with barbecued, grilled, or roast meats.

**PREP** 15 MINS, PLUS STANDING
**COOK** 30 MINS ❖ **SERVES** 6

2 **aubergines**, thinly sliced lengthways
**salt** and freshly ground **black pepper**
2 **garlic cloves**, peeled and chopped
1 tbsp **balsamic vinegar**
2 tbsp **extra virgin olive oil**, plus extra for brushing
4 **courgettes**, trimmed and sliced
**mint** leaves, to garnish

1 Sprinkle the aubergine slices with a little salt and set aside for 30 minutes.

2 For the dressing, whisk together the garlic, vinegar, and oil, and season to taste. Set aside.

3 Preheat a ridged cast-iron grill pan until smoking hot. Brush the courgettes with a little oil and season. Grill the courgettes on both sides until tender, then transfer to a large serving platter.

4 Rinse the aubergines and pat dry with kitchen paper. Brush both sides of the aubergines with oil and grill for several minutes on both sides. Add the aubergines to the courgettes and pour over the dressing. Toss in the mint leaves and leave for 15 minutes for the flavours to blend before serving.

## insalata di peperoni rossi
### ✤ *spain* ✤

In this popular Spanish dish, sweet red peppers are gently stewed, then served at room temperature. Leftovers are lovely served with grilled meats, chicken, or fish.

**PREP** 10 MINS ✤ **COOK** 25 MINS ✤ **SERVES** 4

3 tbsp **olive oil**
6 **red peppers**, deseeded and cut into large strips
2 **garlic cloves**, finely chopped
250g (9oz) ripe **tomatoes**, skinned, deseeded, and chopped
2 tbsp chopped **flat-leaf parsley**
**salt** and freshly ground **black pepper**
1 tbsp **sherry vinegar**

1 Heat the oil in a large frying pan, add the peppers and garlic, and fry over a low heat for 5 minutes, stirring, then add the tomatoes. Increase the heat, bring to simmering point, then reduce the heat to low, cover, and cook for 12–15 minutes.

2 Stir in the parsley, season well, and cook for a further 2 minutes. Using a slotted spoon, remove the peppers and arrange in a serving dish.

3 Add the vinegar to the pan, increase the heat, and simmer the sauce for 5–7 minutes, or until it has reduced and thickened. Pour the sauce over the peppers and allow to cool.

### prepare ahead
The dish can be made up to 2 days in advance and chilled until ready to use.

### variation
**Red pepper dressing** In a food processor, process leftover peppers with a little sherry or wine vinegar and enough oil to make a dressing for a warm potato salad.

## parmigiana di melanzane
### ✤ *italy* ✤

Aubergine parmigiana is one of Italy's most popular dishes and a great choice for vegetarians. Serve with a simple salad or grilled meats.

**PREP** 40 MINS ✤ **COOK** 30 MINS ✤ **SERVES** 4

2 large **eggs**
**salt** and freshly ground **black pepper**
45g (1½oz) **plain flour**
2 **aubergines**, thinly sliced lengthways
4 tbsp **sunflower oil**
600ml (1 pint) **tomato sauce**
60g (2oz) **Parmesan cheese**, grated
a bunch of **basil** (reserve a few leaves, to garnish)
300g (10oz) **mozzarella cheese**, sliced

1 Preheat the oven to 160°C (325°F/Gas 3). Beat the eggs in a shallow bowl and season. Place the flour on a plate. Coat an aubergine slice in the flour, shaking off the excess, then tip it into the egg and let the excess drip back into the bowl. Repeat with the remaining slices.

2 Heat the oil in a large frying pan over a medium heat. Working in batches if necessary, fry the aubergine slices for 5 minutes on each side, or until golden. Drain well on kitchen paper, then continue until all the slices are fried.

3 Layer the tomato sauce, aubergine slices, Parmesan, basil, and mozzarella in a shallow ovenproof serving dish. Continue layering until all the ingredients are used, finishing with a layer of tomato sauce and the cheese on top. Season to taste.

4 Place the dish on a baking tray and bake for 30 minutes, or until the sauce is bubbling and the cheese has melted. Top with extra basil leaves and serve hot.

### prepare ahead
Steps 1 and 2 can be done a day in advance. Alternatively, the entire dish can be assembled a day in advance and baked just before ready to serve. It can be frozen, assembled in an ovenproof dish for up to 1 month; bake as in step 4.

### variation
**Courgette parmigiana** Substitute the same weight of aubergines with courgettes, thickly sliced lengthways.

# *essential*
# aubergines

Master the art of cooking aubergines and you will be rewarded with some of the best dishes from the Mediterranean.

**A bitter, inedible fruit** in its raw state, once cooked an aubergine becomes tender and velvety. It can absorb all flavours, from simple lemon and garlic dressings to complex aromatic ragùs, and spicy sauces. The transformation is not instantaneous – cooking aubergines takes time and patience. Be aware that they are also gluttons for olive oil. Salting before cooking will control the amount of oil they absorb, as will painting on or drizzling the oil, and adding a touch more at the end of cooking.

**Small** aubergines are charming. Pick similar-looking fruit when planning a dish and cut or slice as evenly as possible.

**Striped Italian** aubergines are great for preparing Parmigiana and Moussaka.

**Medium, round** aubergines are best for stuffing and baking.

**White Italian** aubergines are less bitter than most and are good for slicing and grilling, and ratatouille.

**Large, deep purple** aubergines are the most common variety. Make sure they are shiny, smooth, and heavy. They are perfect for baba ganoush and purées.

**Violetta di Firenze** is a prized heirloom variety, which looks beautiful and has a fine flavour.

# mahshi felfel
### ✷ *middle east* ✷

Called *mahshi* in Arabic and *dolma* in Turkish, stuffed vegetables and fruit are common throughout the eastern Mediterranean region, particularly in Turkey and Lebanon.

**PREP** 30 MINS ✷ **COOK** 30 MINS ✷ **SERVES** 4

2 tbsp **currants**

50ml (2fl oz) **olive oil**, plus 2 tbsp extra

2 **onions**, finely chopped

1 tsp **sugar**, plus a little extra

2 tbsp **pine nuts**

2 tsp ground **cinnamon**

1–2 tsp **dried mint**

½ tsp **allspice**

175g (6oz) **short-grain rice**, washed and drained

salt and freshly ground **black pepper**

small bunch of **flat-leaf parsley**, chopped

small bunch of **dill**, finely chopped

small bunch of **fresh mint**, finely chopped

2 **tomatoes**

4 colourful **peppers**, stalks removed and deseeded, but kept whole

juice of 1 **lemon**

1 tbsp **pomegranate syrup**

1 **lemon**, cut into wedges

1 Place the currants in a small bowl. Pour over enough boiling water to cover them well and leave to soften for 5–10 minutes. Drain and set aside.

2 Heat 2 tablespoons of the oil in a heavy-based pan and stir in the onions and sugar. When the onions begins to colour, stir in the pine nuts and currants, until the nuts turn golden. Add the cinnamon, mint, and allspice. Stir in the rice, coating it well in the spices. Pour in enough water to cover the rice and season. Bring to the boil, reduce the heat, and simmer until the water has been absorbed. Turn off the heat and cover the rice with a kitchen towel. Leave for 10 minutes, then toss in the fresh herbs.

3 Slice off the ends of the tomatoes and reserve. Cut the rest of the tomatoes into fine slices. Stuff the rice into the peppers and seal with the tomato lids. Place upright in a heavy-based pot.

4 In a bowl, mix together 50ml (2fl oz) oil and the lemon juice with 200ml (7fl oz) cold water. Pour it over and around the peppers and sprinkle over a little sugar. Bring to the boil, reduce the heat, cover the pan, and cook for 25–30 minutes, until the peppers are tender.

5 Place the peppers on a plate and arrange the tomato slices around them, drizzle the pomegranate syrup over the top, and serve with lemon wedges.

# peperonata
### ✷ *italy* ✷

A true taste of summer, this sweet pepper and tomato stew is a rustic Italian classic. For a more substantial dish, add diced boiled potatoes and black olives.

**PREP** 10 MINS ✷ **COOK** 40 MINS ✷ **SERVES** 2–3

2 tbsp **olive oil**

1 mild **onion**, finely sliced

1 **garlic clove**, crushed (optional)

2 large **red peppers** or 1 red and 1 yellow pepper, halved, cored, deseeded, white ribs removed, and cut into strips

salt and freshly ground **black pepper**

4 ripe **tomatoes**, chopped

a few **basil** leaves, rolled and snipped

1 Pour the oil into a non-stick frying pan over a medium heat. Stir in the onion and cook for 5–8 minutes, until soft, stirring frequently. Add the garlic, if using, then stir in the peppers, season, and soften for 5 minutes, stirring often.

2 Add the tomatoes, stir well, and cover partially. Cook for 20–30 minutes until just soft but not too mushy, stirring occasionally. Season to taste and stir in the basil. Serve warm or at room temperature.

*how to serve*
Serve it as an antipasto, a side dish with lamb, chicken, or fish, a pasta sauce, or a topping for bruschetta.

# ratatouille

❖ *provence* ❖

It's worth spending a little time over this wonderful vegetable stew from Provence. Precooking the vegetables separately, and draining them, keeps their flavours and textures distinctive. Adding peppery basil just before serving makes it more lively.

**PREP** 15 MINS ❖ **COOK** 1 HR ❖ **SERVES** 4

### ingredients
2 large **red peppers**, halved and deseeded
6 tbsp **olive oil**
2 large mild **onions**, peeled and thinly sliced
**sea salt** and freshly ground **black pepper**
1–2 **garlic cloves**, crushed
2 tsp **fresh thyme leaves** or 1 tsp **dried thyme**
1 tsp **fresh oregano leaves** or ½ tsp **dried oregano**
2 medium **aubergines**, cut into 2.5cm (1in) cubes
4 small to medium **courgettes**, cut into 1cm (½in) thick slices
4 medium **tomatoes**, blanched, peeled, deseeded, and chopped
1½ tbsp snipped **flat-leaf parsley**
a few **basil leaves**, torn, to garnish

1 **Preheat the oven** to 240°C (475°F/Gas 9). Place the peppers, cut sides down, on a layer of foil on a baking tray. Roast for 10 minutes, or until the skin chars and loosens. Lift out carefully, wrap in cling film, and leave to cool.

2 **When cool enough** to handle, peel and cut the peppers into strips lengthways. Reserve.

3 **In a pan, heat 3 tablespoons of the oil.** Fry the onions over a medium heat, turning, for 5 minutes. Season, add the garlic, thyme, and oregano, and fry for 8–10 minutes, until the onions are soft and golden, then remove. Add 1 tablespoon of the oil to the pan and fry the aubergines over a medium heat, turning, for 8–10 minutes, until soft and golden. Drain on kitchen paper.

4 **Heat 1 tablespoon of the oil** in another pan, fry the courgettes over a medium heat, turning frequently, for 5–8 minutes, until softened. Spread on a plate lined with kitchen paper.

5 **Wipe the first pan**. Heat the remaining oil and add the onions and tomatoes. Stir, then add the peppers, aubergines, and courgettes. Season lightly and stir in the parsley. Moisten with 100ml (3½fl oz) water. Cover and cook over a low heat for 15–20 minutes. Adjust the seasoning, scatter over the basil, and serve hot or warm.

# tomates confites

*❖ provence ❖*

These tomatoes have a great texture and plenty of flavour, and taste amazing when served with white meat or fish, in an omelette, or stirred into pasta or couscous.

**PREP** 25 MINS ❖ **COOK** 3 HRS ❖ **SERVES** 4

1kg (2¼lb) evenly-sized medium firm ripe **tomatoes**
**coarse sea salt** and freshly ground **black pepper**
3–4 tbsp **olive oil**
1 tsp **sugar**
a few **basil leaves**

1 Place a sieve over a bowl and have a large colander ready on a draining board or in the sink. Wash and quarter the tomatoes. Squeeze firmly over the sieve, and using a teaspoon, ease out of most of the seeds and some pulp. Place the tomatoes in the colander.

2 Sprinkle a tablespoon of salt over the tomatoes, stir, and leave to drain for at least 20 minutes. Discard the contents of the sieve and reserve the juices in the bowl.

3 Preheat the oven to 220°C (425°F/Gas 7). Lightly oil a large gratin dish, at least 25cm x 30cm (10in x 12in), and pack the tomatoes in a single layer. Season with a little pepper and sprinkle over the sugar. Drizzle with a little olive oil. Bake for 40–50 minutes, until slightly charred and wilting.

4 Carefully take the dish out of the oven, tilt, and scoop out the liquid using a spoon. Add to the juice in the bowl. Stir the tomatoes and drizzle with a little more oil. Return to the oven. Reduce the heat to 160°C (325°F/Gas 3) and bake for about 1 hour.

5 Take the dish out and scoop out any excess liquid using a spoon. Reserve. Stir, adjust the seasoning, then snip over the basil.

6 Return the tomatoes to the oven. Turn off the heat and leave in the oven for at least 1 hour. Adjust the seasoning, drizzle over a little oil, and snip over a few basil leaves.

**cook's tip**

The tomatoes shrink a lot in the oven, so transfer them to a smaller dish before serving. You can use the tomato juices in a sauce or soup. If you have 2 ovenproof dishes, double the quantities and store in the fridge. The tomatoes will keep for 3–4 days in the fridge, longer in a jar covered with olive oil.

# tomates à la provençale

*❖ provence ❖*

A perfect side dish for roast lamb or chicken, these pretty tomatoes smell as good as they look, and also make a great starter. This dish is very inviting in winter when you might add a little sugar to deepen the flavours.

**PREP** 20 MINS ❖ **COOK** 25-30 MINS ❖ **SERVES** 4

4 medium–large firm ripe **tomatoes**
**salt** and freshly ground **black pepper**
3–4 heaped tbsp **breadcrumbs**, made from whizzed toasted bread
4 tbsp **olive oil**
2 **garlic cloves**, crushed
3 tbsp finely chopped **flat-leaf parsley**
1 tbsp finely snipped fresh, or 1 tsp dried, **oregano** or **marjoram**
pinch of **sugar** (optional)
2–3 **basil leaves**, to finish

1 Halve the tomatoes. Using a small pointed teaspoon, scoop out some of the seeds and pulp, and discard. Sprinkle with a little salt. Place upside down on kitchen towel and let drain for at least 15 minutes.

2 Preheat the oven to 190°C (375°F/Gas 5). In a bowl, mix the breadcrumbs, oil, garlic, and herbs. Season lightly and add the sugar, if using.

3 Using the teaspoon, spread the mixture into the tomatoes, patting it in evenly.

4 Place the tomatoes in a gratin dish large enough to accommodate them side by side, and still leave a little space between them.

5 Bake for 25–30 minutes, or until the tomatoes are tender but still hold their shape and the filling is golden. Snip over the basil leaves and serve warm or at room temperature.

# *essential*
# tomatoes

It is hard to imagine Mediterranean cooking without this staple, colourful fruit, but the tomato is a relative newcomer to the region.

**Just how and when** tomatoes arrived is not certain, but it was probably in small quantities in the holds of Spanish ships returning from South America. By the 17th century, tomatoes were thriving in Naples and in Southern Italy. Since then they have flourished throughout the whole Mediterranean region. Turkey, Egypt, Italy, and Spain are amongst the world's top ten tomato producers. Choose the right tomatoes for your recipe. For salads, pick them ripe, sweet smelling, and a little soft. For stuffing, choose firm, thicker-skinned, similar sized varieties. Don't refrigerate tomatoes unless they are almost over-ripe and don't dismiss canned and bottled tomatoes – local cooks use them a lot.

**Costoluto Fiorentino**, from Florence, is a well-flavoured, versatile, and traditional tomato.

**Montserrat**, from Spain, has a very sweet, thick juice and provides plenty of fragrance.

**Pantano Romanesco**, with an abundance of rich flavour, is a favourite for sauces.

**Green tomatoes** have a sharp taste and are superb for frying and making jam.

**Yellow tomatoes** aren't sweet or intensely flavoured. Use them to add variety to the appearance of dishes.

**Roma and Olivade** are attractive plum tomatoes for sauces, and are great for slicing in salads and sandwiches.

**Cuor di Bue**, from Liguria, is slightly heart-shaped and excellent for pasta sauces.

**Cherry tomatoes** are small and bite-sized – perfect to have in a bowl on the table. They cook quickly, and can be used for topping pizza and crostini, or pan-fry them for a quick side vegetable.

**San Marsano** is a favourite for canning. It is fleshy and packed full of flavour.

**Plum tomatoes** have a slightly oval shape with thick, solid flesh. They are made for processing.

# basal bi tamer hindi

❖ *middle east* ❖

This medieval Arab recipe combines sweet honey with sour tamarind. Popular in Egypt and parts of North Africa, it is usually prepared with shallots or spring onion bulbs and is served with grilled or roasted meat and poultry.

**PREP** 5 MINS ❖ **COOK** 25 MINS ❖ **SERVES** 4

2–3 tbsp **olive oil**

450g (1lb) **shallots**, small **onions**, or **spring onion bulbs**, peeled and left whole

1 tbsp **tamarind paste**

1 tbsp **honey** or **brown sugar**

**salt**

small bunch of **coriander**, finely chopped

1 Heat the oil in a lidded heavy-based pan. Add the shallots and cook for 4–5 minutes, until they begin to brown.

2 Add the tamarind and honey, and enough cold water to just cover the base of the pan. Reduce the heat and cook gently, covered, for 15–20 minutes, until the onions are soft and the liquid has reduced to a sticky sauce.

3 Remove from the heat and season with a little salt. Transfer the onions to a serving dish and garnish with the coriander.

### cook's tip

Tamarind is derived from the fruit of the evergreen tamarind tree. It is most commonly available in compressed sticky blocks, or as a smooth, concentrated paste.

# cebollitas en adobo

❖ *spain* ❖

Baby onions stewed with olive oil in a fragrant sweet and sour sauce make a lively accompaniment to grilled meat, roast chicken, or a plain potato tortilla.

**PREP** 15-20 MINS ❖ **COOK** 20 MINS ❖ **SERVES** 4

about 500g (1lb 2oz) small **pickling onions** or **shallots**, peeled

3 **garlic cloves**, peeled

1–2 **bay leaves**

6 **black peppercorns**, crushed

1 tsp **salt**

1–2 **cloves**

3–4 tbsp **olive oil**

2 tbsp **raisins**, soaked to swell

2 tbsp **pimentón dulce** (mild Spanish paprika)

100ml (3½fl oz) **dry sherry** or **white wine**

1 tbsp **sherry vinegar**

a little **sugar** (optional)

1 In a large pan, place the onions, whole garlic, bay leaves, peppercorns, salt, and cloves with the oil. Toss over for 2–3 minutes on a gentle heat to start the cooking process without letting the onions brown.

2 Add the drained raisins, paprika, sherry, and enough cold water to cover the onions halfway. Bring to the boil, reduce the heat, cover, and cook gently until the onions are perfectly tender.

3 Add the vinegar, bring to the boil, check the seasoning, and add the sugar, if using. Serve warm or cold.

*how to serve*

Serve as a tapa with cos lettuce leaves, slices of Manchego cheese, and a few slivers of Serrano or Ibérico ham or chorizo.

## haricots verts en persillade

❖ *provence* ❖

Very fine French green beans are best for this recipe, but the robust parsley dressing can also work its magic on larger beans. The cooking time varies depending on the size of the beans.

**PREP** 10 MINS ❖ **COOK** 15 MINS ❖ **SERVES** 4

500g (1lb 2oz) fine **green beans**, topped and tailed
**sea salt** and freshly ground **black pepper**

### For the persillade
2 tbsp chopped **flat-leaf parsley**
1 **garlic** clove, crushed
2½ tbsp **extra virgin olive oil**

1 In a large saucepan of lightly salted boiling water, add the beans and cook for 8–10 minutes, or until tender but not soft. Drain well and refresh under cold running water. Keep warm.

2 Meanwhile, combine the parsley, garlic, and oil in a small bowl. Season well.

3 Tip the beans into a serving bowl, stir to coat with the persillade, and serve warm.

#### variations

**Green beans and persillade salad** You can serve the beans cold as a salad. Toss while still warm. Once cold, drizzle over 1 tablespoon of lemon juice or 2 teaspoons of balsamic vinegar, toss again, and serve.

**Persillade with anchovies and citrus zest** To add zing to persillade, add a few drained and mashed anchovies, and a little lemon or orange zest. Persillade is a good way to dress boiled new potatoes and rice.

## asperges rôties à l'aïoli

❖ *provence* ❖

The first of the new season's asparagus is celebrated in Provence every spring with *foires aux asperges* – asparagus fairs. This starter can be made using only green asparagus, but you can also include white and purple spears.

**PREP** 10 MINS ❖ **COOK** 20 MINS ❖ **SERVES** 4

24 **asparagus spears**, including at least 12 green spears
**salt** and freshly ground **black pepper**
3 tbsp **olive oil**
about 6 tbsp **aïoli** (see p152)
1 tbsp finely snipped **basil**
1 tbsp finely snipped **dill**
1 **tomato**, blanched, peeled, deseeded, and finely chopped

1 Trim the asparagus. In a large frying pan, add water to a depth of 5cm (2in) and bring to the boil. Reduce the heat to medium-high and add a little salt. Blanch the asparagus, starting with the white and purple spears, if using, for 7 minutes. Then add the green spears and cook for a further 3 minutes. Drain and refresh under cold running water.

2 Dry the pan and add the oil. Fry the asparagus in a single layer, in batches, for 5 minutes, until a little charred. Remove from the pan and arrange them on plates.

3 Place a generous tablespoon of aïoli on each plate and scatter over the basil, dill, and tomato. Season with a little pepper and serve immediately.

# fave e cicoria

*✦ italy ✦*

The traditional midday meal of Puglia, this smooth, unsalted, porridge-like purée is made using *fave* with an accompaniment of a spoonful of chicory, dandelion, or any of the edible greens available from the wild in spring.

**PREP** 15 MINS, PLUS OVERNIGHT SOAKING
**COOK** 3¼–4¼ HRS ✦ **SERVES** 4–6

500g (1lb 2oz) dried, split **broad beans**

1 large **floury potato,** peeled and diced

2–3 heads of red **chicory** or frizzy endive

4–5 tbsp **olive oil**, plus 2–3 tbsp extra for frying

2 **garlic** cloves, chopped

½ tsp crumbled **chilli**

**salt**

1–2 tbsp fresh **breadcrumbs**

1 tsp fresh or dried **thyme** leaves

1 Soak the beans overnight in cold water. Drain and transfer the beans to a large saucepan. Pour in twice the volume of cold water into the pan.

2 Bring to the boil, then, using a slotted spoon, skim off any grey foam. Add the potato and bring to the boil, then reduce the heat. Cook gently, stirring occasionally. Add more boiling water, if required. Leave to simmer for 3–4 hours, until the beans have collapsed to a soft golden mush.

3 Separate out the chicory leaves and rinse, but do not pat dry. Chop roughly and cook in a lidded pan with the oil, garlic, chilli, and a pinch of salt for 10 minutes, or until tender. Allow the juices to evaporate until reduced to an oily dressing.

4 In a pan, heat the oil, add breadcrumbs and thyme, and fry until the crisp and just browned.

5 Ladle the bean purée into serving bowls, top with a swirl of greens and a spoonful of the breadcrumb topping, or serve in separate bowls.

**cook's tips**

Any leftovers may be used to make refried fava beans. In a bowl, fold the purée with fried onion, chilli, and parsley. In a pan, heat some olive oil and ladle the purée to form a thick, crisp-crusted pancake.

Unskinned dried broad beans need to be thoroughly soaked before they can be popped out of their skins and split.

# carottes au cumin

*✦ provence ✦*

The cumin seeds add North African flavour to the tender caramelized carrots in this delicious dish.

**PREP** 5 MINS ✦ **COOK** 25–30 MINS ✦ **SERVES** 4

500g (1lb 2oz) large **organic carrots,** scraped and cut on the slant into 8cm (3¼in) thick slices

**salt** and freshly ground **black pepper**

2 tbsp **olive oil**

30g (1oz) **unsalted butter**

1 heaped tsp **cumin seeds**

1 scant tbsp **coriander leaves**, to garnish (optional)

1 Drop the carrots into a pan of fast-boiling, lightly salted water. Cook for 6–8 minutes, then drain well.

2 Return the pan to a low heat. Add the oil, swirl, and add half the butter. Sprinkle in the cumin, stir, and add the carrots. Season to taste and stir to coat the carrots. Cover the pan and cook for about 15 minutes until tender, shaking the pan a few times.

3 Remove the lid, increase the heat, add the rest of the butter, and cook for 2–3 minutes, stirring well. If you like, snip over some coriander leaves just before serving.

*how to serve*

These carrots can also be served cold as a starter, antipasto, or part of a buffet. Sprinkle with a little lemon juice, if you like.

# tostadas de garbanzos con espinacas

❖ *spain* ❖

This quick classic Spanish combination of chickpeas and spinach makes a delicious vegetarian supper when heaped on robust country bread crisped in olive oil.

**PREP** 5 MINS ❖ **COOK** 15-20 MINS
**SERVES** 4

3 tbsp **olive oil**
1 large **mild onion**, finely chopped
2-3 **garlic** cloves, crushed

1 tsp **cumin seeds**
1 tsp **ground cumin**
1 tsp **smoked pimentón** (Spanish paprika)
**salt** and freshly ground **black pepper**
500g (1lb 2oz) fresh **spinach** leaves, rinsed and drained
240g can **chickpeas**, rinsed and drained
1 tbsp **Spanish sherry vinegar**, plus a little more (optional)
2-4 slices of **sourdough bread**, halved
1 heaped tbsp finely snipped **flat-leaf parsley**

1 Heat 2 tablespoons of the oil in a large frying pan over a medium heat. Add the onion and fry for 2-3 minutes, until soft. Stir in the garlic and fry gently for 2-3 minutes, then stir in the cumin and paprika and fry until the spices smell fragrant, stirring frequently. Season lightly.

2 Add the spinach and fry for 2-3 minutes. Stir in the chickpeas and vinegar, then add 120ml (4fl oz) cold water and simmer. Reduce the heat. Cover and cook for 5-8 minutes, shaking the pan occasionally.

3 Meanwhile, in a frying pan, heat the remaining oil over a medium-high heat. Add the bread and fry until golden all over. Drain on a double layer of kitchen paper.

4 Remove the lid. Season and stir in a few drops of vinegar, if you like. Stir in the parsley and spoon on the bread to serve.

## variation

**Haricot beans and spinach toasts** Replace the chickpeas with the same amount of cooked white haricot beans. If you like, you can also add a small can of chopped tomatoes at the same time as the spinach.

# *a taste of*
# TURKEY

When you take a ferry for a quick ride across the Bosphorus, you can sip a glass of black çay and relish the fact that you are crossing continents. At the northeast corner of the Mediterranean, Turkey is a huge land bridge between Europe and Asia. Produce is abundant, colourful, and diverse. In the many markets, seasonal ingredients are shiny, fresh, and many are conveniently prepared – wet walnut kernels, plump artichoke bottoms in buckets of brine, and ready-to-fill supple vine leaves. From frugal soups to exquisite dishes inspired by the Ottoman court, you will be made offers you cannot resist. People go out of their way to show you their favourite restaurant for kalamar or stuffed vine leaves, or freshly baked baklava. They will give you their mother's recipe for imam bayıldı or purslane stew with garlic yogurt sauce. The sharing of food creates a common language.

Marmaris on Turkey's Western Mediterranean coast has a lovely harbour, a very large marina, and is a hugely popular holiday resort.

Beşiktaş is a busy residential district on the European side of the Bosphorus. Every Saturday there's a market selling food, clothing, textiles and other products.

**Dried apricots** are the preferred fruit for savoury and sweet dishes. Thanks to its climate and terrain, Turkey is the largest apricot-producing country in the world.

**Beyaz peynir** means white cheese, and like feta it comes in many varieties – fresh and unsalted, preserved in brine, soft or firm.

**Aubergine** is used in more Turkish dishes than in any other country in the region. It is pickled, fried, baked, smoked, stuffed, poached in sugar syrup to make jam, or hollowed out to dry on strings.

**Tea** is the national drink, drunk without milk but usually with sugar in pretty tulip-shaped glasses.

**Kırmızı acı biber**, chopped dried chilli flakes, are a ubiquitous condiment. Sometimes called Aleppo pepper, they are sometimes hot, sometimes mild.

**Kebabs** are everywhere – and their aroma is hard to resist.

**Kahve**, very finely ground Arabica coffee, is served black, and poured piping hot from a copper cezwe boiling pot, with plenty of grounds languishing at the bottom of the cup.

Istanbul's spice bazaar is the place to find all manner of delights – spices, oils, pastries, sweets, nuts, dried fruit, honeycombs, figs, dried beans, caviar, cheeses, as well as herbal medicines and magic potions.

# A special Turkish breakfast

Turkey's daily love affair with food begins with kahvaltı, literally meaning "under coffee" – what you eat before coffee – while drinking black tea. Breakfast is a serious meal. Boiled eggs or menemem, eggs with peppers and tomatoes, white breads, and simit, the round rings with sesame seeds. There may be regional variations but the spread will often include tahin pekmez, a combination of tahini and grape syrup, white cheese, honey, süzme (strained yogurt), olives, tomato, cucumber, and honey. Cigar-shaped boreks are a favourite extra.

**Black tea**

**Sıgarı böreği**
page 210

**Shakshouka**
page 77

**Feta cheese**

Simit

Tahin pekmez

Plain yogurt drizzled with honey

# radicchio alla trevigiana

*italy*

Radicchio has a pleasing, slightly bitter flavour and is refreshing in salads. In this Italian recipe, it is cooked and gently caramelized until richly bitter-sweet.

**PREP** 5 MINS ❖ **COOK** 20 MINS ❖ **SERVES** 4

3 tbsp **olive oil**
white part of 1 large **spring onion**, chopped
1 **garlic clove**, crushed
4 heads of **radicchio**, trimmed at the base and quartered
**salt** and freshly ground **black pepper**
1 tbsp **balsamic vinegar**
1–2 tsp **caster sugar**

1 In a frying pan, heat the olive oil, add the spring onion and garlic, and cook over a medium heat, until softened and golden.

2 Spread the radicchio in the pan. Cook for 3 minutes, then turn it over using tongs, and cook for a further 3 minutes. Season. Add about 3–4 tablespoons of cold water, cover, and simmer for 10 minutes.

3 Remove the lid, increase the heat, then add the balsamic vinegar and sugar. Cook for 2–3 minutes, turn the radicchio over, and cook for a further 2 minutes. Serve hot.

**variation**

**Braised radicchio with anchovies and raisins** Add a couple of drained and chopped anchovies and a tablespoon of raisins to the radicchio before sprinkling with water.

# tian aux courgettes

*provence*

Courgette gratin makes a simple yet satisfying main course. Serve it with a side salad and some cured ham or salami.

**PREP** 20 MINS ❖ **COOK** 1¼ HRS ❖ **SERVES** 6

2kg (4½lb) **courgette**, diced
4 tbsp **olive oil**
115g (4oz) **Gruyère cheese**, grated
120ml (4fl oz) **light cream**
½ tsp grated **nutmeg**
1 tsp dried **sage leaves**
**salt** and freshly ground **black pepper**

1 Place the courgette with the oil in a soup pot or very large saucepan. Cover and cook over a medium heat, stirring occasionally, for 15–20 minutes, or until tender. Turn out the courgette into a colander and let it stand for 30 minutes to drain off the excess moisture.

2 Preheat the oven to 200°C (400°F/Gas 6). Gently press down the drained courgettes with the flat side of a wide slotted spoon, then transfer to a tian or gratin dish. Add half the cheese, the cream, nutmeg, and sage leaves, and stir well to mix. Season.

3 Spread out and smooth the surface with the back of a fork. Sprinkle with the remaining cheese. Bake for 15–20 minutes, until golden. Serve hot.

*how to serve*
Perfect with roasts, this dish can also be served at room temperature on its own as an antipasto.

# slada bata halwa

### *north africa*

In Morocco and Tunisia, sweet potatoes are often cooked in tagines, combined with herbs and spices, and served as a side dish or salad. The combination of green olives and preserved lemon is typically Moroccan.

**PREP** 15 MINS ❖ **COOK** 20 MINS ❖ **SERVES** 4

3–4 tbsp **olive oil**

1 **onion**, coarsely chopped

1 tsp cumin seeds

25g (scant 1oz) fresh root **ginger**, peeled and finely chopped

500g (1lb 2oz) **sweet potatoes**, peeled and cut into bite-sized cubes

½ tsp **pimentón** (Spanish paprika)

**salt** and freshly ground **black pepper**

8–10 pitted **green olives**

peel of 1 **preserved lemon**, finely chopped

juice of ½ **lemon**

small bunch of **flat-leaf parsley**, finely chopped

small bunch of **coriander**, finely chopped

1 Heat the oil in a tagine pot or heavy-based pan. Stir in the onion and cook for 1–2 minutes, until it begins to colour. Add the cumin and ginger, and fry until fragrant.

2 Toss in the sweet potatoes along with the paprika and pour in cold enough water to just cover the base of the pot. Cover and cook gently for 10–12 minutes, until tender but firm, and the liquid has reduced.

3 Season to taste and add the olives, lemon, and lemon juice. Cover and cook for a further 5 minutes to let the flavours combine.

4 Stir in half the herbs and transfer the mixture to a serving dish. Garnish with the rest of the herbs and serve warm or at room temperature.

# battata hara

### *middle east*

The variations of this spicy potato dish can be fiery with extra chillies, tangy with preserved lemon, or refreshing with chopped mint, parsley, and dill. This version is more common in Egypt, Jordan, Syria, and Lebanon.

**PREP** 20 MINS ❖ **COOK** 10 MINS ❖ **SERVES** 4

350g (12oz) **new potatoes**

2–3 tbsp **olive oil**

3–4 **garlic cloves**, finely chopped

2 fresh or dried **red chillies**, deseeded and finely chopped

1–2 tsp **cumin seeds**

2 tsp ground **turmeric**

juice of 1–2 **lemons**

**salt** and freshly ground **black pepper**

bunch of **coriander**, finely chopped

1 **lime**, cut into quarters

1 Place the potatoes in a large pan with plenty of water and bring to the boil. Boil them for about 10 minutes, until cooked through but still firm. Drain and refresh under cold running water and peel off the skins. Place the potatoes on a wooden board and cut them into bite-sized pieces.

2 Heat the oil in a heavy-based pan. Stir in the garlic, chillies, and cumin seeds, and cook for 2–3 minutes, until the seeds begin to colour. Add the turmeric, toss in the potatoes, and mix well to coat. Pour in the lemon juice and cook gently for 4–5 minutes. Then season to taste and stir in half the coriander.

3 Remove from the heat and transfer the potatoes to a serving dish. Garnish with the remaining coriander and serve with lime wedges to squeeze over.

### *how to serve*

Serve as part of a mezze spread, as an accompaniment to grilled and roasted meat and fish, or on its own with a dollop of garlic-flavoured yogurt.

# champiñones al ajillo

❖ *s p a i n* ❖

A popular, simple tapas dish of garlic mushrooms to enjoy with a glass of chilled, crisp rosé wine, or a copita of dry sherry or manzanilla.

**PREP** 5 MINS ❖ **COOK** 10 MINS ❖ **SERVES** 4

3 tbsp **olive oil**

225–250g (8–9oz) **brown-cap mushrooms**, stems removed, and halved or quartered if large

**salt** and freshly ground **black pepper**

3–4 **garlic cloves**, crushed

1–2 tbsp **dry sherry**

1 tsp **smoked pimentón** (Spanish paprika), or ½ tsp chilli powder

2 tsp **sherry vinegar**

1½ tbsp snipped **flat-leaf parsley**

4 **lemon wedges**, to serve

1 Heat the oil in a frying pan. Fry the mushrooms over a medium-high heat, stirring frequently, for 2–3 minutes, and season well.

2 Add the garlic, sherry, a splash of cold water, and the paprika. Reduce the heat and cook for 5 minutes, stirring occasionally, until the mushrooms are just cooked.

3 Sprinkle over the sherry vinegar, scatter over the parsley, and stir well. Remove from the heat and transfer to a serving dish. Serve with lemon wedges and chunks of fresh crusty bread.

**variation**

**Mushrooms with garlic and ham**  To make this tapas dish more elaborate, cut a slice of Serrano ham into pieces. Stir the ham into the mushrooms at the same time as you add the sherry vinegar and parsley.

# patatas bravas

❖ *s p a i n* ❖

This classic tapas dish features cubes of potatoes mixed with a spicy sauce. Be generous with the flat-leaf parsley as it looks great and adds contrasting taste and texture.

**PREP** 15 MINS ❖ **COOK** 1 HR ❖ **SERVES** 4

6 tbsp **olive oil**

700g (1½lb) **white potatoes**, peeled and cut into 2cm (¾in) cubes

2 **onions**, finely chopped

1 tsp **dried chilli flakes**

2 tbsp **dry sherry**

grated zest of 1 **lemon**

4 **garlic cloves**, grated or finely chopped

200g can chopped **tomatoes**

small handful of **flat-leaf parsley**, chopped

**salt** and freshly ground **black pepper**

1 Preheat the oven to 200°C (400°F/Gas 6). Heat half the oil in a non-stick frying pan, add the potatoes, and cook over a low heat for 20 minutes, or until starting to brown, turning frequently. Add the onions and cook for a further 5 minutes.

2 Add the chilli, sherry, lemon zest, and garlic. Reduce for 2 minutes before adding the tomatoes and parsley. Season, combine well, and cook over a medium heat for 10 minutes, stirring occasionally.

3 Stir in the remaining oil, place all the ingredients in a shallow baking dish, and bake in the oven for 30 minutes, or until cooked. Serve hot with a selection of tapas dishes.

**variation**

**Potato, parsnip, and celery bake**  Prepare in the same way, but cook 350g (12oz) potatoes and 350g (12oz) parsnips, both peeled and cut into 2cm (¾in) cubes, instead of all potatoes. Add 2 thinly sliced celery sticks at the same time. Add the zest of 1 orange instead of lemon, and 2 tablespoons of chopped fresh thyme as well as the parsley.

*how to serve*
You can also serve this dish as a starter for 2, on a bed of lightly dressed salad leaves or on a slice of buttered toast.

# broccoli stuffato
❖ *italy* ❖

Gentle braising in its own juices with olive oil – a technique much favoured in southern Italy – enhances the delicate, mustardy flavour of the brassica. The broccoli is deliciously soft and bathed in its own aromatic oil.

**PREP** 10–15 MINS ❖ **COOK** 25–30 MINS
**SERVES** 4–6

750g (1lb 10oz) large-head **broccoli** or **green cauliflower**
5–6 **garlic cloves**, left unpeeled
4–5 tbsp **extra virgin olive oil**
2–3 dried **red chillies**, plus extra (optional)
**salt**

1 Divide the broccoli into small florets. Trim the stalks and cut into short lengths. Blanch in salted water for 3 minutes, then drain.

2 Thread the garlic cloves onto a toothpick to make them easier to remove. Heat the oil with the chillies and the garlic in a lidded saucepan. Remove and discard the chillies, then stir in the broccoli. Reduce the heat, season with a little salt, cover tightly with the lid, and cook gently, stirring occasionally, for 25–30 minutes.

3 Remove from the heat and serve with or without the garlic.

### cook's tip

*Peperoncini*, tiny red chillies dried in the sun, take the place of imported peppercorns in southern Italy's traditional *cucina povera*, the cooking of the poor, which means making the best of what's grown or gathered in season. It is a style equally relished by the region's rich.

# tian de pommes de terre
❖ *provence* ❖

Flavoured with garlic and enriched with cream, this gratin is a modern version of a frugal dish of old Provence called *lou tian de poumo* – potatoes cooked in the hearth in a garlic-rubbed pan.

**PREP** 30 MINS ❖ **COOK** 50 MINS ❖ **SERVES** 6

1.35kg (3lb) large **waxy potatoes**
6 **garlic** cloves, crushed
leaves from 6 sprigs of **flat-leaf parsley**
30g (1oz) **unsalted butter**, plus extra for greasing
1 tsp **thyme leaves**, chopped
100ml (3½fl oz) **milk**
100ml (3½fl oz) **single cream**
75g (2½oz) **Gruyère cheese**, grated
½ tsp grated **nutmeg**
**salt** and freshly ground **black pepper**

1 Preheat the oven to 190°C (375°F/Gas 5). Lightly grease a tian or gratin dish. In a large saucepan, bring plenty of lightly salted water to the boil. Peel the potatoes and cut into 1cm (½in) slices. Add them to the pan, return to the boil, and boil gently for 15 minutes. Stir gently from time to time. The potatoes should be almost cooked but still a little firm. Drain in a colander.

2 Meanwhile, finely chop together the garlic and parsley. Melt the butter in a medium saucepan, add the garlic, parsley, and thyme, and stir over a medium heat for 2 minutes. Add the milk and cream. Bring to the boil, then immediately remove from the heat. Stir in half the cheese and the nutmeg. Season with a little salt and plenty of pepper.

3 Spread the potato slices in the gratin dish, then spoon over the cream and cheese sauce. Scatter over the rest of the cheese. Bake for 30 minutes, until golden. Serve hot.

### variation

**Potato and mushroom gratin** For a deeper flavoured gratin, soak 20g (¾oz) dried mushrooms in just off-the-boil water for 15 minutes to plump them up, then drain and chop. Add to the potatoes together with drained, chopped anchovy fillets before baking.

# breads and
# bread dishes

# fatayer bi zahtar

### *middle east*

These little flatbreads sprinkled with a blend of herbs are popular as street food in Lebanon, Syria, and Jordan. They are often enjoyed on their own as a snack, or as an accompaniment to mezze dishes.

**PREP** 1½ HRS, PLUS RISING ❖ **COOK** 10 MINS
**SERVES** 4–6

7g **dried yeast**
½ tsp **sugar**
450g (1lb) **strong bread flour**, plus extra for dusting
½ tsp **salt**
2–3 tbsp **olive oil**, plus extra for greasing
3–4 tbsp **zahtar**
**coarse salt**

1 In a small bowl, dissolve the yeast and the sugar in a mixture of 4ml boiling water and 6ml cold water. Leave to cream for 10 minutes, or until frothy.

2 In another bowl, sift the flour with the salt. Make a well in the centre and add the creamed yeast. Add 300ml (10fl oz) lukewarm water and draw the flour in from the sides to form a dough.

3 Turn out the dough onto a floured surface and knead well for about 10 minutes, until it is smooth and elastic. Pour a drop of the oil into the base of the bowl, roll the dough in it, and cover with a damp cloth or cling film. Leave the dough to rise for about 1 hour, until it has doubled in size.

4 Preheat the oven to 200°C (400°F/Gas 6). In a small bowl, mix together the zahtar with the oil and bind it to a paste. Knock back the dough and knead it lightly, then divide the dough into about 20 parts. Knead each part into a ball, flatten and stretch it, and smear it with some of the zahtar paste.

5 Place the flatbreads on lightly greased baking trays and bake for about 10 minutes, until golden brown. Sprinkle over a little salt and serve warm.

### variation

**Fatayer with herbs** Instead of zahtar, you can combine dried thyme or oregano with crushed dried chillies and olive oil, or use a combination of sumac, dried mint, and sesame seeds, or a crushed olive paste.

# khubz

### *middle east*

This traditional pitta bread is a staple in Lebanon, Syria, Jordan, and Egypt. It is delicious drizzled with butter or honey for breakfast, sprinkled with feta and pickles as a snack, and used as a base for "fatta" dishes.

**PREP** 4–6 HRS, PLUS RISING AND PROVING
**COOK** 8 MINS ❖ **SERVES** 6–8

7g **dried yeast**
½ tsp **sugar**
450g (1lb) **strong bread flour**, or a mix of plain and wholemeal flours, plus extra for dusting
½ tsp **salt**
**sunflower oil**, for greasing

1 In a small bowl, dissolve the yeast with the sugar in 50ml (1¾fl oz) lukewarm water and leave to cream for 15 minutes, or until frothy.

2 In a separate bowl, sift the flour with the salt. Make a well in the centre and pour in the yeast mixture and 250ml (9fl oz) lukewarm water. Draw the flour in from the sides and knead the mixture into a pliable dough. Turn the dough out onto a lightly floured surface and knead until it is smooth and elastic. Pour a drop of the oil into the base of the bowl and roll the dough in it to coat the surface. Cover the bowl with a damp cloth and leave the dough to rise in a warm place, for at least 2 hours or overnight, until it has doubled in size.

3 Knock back the dough and knead again lightly. Divide the dough into small balls. Flatten the balls with the palm of your hand so that they resemble thick oval discs.

4 Dust a clean cloth with flour and place the flattened ovals of dough on top, leaving enough room to expand between them. Dust with flour and lay another clean cloth on top. Leave to prove for 1–2 hours.

5 Preheat the oven to 220°C (425°F/Gas 7). Place several baking sheets in the oven to heat. Lightly grease with oil and place the bread ovals on them. Sprinkle lightly with water and bake for 6–8 minutes, until they are lightly browned but not too firm and slightly hollow inside. Place the flatbreads on a wire rack and serve while still warm, or leave to cool and wrap them in a clean, dry cloth to keep soft.

# khubz bil hummus

### ❖ *north africa* ❖

Best eaten on the day they are made, these spiced breads are good as they are, or lightly chargrilled. They are a delicious accompaniment for lamb koftas, hummus, black olive tapenade, and salads.

**PREP** 25 MINS, PLUS RISING
**COOK** 15 MINS ❖ **MAKES** 8

1½ tsp **cumin seeds**, plus extra for topping
1½ tsp **ground coriander**
450g (1lb) **strong white flour**, plus extra for dusting
1 tsp fast-action **dried yeast**
1 tsp **salt**
small bunch of **coriander leaves**, roughly chopped
200g can **chickpeas**, drained and roughly crushed
150g (5½oz) **plain yogurt**
1 tbsp **olive oil**, plus extra for greasing

1 Dry-fry the cumin and ground coriander in a pan for 1 minute, until fragrant. Mix the flour, yeast, and salt in a large bowl. Stir in the toasted spices, coriander leaves, and chickpeas. Make a well in the middle, pour in the yogurt, oil, and 300ml (10fl oz) warm water. Bring together quickly to form a sticky dough. Set aside for 10 minutes.

2 Turn out the dough onto a lightly floured surface. Knead for 5 minutes. Shape into a ball and place in a large oiled bowl. Cover loosely with oiled cling film and leave to rise in a warm place for 1 hour, or until doubled in size.

3 Preheat the oven to 220°C (425°F/Gas 7). Turn out the dough onto a floured surface and cut into 8 even-sized pieces. Using a rolling pin, flatten out into ovals about 5mm (¼in) thick. Lightly dust 2 large baking trays with flour. Place the ovals on the baking trays, brush with a little oil, and scatter over a few cumin seeds. Transfer to the oven and bake for 15 minutes, or until the breads are golden and puffed up. Serve with black olive tapenade (see p14).

# kesra

*✦ Morocco ✦*

This leavened country bread is served with every meal in the Middle East to scoop up delicious sauces and juices. In Morocco, it is often served for breakfast, dipped in olive oil or drizzled with honey.

**PREP** 20 MINS, PLUS RISING  ✦  **COOK** 30 MINS
**SERVES** 6-8

½ tsp **dried yeast**
1 scant tsp **sugar**
450g (1lb) **unbleached white flour**, plus extra for dusting
60g (2oz) **cornmeal**, plus 1 tbsp for dusting
1 scant tsp **salt**
2 tbsp **melted butter** or **ghee**
**sesame seeds**, for sprinkling

1 In a small bowl, dissolve the yeast with the sugar in 50ml (1¾oz) lukewarm water and leave to cream for 10 minutes, or until frothy.

2 Sift the flour and cornmeal with the salt in a large bowl. Make a well in the middle and pour in the dissolved yeast and butter. Gradually add 450ml (15fl oz) lukewarm water. Using your hands, draw in the flour from the sides and form the mixture into a dough. Add more flour if the dough is too sticky. On a floured surface, knead the dough until smooth and elastic.

3 Divide the dough into two parts and roll each part into a ball. Flatten the balls and stretch into circles, about 20cm (8in) in diameter. Lightly oil 2 baking trays and dust with cornmeal. Place the circles on the baking trays and sprinkle with sesame seeds. Cover with a damp cloth and leave to rise in a warm place for about 1–2 hours, until doubled in size.

4 Preheat the oven to 220°C (425°F/Gas 7). Bake the dough circles for 15 minutes. Reduce the heat to 180°C (350°F/Gas 4) and bake for a further 15 minutes, until the loaves are crusty, golden, and sound hollow when tapped on the base.

# ciabatta

*✦ italy ✦*

This classic soft Italian bread is made using a starter that is left to rise overnight. Serve with soup, Italian cheeses, or simply dipped into olive oil and balsamic vinegar.

**PREP** 30 MINS, PLUS RISING
**COOK** 40 MINS  ✦  **MAKES** 1 LOAF

### For the starter
175g (6oz) (Italian) "00" flour
¼ tsp fast-action **dried yeast**

### For the dough
450g (1lb) (Italian) "00" flour
1½ tsp fast-action **dried yeast**
2 tsp **olive oil**, plus extra for greasing
1 tsp **salt**

1 For the starter, place the flour, yeast, and 100ml (3½fl oz) lukewarm water in a bowl. Mix well for 2–3 minutes until the mixture forms a ball. Place in a lightly oiled bowl, roll around the bowl to coat in the oil, cover, and leave overnight in a warm place.

2 For the dough, mix the flour, yeast, oil, salt, and 350ml (12fl oz) lukewarm water. Once combined, add the starter and continue kneading until you have a wet, sticky dough.

3 Place the dough in a lightly oiled bowl. Roll it around the bowl to coat in the oil, then leave to rise in a warm place for 2 hours, or until doubled in size.

4 Preheat the oven to 220°C (425°F/Gas 7). Knock back the dough and knead for 10 minutes, or until smooth and elastic. Mould the dough into a slipper shape and place it on an oiled baking tray. Bake for 10 minutes, then reduce the oven temperature to 190°C (375°F/Gas 5) and bake for a further 30 minutes, or until a crust forms and the loaf sounds hollow when tapped on the base. Remove from the oven and cool on a wire rack.

# fougasse aux olives

❖ *provence* ❖

Fougasse is the traditional bread of Provence and a close relative of the Italian focaccia. Black olives are probably the most popular and traditional flavouring, but green olives and herbs can also be used.

**PREP** 50 MINS, PLUS RISING AND PROVING
**COOK** 15 MINS ❖ **MAKES** 4 LOAVES

bread flour, for dusting
300g (10oz) small **black olives**, pitted
1 **egg yolk**

**For the fougasse dough**
500g (1lb 2oz) **bread flour**, plus extra for dusting
500g (1lb 2oz) **wholemeal bread flour**
1 tbsp **salt**
20g (¾oz) **dried yeast**
175ml (6fl oz) **olive oil**

1 For the dough, sift the 2 types of flour onto a clean work surface in a pile. Mix in the salt and make a well in the centre.

2 In a cup, mix the yeast with 150ml (5fl oz) lukewarm water. Pour the yeast mixture into the well. Work in a little of the flour. Add the oil, a little at a time, and continue working the ingredients together. Add more water as needed – up to 250ml (9fl oz) – to make a soft paste.

3 On a floured surface, knead the dough for 5–6 minutes, until smooth and elastic. Place the dough in a large bowl, cover with a clean, damp kitchen towel or with cling film, and leave to rise in a warm, draught-free place for about 1½ hours, or until doubled in size.

4 Turn out the dough onto a lightly floured surface. Punch down the dough with the side of your hand, then bring back together. Cover again and leave to rest for 20–30 minutes before using.

5 Divide the dough into 4 pieces. On a lightly floured surface, roll out each piece into an oval shape, 20 x 30cm (8 x 12in) in size. Take one of the ovals and place one-quarter of the black olives on one half. Brush the other half with water and fold over to cover the olives. Press down the dough edges with your fingertips to seal. Make a few parallel slashes in the top. Repeat to make 3 more loaves.

6 Cover with a damp kitchen towel and leave to prove in a warm place for about 30 minutes, until the dough feels a little springy when gently pressed down with the thumb.

7 Preheat the oven to 230°C (450°F/Gas 8). Place the loaves on a non-stick baking tray, leaving plenty of space between them. In a cup, mix the egg yolk with 1 tablespoon of cold water. Brush the egg wash lightly over the loaves and bake them for 15 minutes. Leave to cool on a wire rack for at least 15 minutes before serving.

## cook's tip

To make the dough using a heavy-duty electric mixer equipped with a dough hook, sift the 2 types of flour into the bowl. With the motor running, add the salt and yeast mixture, then add the oil, beat, and knead for 5 minutes.

## variations

**Aniseed or fennel seed fougasse** For aniseed fougasse, add 2 teaspoons of pastis or 1 teaspoon of aniseed to the dough after working in the yeast. For fennel seed fougasse, add 1 teaspoon of fennel seeds.

**Bacon fougasse** Blanch 100g (3½oz) smoked lardons or pancetta in boiling water for 2 minutes. Drain, then sauté with 2 teaspoons of olive oil until crisp. Add to the loaves instead of olives.

**Anchovy fougasse** After adding the yeast mixture, work in 1 scant tablespoon of finely chopped fresh thyme or rosemary, or a mixture of herbs: thyme, rosemary, oregano, marjoram, and savoury. Finely chop 3 drained anchovy fillets and add to the loaves instead of olives.

# pan bagna

❖ *provence* ❖

*Pan bagna*, literally "bathed bread", is the original Provençal sandwich. It makes a perfect light bite or substantial snack.

**PREP** 10 MINS ❖ **SERVES** 4

4 large, crusty **white bread rolls**
6 ripe, medium **tomatoes**, sliced
½ small **red pepper**, cut into thin strips
3 **spring onions**, white parts only, sliced
4 hard-boiled **eggs**, peeled and sliced crossways
leaves from 1 small **celery** head, chopped
16 small **black olives**, pitted, kept whole or halved

**For the vinaigrette**
6 **anchovy** fillets, packed in oil or salt
12 tbsp **olive oil**
2½ tbsp **red** or **white wine vinegar**
**salt** and freshly ground **black pepper**

1 For the vinaigrette, drain and rinse the anchovy fillets, pat dry on kitchen paper, and chop finely. Place in a bowl and add the oil and vinegar. Stir well and season.

2 On a work surface, slice the bread rolls horizontally in half and place cut-sides up. Place a spoonful of vinaigrette on the bottom half of each roll and spread well. Add the tomatoes, red pepper, spring onions, eggs, celery leaves, and olives. Season lightly. Spread the remaining vinaigrette over the top. Add the top half of each roll. Set on plates and press down each sandwich gently but firmly. Leave for 2–3 minutes, then cut in half and serve.

# crostini napolitana
### ❖ *italy* ❖

A classic Italian appetizer, these crostini are best prepared using fresh mozzarella, slightly squishy ripe tomatoes, and Gaeta olives. They are easy to make at home and are traditionally enjoyed with soup.

**PREP** 15 MINS ❖ **COOK** 4–5 MINS ❖ **MAKES** 4

2 large, very ripe **tomatoes**
175g (6oz) fresh **buffalo mozzarella**
4 thick slices of **focaccia, ciabatta,** or **toasting bread**
4 **anchovy fillets**, drained and patted dry
freshly ground **black pepper**
2–3 tbsp **fruity olive oil**, plus extra for greasing
6 **pitted black olives**, to finish
leaves from a few sprigs of **fresh oregano**

1 Blanch the tomatoes in a pan of boiling water for 1–2 minutes, then drain and refresh in cold water. Peel the skins, then quarter, remove the seeds, and finely chop.

2 Preheat the oven to 230°C (450°F/Gas 8) or the grill to high. Cut the mozzarella and arrange evenly on each slice of bread and cover with a layer of tomato. Place the anchovies between 2 layers of kitchen paper or cling film and flatten lengthways with a rolling pin. Cut each fillet crossways. Place 2 halved fillets on each slice of bread. Season generously with pepper.

3 Lightly grease a baking sheet. Place the slices of bread on the sheet and drizzle with oil. Bake for 7–8 minutes, or grill for 2–3 minutes, until the mozzarella is melting and bubbling. The crostini should be crisp outside but soft inside. Place 3 olive halves on top, scatter over the oregano, and allow to cool for 5 minutes before serving.

### variation

**Crostini with prosciutto** Bake or grill the bread with the mozzarella thickly spread on top. After cooking, sprinkle over a little oregano, top with sliced Prosciutto, drizzle with extra virgin olive oil, and season with black pepper.

# crostini di fave
### ❖ *italy* ❖

Ideal for parties or as an appetizer with drinks, this Italian-style bread has a crunchy base and soft, melt-in-the-mouth topping.

**PREP** 15 MINS ❖ **COOK** 15 MINS ❖ **MAKES** 12

½ **focaccia, ciabatta,** or **toasting bread**
3 tbsp **extra virgin olive oil**
**salt** and freshly ground **black pepper**
100g (3½oz) podded **broad beans**
1 small **shallot**
1 **garlic clove**
small bunch of **tarragon**

1 Preheat the oven to 150°C (300°F/Gas 2). Cut the bread on the diagonal into 12 thin slices and brush both sides with 2 tablespoons of the oil. Season well. Place the bread flat on a baking tray and bake for 15 minutes, or until crisp all the way through.

2 Meanwhile, blanch the beans in a pan of boiling water for 2 minutes, then drain and refresh in cold water. Remove the tough outer skin and discard. Keep a few beans aside for garnish. Place the remainder in a food processor with the shallot, garlic, the remaining oil, and tarragon. Process to form a thick paste. Season to taste.

3 Spread onto the prepared crostini just before serving. Garnish with the reserved beans and a grinding of pepper.

# essential
# cheese

Cheese has long been a Mediterranean staple
and people have turned goat's and ewe's milk
into simple cheeses since biblical times.

**Making small farmhouse cheeses**, which you then take to market, is
traditional in Italy, the South of France, and the Spanish peninsula. Italy
has always used more cheese in cooking than any other country – in
desserts as well as savoury dishes. Expensive artisan cheeses, made by
hand or in small dairies, are gaining in popularity. More and more, cheeses
are enjoyed for their individual flavours, not just as a source of protein.

**Kasseri** is a Greek-Turkish cheese
made from ewe's milk with goat's
milk mixed in. Creamy coloured,
it has a mild, buttery taste, a good
salty flavour and a sweet after-taste.

**Garrotxa** is a goat's milk hard
cheese from Catalonia. With a
mild, earthy flavour and a nice
tang, it is typical of the Spanish
cheese renaissance – artisan
dairies rediscovering traditional
cheeses.

**Halloumi** from Cyprus is
distinctively salty, delicious
fried, and very good raw with
black olives and watermelon.

**Pecorino** is the Italian name for
ewe's milk cheeses. Creamy,
crumbly or firm, it differs from
area to area.

**Manchego**, the best known
of Spanish cheeses, is made
from the milk of ewes from
La Mancha. Its nutty flavour
becomes sharper as the
cheese ages.

**Fromages de chèvre** have
been made in the
farms of Provence for
centuries. Soft when
fresh, drier as they
mature, they can
be covered in ash,
aromatic herbs,
or leaves.

**Cabrales** is a mixed milk semi-hard Spanish blue cheese with a great aroma, a buttery texture, and a good sharp taste.

**Roquefort**, a famous blue ewe's milk cheese, is made in the Midi-Pyrénées region. Its complex flavours are mouth-watering.

**Feta**, a brined curd cheese, is made all over the Eastern Mediterranean from ewe's milk and a little goat's milk. Keep it in brine or milk once opened, as it soon turns dry and sour.

**Ricotta** is a whey cheese made from milk left after cheese-making. It is very light and blends well with eggs in baking and desserts.

# crostini di fegatini

*❖ t u s c a n y ❖*

These chicken liver toasts are a Tuscan tradition. Originally, the cooked chicken livers were spread on stale bread which was softened by the meaty juices.

**PREP** 15 MINS ❖ **COOK** 25 MINS ❖ **SERVES** 4-6

2 tbsp **olive oil**

1 **mild onion**, finely chopped

1 **garlic clove**, crushed

250g (9oz) **chicken livers**, deveined, trimmed, rinsed and patted dry with kitchen paper

150ml (5fl oz) **white wine**

pinch of **caster sugar**

2 **anchovy fillets**, drained and chopped

½–1 tsp **dried sage**

1 tbsp **capers**, rinsed and drained

**salt** and freshly ground **black pepper**

1 tbsp **butter**, softened

1 tbsp snipped **flat-leaf parsley**

½ **focaccia, ciabatta,** or **toasting bread**, halved lengthways, then crossways into 4–6 chunky slices

1 Heat the oil in a medium frying pan. Add the onion and garlic, and cook over a medium heat for 5 minutes, stirring frequently, until softened. Add the chicken livers, increase the heat, and cook for 3–5 minutes until well-browned.

2 Add the wine, sugar, anchovies, sage, and capers. Reduce the heat, season, and cook for 15 minutes, stirring occasionally, until soft. Stir in the butter and parsley.

3 Meanwhile, toast the bread, in a toaster or on a baking sheet in a medium oven for 15 minutes.

4 Transfer the mixture to a food processor and pulse briefly, or mash well with a fork – the mixture should not become too smooth. Taste and adjust the seasoning with a little pepper, if necessary. Spread the mixture thickly on the toast and serve hot.

### prepare ahead

You can prepare the chicken livers ahead and refrigerate in an airtight container. Reheat them gently before serving.

### variation

**Crostini di fegatini with balsamic vinegar**
Add a tablespoon of balsamic vinegar at the same time as the butter and parsley.

# crostini di melanzane

*❖ i t a l y ❖*

These crisp crostini with a deliciously savoury topping make an elegant appetizer. The creamy tartness of goat's cheese combines wonderfully with aubergine.

**PREP** 10 MINS ❖ **COOK** 20 MINS ❖ **MAKES** 12

12 slices of **focaccia, ciabatta,** or **toasting bread**

2 tbsp **olive oil**, plus extra for brushing

1 **garlic clove**, cut in half

1 firm **aubergine**

2 tbsp chopped **mint leaves**

1 tbsp **balsamic vinegar**

**salt** and freshly ground **black pepper**

60g (2oz) **soft goat's cheese**

1 Preheat the oven to 180°C (350°F/Gas 4). Brush the bread on both sides with oil, then toast for 10 minutes, or until crisp, turning once. Cut the garlic in half and rub the cut side over each slice.

2 Preheat the grill. Slice the aubergine into 5mm (¼in) thick rounds, brush each side with oil, then grill on both sides until cooked.

3 Halve or quarter the aubergine slices, and place in a bowl. Add the remaining oil, mint, and balsamic vinegar, toss, and season to taste.

4 Spread the crostini with goat's cheese, top with the slices of aubergine, and serve immediately.

# croutons

*provence*

A must-have with fish soups, these golden, crunchy cubes are a Provence essential and a welcome addition to salads. You can add a small pinch of dried thyme, summer savory, or oregano to the oil before frying.

**PREP** 5 MINS ❖ **COOK** 5–10 MINS ❖ **SERVES** 4

1 **garlic clove**, cut in half

2 tbsp **olive oil**

2 thick slices tight-textured **toasting bread**, crusts removed, and cut into 12–16 squares each

1 Rub a frying pan with the cut sides of the garlic. Heat the oil in the pan over a medium-high heat. Line a plate with a double layer of kitchen paper.

2 Fry the croutons in the oil, stirring and tossing frequently, until golden all over. Remove from the pan and lay them on the prepared plate to drain. Store for up to 2 days in an airtight container.

# croûtes

*provence*

This thin, crisp *pain de campagne* or sourdough bread is perfect for dipping or spreading with tapenade, rouille, pesto, goat's cheese, and other Mediterranean delights.

**PREP** 5 MINS ❖ **COOK** 5 MINS ❖ **SERVES** 4

8 thin slices of **artisan baguette**, **country bread**, or **ciabatta**

2 tbsp **olive oil**

1 Preheat the oven to 220°C (425°F/Gas 7). Lightly brush one side of the bread slices with a little oil. Place them, oiled-sides down, on a non-stick baking tray. Lightly brush the tops of the slices with the remaining oil.

2 Bake the croûtes for 5 minutes, or until golden. Then turn off the heat. Turn the slices over and leave in the warm oven for 1–2 minutes, with the door slightly open, to crisp up. These can be stored for up to 2 days in an airtight container.

# polpette di lupo

*italy*

Not "wolf meatballs" as their name suggests, these crisp, cheesy morsels are a Puglian speciality. Prepared with hard durum wheat bread which dries out gradually, they are usually served as an antipasto with tomato sauce.

**PREP** 10 MINS ❖ **COOK** 5 MINS ❖ **SERVES** 4

2 **garlic cloves**, crushed and coarsely chopped

500g (1lb 2oz) **torn bread**, soaked in milk

60g (2oz) grated **Parmesan**, **Grana Padano**, or any hard cheese

2 tbsp chopped **flat-leaf parsley**

2 **eggs**

2 tbsp **milk**

**salt** and freshly ground **black pepper**

**olive oil**, for frying

**tomato sauce**, to serve

**peperoncini** or **dried chillies**, to serve

1 Work the first seven ingredients together until smooth. With damp hands, form the mixture into small marble-sized balls.

2 Heat the oil in a saucepan, filling it about half way. Fry the balls in batches until brown all over. Do not overcrowd the pan. Remove the balls using a slotted spoon and drain on kitchen paper. Serve with fresh tomato sauce mixed with a little flaked peperoncino or dried chillies.

**variation**

**Meat polpettine** To make a meat version, replace half the breadcrumbs with minced beef or pork.

# fattoush
### *middle east*

This tangy toasted bread salad is enjoyed throughout Lebanon, Syria, and Jordan. You can vary the salad ingredients, but sumac, pomegranate syrup, and toasted flatbread are essential components of this traditional dish.

**PREP** 15 MINS ❖ **SERVES** 4-6

handful of fresh **lettuce leaves**
2–3 **tomatoes**, skinned and sliced
1 **red or green pepper**, seeded and sliced
4–5 **spring onions**, trimmed and sliced
small bunch of **flat-leaf parsley**, coarsely chopped
2 thin **flatbreads**, such as pitta breads
2–3 tbsp **olive oil**
juice of 1 **lemon**
1–2 **garlic cloves**, crushed
1 tsp **cumin seeds**, crushed
**salt** and freshly ground **black pepper**
1–2 tbsp **pomegranate syrup**
2 tsp **sumac**

1 Arrange the lettuce leaves, tomatoes, peppers, and spring onions in a wide, shallow bowl and sprinkle the parsley over the top. Lightly toast the flatbreads, break them into bite-sized pieces, and scatter them over the salad.

2 In a small bowl, combine the oil and lemon juice with the garlic and cumin seeds.Season well and pour over the salad. Drizzle the pomegranate syrup over the top and sprinkle with sumac. Toss the salad gently just before serving.

# panzanella
### *italy*

This popular Italian dish is a great way to use up leftover ciabatta. You can serve it with cold meats or on a cheese platter.

**PREP** 25 MINS, PLUS MARINATING
**SERVES** 4

½ loaf **ciabatta**, about 300g (10oz), cut into bite-sized pieces
400g (14oz) small, ripe **plum tomatoes**, quartered or cut into chunks
½ **red onion**, thinly sliced
½ **cucumber**, peeled and cut into chunks
1 tbsp **red wine vinegar**

3 tbsp **extra virgin olive oil**
**salt** and freshly ground **black pepper**
small bunch of **flat-leaf parsley**, coarsely chopped
8 **basil leaves**, torn into small pieces

1 Place the bread, tomatoes, onion, and cucumber in a serving bowl. Add the vinegar and oil, season to taste, then mix well. Set aside for 30–40 minutes, mixing thoroughly once or twice to ensure the bread pieces soak up the dressing and all the juices from the tomatoes and cucumber.

2 Scatter the herbs over the salad just before serving.

### *how to serve*
You can serve fattoush as a mezze dish with crumbled feta, pickles, and a dip, or as an accompaniment to grilled or roasted meat and poultry.

# fattet hummus
### ❖ *middle east* ❖

This simple dish of spicy chickpeas on toasted flatbread is a Middle Eastern "fatta" dish that uses day-old bread. It is popular as both a street snack and a family meal at home, and may be enjoyed at any time of the day.

**PREP** 15 MINS, PLUS OVERNIGHT SOAKING
**COOK** 1 HR ❖ **SERVES** 4-6

250g (9oz) **dried chickpeas**, soaked overnight
2 **bay leaves**
3-4 **black peppercorns**
600ml (1 pint) thick, creamy **yogurt**
3-4 **garlic cloves**, crushed
salt and freshly ground **black pepper**
3-4 **pitta breads**
1 large **red onion**, roughly chopped
2-3 tbsp **olive oil**
juice of 1 **lemon**
1-2 tsp **cumin seeds**
1-2 tsp **pimentón** (Spanish paprika)
   or finely chopped **dried chillies**
2 tsp dried **mint**

1 Drain the chickpeas and tip them into a pan. Cover with plenty of cold water and bring to the boil. Add the bay leaves and peppercorns, reduce the heat, and simmer for 1 hour, until tender.

2 Meanwhile, in a bowl, beat the yogurt with half the garlic and season. Toast the bread, break it up into bite-sized pieces, and arrange on a serving dish.

3 Drain the chickpeas and reserve about 4 tablespoons of the cooking liquid. While still hot, tip the chickpeas into a bowl. Remove the bay leaves and add the onion, oil, lemon juice, the remaining garlic, cumin seeds, paprika, and mint, reserving a little mint.

4 Moisten the bread with the reserved cooking liquid and spread the chickpeas over. Spoon the yogurt over the top and sprinkle with the reserved mint.

**variation**

**Fattet hummus with pine nuts** Roast 2 tablespoons of pine nuts in a frying pan until they turn golden brown and have a nutty aroma. Add 1 tablespoon of butter, allow it to melt, and pour the mixture over the yogurt. Serve immediately, while the chickpeas are still warm.

# açorda de mariscos
### ❖ *portugal* ❖

Somewhere between a paella and a bread soup, Portugal's *açorda* is a nourishing family dish, and the first one that Portuguese babies share with their parents. Fresh coriander is the only essential flavouring.

**PREP** 35 MINS, PLUS SOAKING
**COOK** 1½ HRS ❖ **SERVES** 4

350g (12oz) two-day-old **sourdough bread**
100ml (3½fl oz) **olive oil**
1 large or 2 medium **onions**, finely sliced
**salt**
500g (1lb 2 oz) **tomatoes**, skinned and diced
3-4 **garlic cloves**, roughly chopped
½ tsp **black peppercorns**, crushed
½ tsp **coriander seeds**, crushed
½ tsp **dried oregano**
150g (5½oz) diced **monkfish** or other firm white fish
150g (5½oz) raw **shrimps**, **prawns**, or **mussels**
handful of **coriander leaves**, roughly chopped, to garnish

1 Tear the bread into bite-sized pieces and soak in water for 2-3 hours. Squeeze the bread with your hands to remove the excess water.

2 Heat half the oil in a frying pan, add the onion, season lightly with salt, and fry gently for 30 minutes, until soft and golden.

3 In a deep-sided saucepan, cook the tomatoes, garlic in the remaining oil. Then add the peppercorns, coriander seeds, and oregano, and cook until the juices are reduced by half and the sauce is thick.

4 Push the sauce through a sieve and return it to the pan. Bring to the boil and stir in the bread pieces. Add about 750ml (1¼ pints) cold water and bring to the boil. Reduce the heat and simmer for a further 20 minutes, until you have a soft, well-flavoured bread pap.

5 Add the fish to the onions in the frying pan and cook for 2-3 minutes until the fish begins to turn opaque. Stir in the bread pap, toss to separate the crumbs a little, and cook for a few minutes, until the base begins to crisp. Whisk lightly to blend, then fry again – this final crisping is not essential, but it heightens the flavour. Sprinkle with plenty of coriander and serve immediately.

# a taste of
# PROVENCE

In many ways Provence is a microcosm of the Mediterranean region: colonized by the Greeks who founded Marseilles around 600BC, it was occupied by the Romans who gave it its name. Its original cooking style was frugal – a soil too poor for large-scale agriculture, but plentiful with vines and olive trees, figs, wild birds and game, plenty of aromatic bushes and trees to attract honeybees, and good grazing for goats and sheep. There were plenty of fish in the rivers and seafood along the coast. Wines, olives, and salt from the Camargue helped the balance of trade, then spices, raisins, and lemons gradually came in, and eventually tomatoes and peppers. Well into the 19th century, Provence remained cut off from the rest of France by the Alps. It was much closer to the Italian peninsula with which it shares ingredients and recipe families.

**Charentais melon** is vibrantly orange-fleshed, sweet, fragrant, and tender. Cavaillon, in central Provence, is hailed to be the French melon capital.

Marseille, France's second largest city, is a dynamic place, with an excellent infrastructure, new businesses, and plenty of exciting attractions.

A market in Provence is always a treat for the eyes: baby artichokes, healthy greens, tomatoes on the vine or ribbed and rustic-looking, fresh green asparagus. Displays look like casual works of art.

**Lemons** have their own city, Menton – a top producer of prized bright yellow fruits, with good acidity and a peel rich in essential oils.

**Saucisson sec** from Arles is the best-known local dry salami and is made from a mixture of meats gently flavoured with spices. The precise recipe is a well-kept secret.

**Honeys** of varying colours, flavours, and consistencies are a local treat.

**Lavender** proliferates from the middle of June. The scented fields of purple or mauve under a deep blue sky sum up the magic of Provence.

**Banon** is a soft, mildly pungent unpasteurized goat's cheese wrapped in chestnut or vine leaves. Market-goers take their time to smell, handle, and choose the best cheese to buy on the market.

**Sea salt** has been harvested since antiquity in the Camargue swamps of the Rhone delta. Fleur de sel, the top layer of surface salt crystals, is highly prized.

# A Provençal dinner by the sea

A glass of pale, dry Côtes de Provence rosé, black tapenade, and golden aïoli are put on the table with crudités and thin crisp slices of toasted baguette. Steamed baby new potatoes are perfect for dipping into the aïoli. The main course is a classic Mediterranean favourite, sea bass cooked in a salt crust, with a side dish of al dente green beans and fresh fougasse bread. For dessert, soft fresh cheese with a dribbling of local honey is served with figs and other fruit.

**Haricots verts en persillade**
page 240

**Tapenade**
page 14

**Côtes de Provence rosé**

**Rouille**
page 154

**Fougasse**
page 261

**Loup de mer en croûte de sel**
p132

**Brousse au miel
de romarin**
page 285

# all things sweet

# pesche ripiene alla piemontese

*❖ italy ❖*

This classic Italian dessert of baked peaches with amaretti is as delicious as it is easy to prepare and can be served warm or cold. Choose fruits that feel heavy for their size, showing they contain lots of juice.

**PREP** 15–20 MINS
**COOK** 1 HR–1 HR 15 MINS ❖ **SERVES** 6

7 large **peaches**, about 1kg (2¼lb) in total
8–10 **amaretti biscuits**
60g (2oz) **caster sugar**, plus 1–2 tbsp for the cream
1 **egg yolk**
120ml (4fl oz) **double cream**
1–2 tbsp **amaretto liqueur**

1 Immerse 1 peach in boiling water for 10 seconds, then plunge into iced water. Cut the peach in half, using the indentation on one side of the peach as a guide. Using both hands, give a sharp twist to each half to loosen it from the stone. Scoop out the stone using a small knife. Peel the skin from the halves. Discard the stone and skin.

2 Preheat the oven to 180°C (350°F/Gas 4). Using a rolling pin, crush the amaretti biscuits in a plastic food bag and pour into a bowl. Put the 2 peeled peach halves in a food processor and whizz to a thick, smooth purée.

3 Transfer the purée to a large bowl, scraping it from the food processor using a spatula. Add the sugar, egg yolk, and amaretti crumbs to the purée. Mix well.

4 Set the peach halves, cut-side up, in a baking dish. Spoon some filling into each half and bake for 1–1¼ hours, until tender. Meanwhile, whip the cream with the remaining sugar and liqueur until stiff peaks form. Transfer the hot peaches to individual serving plates and spoon over any juices. Serve the flavoured cream in a separate bowl.

# salade d'oranges à la marocaine

*❖ middle east ❖*

Slices of fresh orange are made more exotic and flavoursome with rosewater, pomegranate seeds, and pistachio nuts.

**PREP** 15 MINS ❖ **SERVES** 4

4 **oranges**
1–2 tbsp **runny honey**
2 tbsp **rosewater**
good pinch of ground **cinnamon**
seeds from 1 **pomegranate**
small handful of chopped **pistachios** (optional)
handful of **mint leaves**, to decorate

1 Slice off the top and bottom from each orange and place on a chopping board. Carefully slice off the skin and pith, leaving as much flesh as possible, and following the sides of the orange so you keep the shape of the fruit. Slice the oranges horizontally into thin strips, discarding any pips as you come across them. Arrange the orange slices on a serving platter. Pour over any remaining juice.

2 Drizzle with the honey and rosewater, and sprinkle with the cinnamon. Scatter with the pomegranate seeds and pistachios, if using, then decorate with the mint leaves and serve.

**variation**

**Caramelized oranges and passion fruit**
In a saucepan, put 60g (2oz) sugar with 2 tablespoons of cold water. Stir, then heat gently without stirring, until the sugar melts. Boil rapidly until the sugar syrup turns a rich golden brown. Remove from the heat and add 2 tablespoons of water. Stir over a gentle heat until the caramel dissolves, then leave to cool. Prepare the dish in the same way, but drizzle with the caramel instead of the honey, omit the rosewater, and scatter with passion fruit seeds instead of pomegranate.

# figs and dried fruits

Figs have always been a Mediterranean staple. They are enjoyed fresh during their short season and widely used dried, along with apricots, dates, and raisins.

**One of the first fruits** to be cultivated, figs thrive in warm, dry climates. The Roman legions conquered nations on a diet of figs, cheese, bread, and olives, and no garden was complete without a fig tree. Figs come in many sizes and colours, but everyone will tell you that their local variety is the best. The Mediterraneans love the intense flavours of dried fruit and excel at using them in savoury and sweet dishes. When dried, figs taste differently delicious.

**Fresh figs** have a succulent honeyed flesh spiked with tiny crunchy seeds – a perfect quick dessert with ricotta and honey.

**Apricots** naturally turn brown as they dry. They are as happy dried, with lamb, chicken, and rice, as they are fresh, with soft cheese and honey.

**Dried figs** are great for baking, stuffing, and stewing, and for use in game and poultry dishes.

**Medjool dried dates** from arid North Africa and the Middle East are sweet, fleshy, and an ideal sweetmeat.

# fichi ripieni alla calabrese

*※ italy ※*

This lovely summer recipe of stuffed figs is traditionally made with sweet, white-fleshed Dottato green figs, which are at their best in Calabria during August and September. Vanilla ice cream is a great accompaniment.

**PREP** 5 MINS, PLUS DRYING
**COOK** 35 MINS, PLUS COOLING ❖ **SERVES** 4

115g (4oz) **caster sugar**, plus 1 tbsp extra for filling

zest from ½ **orange**, cut into fine strips

zest from ½ small **lemon**, cut into fine strips

½ tsp ground **cinnamon**

1–2 tbsp **amaretto liqueur**

3 tbsp **walnut**, blanched and chopped

3 tbsp **almonds**, blanched, peeled, and chopped

2 tbsp **grated chocolate** or **cocoa powder**

8 large **ripe figs**

1 In a heavy pan, pour 120ml (4fl oz) cold water, add the sugar, and bring to the boil. Add the orange and lemon zests. Keep boiling gently for about 10 minutes, or until the citrus strips are soft. Drain well in a fine sieve and reserve the syrup. Spread the strips on a plate and keep overnight in a warm place, until thoroughly dried. If you like, cut the longer strips in half.

2 Preheat the oven to 180°C (350°F/Gas 4). Pour the reserved syrup into a small pan, add the cinnamon, and boil gently until slightly reduced. Stir in the liqueur and remove from the heat.

3 For the filling, place the walnuts, almonds, and dried citrus strips in a bowl. Stir in the chocolate and 1 tablespoon of sugar.

4 Slice the figs lengthways to open them up, then fill them with the filling. Close each fig back together. Place the figs side by side in a baking dish. Drizzle over the syrup. Transfer to the oven and bake for 20 minutes, until the figs are soft and slightly caramelized. Leave to cool in the oven for 30 minutes. Serve warm or at room temperature.

# membrillo

*※ spain ※*

Made from puréed quinces, membrillo is an intensely flavoured fruit cheese that is solid enough to slice. It keeps for 12 months or longer and is excellent served with cheeses.

**PREP** 10 MINS, PLUS COOLING AND MATURING
**COOK** 1 HR 20 MINS
**MAKES** 750G–1KG (1LB 10OZ–2¼LB)

1kg (2¼lb) **quinces**, scrubbed and roughly chopped

juice of ½ **lemon**

about 450g (1lb) **granulated sugar** (see step 2)

**oil**, for greasing

1 In a preserving pan or large heavy-based saucepan, place the quinces with 600ml (1 pint) cold water. Add the lemon juice, bring to the boil, and simmer for about 30 minutes. Once the fruit is soft enough, mash it with a potato masher or fork until it becomes a soft, syrupy pulp. Set aside.

2 Strain the pulp in batches over a large, clean bowl, pressing the pulp hard against the sieve with a wooden spoon to extract as much of the purée as possible. You can also use a mouli food mill. Measure the purée. For every 450ml (15fl oz) of purée, you will need 450g (1lb) of sugar.

3 Put the purée back in the pan along with the sugar over a low heat and stir to dissolve the sugar. Bring to the boil and simmer gently for 45–60 minutes, until the purée is reduced to a dark, very thick, glossy paste. It is ready when it makes "plopping" sound, sticks to the wooden spoon, and leaves a trail if the spoon is scraped across the bottom of the pan. Stir frequently near the end of cooking so the paste doesn't catch and burn on the base of the pan.

4 Lightly grease some warm ramekins or moulds with a little oil. Spoon in the paste and level the top. Seal with waxed paper discs and cellophane if leaving in the ramekins, otherwise leave to cool. If you are turning the membrillos out of their ramekins, loosen each with a palette knife, turn out, wrap in waxed paper, and tie with string. Leave to mature in a cool, dark place for 4–6 weeks. Serve thinly sliced with a cheeseboard or platter of cold meats, or as an after-dinner sweetmeat.

# pere al forno al vino di marsala
## ❖ *italy* ❖

This popular Italian dessert can also be made with other firm fruit, such as plums, peaches, or apricots. Serve it with sponge fingers or amaretti biscuits.

**PREP** 10 MINS, PLUS CHILLING
**COOK** 30-50 MINS ❖ **SERVES** 4-6

6 ripe **pears**, peeled and halved
100g (3½oz) **caster sugar**
250ml (9fl oz) **dry Marsala**
1 tsp pure **vanilla extract**
1 **cinnamon stick**
250ml (9fl oz) **double cream** or **whipping cream**
2 tbsp **icing sugar**

1 Preheat the oven to 150°C (300°F/Gas 2). Place the pears in an ovenproof dish, cut-side up, and sprinkle with the caster sugar, Marsala, and vanilla extract, then pour in 250ml (9fl oz) cold water. Add the cinnamon stick.

2 Bake for 30–50 minutes, depending on ripeness, or until tender. Check occasionally and baste with the sugar and Marsala liquid.

3 Meanwhile, in a medium bowl, whip the cream, gradually adding the icing sugar until firm peaks form. Serve the pears warm or chilled, in their syrup, with the whipped cream.

# mishmishiyaa
## ❖ *middle east* ❖

Desserts and sweet snacks prepared with dried fruit are popular throughout the Middle East. This simple purée of apricots is prepared in many households in Lebanon, Syria, and Jordan.

**PREP** 1 HR, PLUS SOAKING AND CHILLING
**COOK** 30 MINS ❖ **SERVES** 4-6

450g (1lb) dried **apricots**
125g (4½oz) **granulated sugar**
200ml (7fl oz) **double cream**
2 tbsp **icing sugar**
1–2 tbsp **orange blossom water**
1–2 tbsp flaked toasted **almonds**

1 Put the apricots in a bowl, pour in about 400ml (14 fl oz) cold water to cover, and leave to soak for 6 hours or overnight.

2 Strain the apricots over a heavy-based pan to collect the water. Heat the strained water with the sugar, stirring continuously, until the sugar has dissolved. Bring the liquid to the boil. Continue to boil for 4–5 minutes to get a thin syrup.

3 Add the apricots and bring the liquid to the boil again. Reduce the heat and simmer the apricots for about 15 minutes, until tender. Leave to cool in the pan.

4 In a food processor, blend the apricots with 150ml (5fl oz) of the syrup to form a smooth purée. Spoon the purée into a wide, shallow serving bowl, or individual bowls, cover with cling film, and chill in the fridge.

5 Before serving, whip the cream until it begins to thicken, then add the icing sugar and orange blossom water. Continue to whip until thick peaks form. Spoon the whipped cream onto the apricot purée. Sprinkle the top with the almonds and serve immediately.

## cook's tip

Some harvested fruit, such as apricots, grapes, and mulberries, is puréed and spread out in thin layers on trays and left to dry in the sun to form "fruit leathers". These "leathers" are sold as sweet snacks in the markets or they can be used to make puddings like this one by soaking in water first to reconstitute them.

# muhallabia
## ❖ *middle east* ❖

The milk puddings of the Middle East are delectable and moreish, often enhanced with the medieval notes of scented, floral waters. The basic recipe remains the same throughout Lebanon, Syria, Jordan, and Turkey.

**PREP** 10 MINS ❖ **COOK** 35 MINS ❖ **SERVES** 6-8

60g (2oz) fine **rice flour**
1 litre (1¾ pints) **milk**
125g (4½oz) **granulated sugar**
2–3 tbsp **rosewater**
2 tbsp **icing sugar**, for dusting
handful of **pistachios**, finely chopped, for sprinkling

1 In a small bowl, combine the rice flour with a little milk to form a loose paste. Pour the remaining milk into a heavy-based pan and stir in the sugar. Bring the milk to the boil, stirring continuously, until the sugar has dissolved.

2 Reduce the heat and stir a spoonful or two of the hot milk into the rice flour paste, then tip the mixture into the pan. Whisk the mixture well to prevent the flour from forming lumps. Bring the milk to the boil again, then stir in the rosewater.

3 Reduce the heat to low and simmer for 20 minutes, stirring, until the mixture is thick and coats the back of the spoon.

4 Pour the mixture into a serving bowl, or individual bowls, and let it cool, allowing a skin to form on top. Chill and, just before serving, dust the tops with icing sugar and sprinkle with pistachios.

## variation

**Muhallabia with orange blossom water**
You can flavour the dish with orange blossom water instead of rosewater, or even combine the two.

### *how to serve*
The chilled pudding is usually garnished with icing sugar and chopped pistachios, or it can be decorated with fresh or crystallized rose petals.

# honey

In the thousands of years before cane sugar became more than a medicinal luxury, honey was the main sweetening agent. An offering to the gods, it was always hailed as nutritious and health-giving.

**Early paintings** in caves near Valencia depict honey gathering, and honey has been held in high esteem around the Mediterranean since time immemorial. It's just as popular now – people in the region have a sweet tooth and desserts, cakes, and pastries without honey would be unthinkable. Where would the Middle East be without baklava, Spain without turrón and tortitas con miel, Provence without calissons and nougat, and Italy without Panforte and struffoli?

**Lavender honey** has a delicate but distinctive flavour, good for biscuits, cakes, and to add to drinks.

**Beeswax combs** come straight from the hive and are filled with honey.

**Orange blossom honey** has a mild citrus flavour and tastes very sweet.

**Rosemary honey** is a Provence favourite with a strong, woody aroma, ideal for savoury recipes.

# brousse au miel de romarin

*provence*

Brousse is a fresh cheese made from whey, often bought as a large round. It has a clean, mild flavour and tastes less salty than most cheeses. If Brousse is difficult to find, very fresh ricotta makes a good alternative.

**PREP** 5 MINS ❖ **SERVES** 4-6

450g (1lb) fresh **Brousse cheese**
bunch of **sweet grapes**, rinsed
8–12 tbsp **rosemary-scented
    runny honey**
freshly ground **black pepper** (optional)

1 Remove the cheese from the fridge about 15 minutes before serving. Cut the cheese into wedges and put on individual plates. (If you have any cheese left over, wrap it in cling film, and keep in the fridge.)

2 Add a few grapes and a good trickle of honey to each serving, then grind over some black pepper, if you like. Serve immediately.

**variation**

**Brousse with other honeys** Rosemary honey is particularly good, but you might also want to try lavender or acacia honey.

**cook's tip**

Leftover Brousse can be added to pasta sauces or mixed with crème fraîche to serve with berries.

# churros

*spain*

These cinnamon- and sugar-sprinkled Spanish snacks take minutes to make and will be devoured just as quickly. Try them dipped in hot chocolate.

**PREP** 10 MINS ❖ **COOK** 5-10 MINS ❖ **SERVES** 2-4

1 tbsp **olive oil**
200g (7oz) **plain flour**
**salt**
1 tsp **baking powder**
1 litre (1¾ pints) **sunflower** or **olive oil,**
    for deep-frying
25g (scant 1oz) **caster sugar**
1 tsp ground **cinnamon**

1 Measure 200ml (7fl oz) boiling water in a jug. Add the olive oil. Sift together the flour, a pinch of salt, and the baking powder into a bowl.

2 Make a well in the centre and slowly pour in the hot liquid, beating continuously, until you have a thick paste; you may not need all the liquid. Leave the mixture to cool and rest for 5 minutes.

3 Pour the sunflower oil into a large, heavy-based saucepan to a depth of at least 10cm (4in) and heat to 170–180°C (340–350°F). Regulate the temperature using an oil thermometer, making sure it remains even, or the churros will burn.

4 Place the cooled mixture into a piping bag fitted with a 2cm (¾in) nozzle. Pipe 7cm (scant 3in) lengths of the dough into the hot oil, using a pair of scissors to snip off the ends. Do not crowd the pan or the temperature of the oil will go down. Cook the churros for 1–2 minutes on each side, turning them when they are golden brown. Remove them from the oil using a slotted spoon and drain on kitchen paper.

5 Mix the sugar and cinnamon together on a plate and toss the churros in the mixture while still hot. Cool for 5–10 minutes before serving while still warm.

**cook's tip**

The thinner the batter, the lighter the results, but frying with a liquid batter takes a little practice.

# flan
*❖ s p a i n ❖*

This softly set, oven-baked egg custard makes its own little pool of caramel sauce when unmoulded. It is much nicer than the packet mix.

**PREP** 35–40 MINS, PLUS COOLING AND CHILLING
**COOK** 30–40 MINS ❖ **SERVES** 4–6

175g (6oz) **caster sugar**
600ml (1 pint) **full-fat milk**
½ **vanilla pod**
1 whole **egg** and 4 **yolks**

1 In a pan, melt 100g (3½oz) of the sugar in 2 tablespoons cold water. Stir over a low heat until the sugar loses its moisture and begins to caramelize and turns chestnut colour. Then pour it into a medium soufflé dish – or divide between individual moulds – rolling it around to coat the bottom. Cool and transfer to the fridge for 10 minutes.

2 Pour the milk into a separate pan, scrape the seeds from the vanilla pod into the milk, and bring to the boil. Remove from the heat as soon as it rises. In a bowl, whisk the egg and yolks with the remaining sugar. Whisk in the hot milk and pour through a sieve into the dish or moulds.

3 Preheat the oven to 160°C (325°F/Gas 3). Set the moulds in a baking tray and pour in enough boiling water to come halfway up the sides. Bake for 40–50 minutes, until the custard is just set but still wobbly in the middle. Check after 20 minutes and reduce the heat if necessary or top up with more boiling water. If the temperature is too high, the custard will curdle and form watery air holes; if the temperature is too low, the custard will take longer to set.

4 Allow the custard to cool and firm up. When ready to serve, unmould it. Reverse the mould onto a small plate, hold it firmly in place and shake once or twice. The custard should drop neatly onto the plate, bringing its own caramel sauce with it. You can also reverse the mould and loosen the edges of the custard with a knife.

### variation

**Chocolate caramel custard** Whisk some of the hot milk with 1 tablespoon of sifted cocoa powder in a cup until dissolved. Stir into the milk and egg mixture before baking.
**Lemon caramel custard** Infuse the rind of 1 lemon in the milk and add the finely grated zest of 1 lemon to the egg mixture.

# torrijas
*❖ s p a i n ❖*

In Spain, this version of French toast is usually served as an indulgent pudding rather than as a breakfast dish.

**PREP** 5 MINS, PLUS STANDING
**COOK** 20 MINS ❖ **SERVES** 4

8 slices of 1–2 day-old **bread roll** or **baguette**
750ml (1¼ pints) **full-fat milk**
3 tbsp **caster sugar**
1 **cinnamon stick**
200ml (7fl oz) **olive oil**, for frying
3 **eggs**, beaten
4 tbsp **icing sugar**, for dusting
**maple syrup**, for drizzling

1 Arrange the bread slices in a wide, shallow dish. Put the milk, sugar, and cinnamon in a saucepan. Bring to the boil, stirring constantly, then pour over the bread. Discard the cinnamon, and leave the bread to stand for 15 minutes, so that it soaks up all the milk. Put the beaten eggs in a shallow bowl.

2 Heat the oil in a frying pan over a medium heat. Using a fork, take a slice of bread and dip it in the egg, making sure both sides are evenly coated. Place in the frying pan and fry on both sides until golden, then repeat with the remaining slices, in batches, as quickly as possible.

3 Drain the slices of bread on kitchen paper and arrange on a plate. When slightly cooled, dust generously with icing sugar and drizzle with maple syrup. Serve warm.

# vanilla cheesecake

❖ *israel* ❖

Cheesecake in its many interpretations came to Israel with the settlers from Eastern Europe. This rich vanilla-flavoured crowd pleaser is best made 1–2 days ahead and refrigerated.

**PREP** 20 MINS ❖ **COOK** 50 MINS
**CHILL** 6 HRS ❖ **SERVES** 10-12

60g (2oz) **unsalted butter**,
  plus extra for greasing

225g (8oz) **digestive biscuits**,
  finely crushed

1 tbsp **demerara sugar**

675g (1½lb) **cream cheese**,
  at room temperature

4 **eggs**, separated

200g (7oz) **caster sugar**

1 tsp **vanilla extract**

500ml (16fl oz) **soured cream**

finely grated zest of 2 **lemons**, to garnish

1 Preheat the oven to 180°C (350°F/Gas 4). Grease and line a 23cm (9in) round springform cake tin with baking parchment. Melt the butter in a pan over a medium heat. Add the biscuit crumbs and demerara sugar, and stir until blended. Press the crumbs into the base of the tin.

2 Beat the cream cheese, egg yolks, 150g (5½oz) of the caster sugar, and vanilla extract in a bowl until blended. In a separate bowl, beat the egg whites until stiff and fold them into the cream cheese mixture. Pour into the tin and smooth the top. Place in the oven and bake for 45 minutes until set. Remove the tin from the oven and leave to stand for 10 minutes.

3 Combine the soured cream and the remaining sugar in a bowl, and beat well. Pour over the cheesecake and smooth the top.

4 Increase the oven temperature to 240°C (475°F/Gas 9) and bake the cheesecake for 5 minutes. Leave to cool on a wire rack, then chill for at least 6 hours. Garnish with the lemon zest and serve.

# tiramisú
### ❖ *italy* ❖

The famous layered dessert of northern Italy needs no introduction. This recipe uses grated chocolate rather than cocoa powder to enhance flavour and appearance.

**PREP** 20 MINS, PLUS SETTING ❖ **SERVES** 6–8

3 large **eggs**
85g (3oz) **caster sugar**
a few drops of **vanilla extract**
225–250g (8–9oz) **mascarpone cheese**
115g (4oz) **crème fraîche**
200–225ml (7–7½fl oz) **cold strong black coffee**
2–3 tbsp **amaretto liqueur** or **brandy**
about 30 **biscuits à la cuillère** (or **savoiardi** or **sponge fingers**)
85g (3oz) good-quality **black chocolate**, chilled and grated
1 tbsp **chocolate shavings**, to finish (optional)

1 Separate the eggs in 2 large bowls. Using an electric whisk, beat the yolks with the sugar and vanilla extract until the mixture becomes pale and creamy. Whisk in the mascarpone until smooth.

2 In a small bowl, whip the crème fraîche until stiff. Add to the mascarpone mixture and whisk in well. Whisk the egg whites until stiff peaks form, then fold gently into the mascarpone cream.

3 In a shallow bowl, combine the coffee and the amaretto. Quickly dip half of the biscuits into the coffee mixture and arrange, flat-side down, in a deep 20 x 30cm (8 x 12in) serving dish.

4 Spread half the mascarpone mixture over the biscuits. Dip the remaining biscuits in coffee and arrange on top. Spread the rest of the mixture on top of the biscuits, smoothing it down with a spatula.

5 Scatter over the grated chocolate. Cover with cling film and keep in the fridge for at least 4 hours before serving. If you like, scatter over a few chocolate shavings just before serving.

# cassata gelato
### ❖ *italy* ❖

This type of cassata is made without a sponge cake. This ice cream version is utterly irresistible.

**PREP** 25 MINS, PLUS 24 HRS FREEZING
**COOK** 10 MINS ❖ **SERVES** 6–8

175g (6oz) **caster sugar**
4 **egg yolks**
1 tsp **vanilla extract**
300ml (10fl oz) **double cream**, lightly whipped
60g (2oz) **glacé cherries**, rinsed and roughly chopped
60g (2oz) dried **apricots**, roughly chopped
60g (2oz) dried **pineapple**, roughly chopped
30g (1oz) **shelled pistachios**, roughly chopped
200g (7oz) fresh **raspberries**

1 Place the sugar in a small saucepan, pour 120ml (4fl oz) cold water, and bring to the boil. Boil rapidly for 5 minutes, or until thick and syrupy.

2 Beat the egg yolks with an electric whisk and slowly drizzle in the hot sugar syrup, until the mixture is thick and pale. Fold in the vanilla extract and whipped cream. Tranfer one-third of the mixture to a separate bowl, and stir in the cherries, dried fruit, and nuts. Cover and chill until needed.

3 Press the raspberries through a sieve to remove the seeds, then stir the purée into the remaining mixture. Pour into a 900ml (1½ pints) mixing bowl. Place a 600ml (1 pint) pudding basin in the centre of the mixture and secure in place with tape. (The raspberry mixture will be forced to rise up the sides of the pudding basin.) Freeze for at least 3–4 hours, or until firm.

4 Remove the tape and pour a little hot water into the pudding basin to release it. Spoon the creamy dried fruit mixture into the centre and level the surface. Cover and freeze overnight.

5 To serve, dip the mixing bowl into warm water for a few seconds, then invert onto a serving plate and remove the bowl. Cut into wedges to serve.

# granita di caffé expresso

❖ *sicily* ❖

This heavenly coffee-flavoured granita is simple to prepare, yet looks impressive. Make sure the texture of the granita is crystallized, like shaved ice.

**PREP** 5 MINS, PLUS COOLING AND FREEZING
**COOK** 5 MINS ❖ **SERVES** 4

100g (3½oz) **caster sugar**
½ tsp pure **vanilla extract**
300ml (10fl oz) very strong **espresso coffee**, chilled

1 Set the freezer to its coldest setting and place 4 freezerproof serving bowls or glasses in the freezer. In a small saucepan, dissolve the sugar in 300ml (10fl oz) cold water over a medium heat. Increase the heat and bring to the boil, then boil for 5 minutes to make a light syrup.

2 Pour the syrup into a shallow, freezerproof dish. Stir in the vanilla extract and coffee, then set aside to cool completely.

3 Transfer to the freezer. Use a fork to break up the frozen chunks every 30 minutes or so. Continue to do this for 4 hours, or until the mixture has the texture of shaved ice, then leave the granita in the freezer until ready to serve.

**prepare ahead**

The granita can be made a few days in advance. You can put some freezerproof serving dishes in the freezer to chill for 1 hour before serving the granitas.

# sorbetto di limone amaro

❖ *italy* ❖

Italians love to eat this delightful, bittersweet lemon sorbet either on its own, as a refreshing sweet treat on a hot day, or as a light dessert after a rich meal.

**PREP** 5–10 MINS, PLUS COOLING AND FREEZING
**COOK** 5 MINS ❖ **SERVES** 4

6 **lemons**
115g (4oz) **caster sugar**
twists of **lemon zest**, to decorate

1 Set the freezer to its coldest setting and place 4 freezerproof serving bowls or glasses in the freezer. Using a cannelle knife or lemon zester with a V-shaped cutter, thinly pare the zest from 4 of the lemons, and set aside. Grate the zest from the remaining 2 lemons. Set this aside separately.

2 In a small pan, dissolve the sugar in 250ml (9fl oz) cold water over a medium heat. Increase the heat and bring to the boil, then continue boiling for 5 minutes, or until the liquid turns into a light syrup.

3 Pour the syrup into a shallow, freezerproof non-metallic bowl. Stir in the pared lemon zest and set aside to cool completely.

4 Squeeze the lemons to make about 250ml (9fl oz) lemon juice. Remove the lemon zest strips from the mixture. Stir in the lemon juice and grated zest.

5 Transfer to the freezer for 1–2 hours, or until frozen around the edges and still slightly slushy in the middle. Every 30 minutes or so, use a fork to break up the frozen granita. Continue for 4 hours, or until the mixture has the texture of shaved ice, then leave the granita in the freezer until ready to serve.

# dondurma

*turkey*

Influenced by the Ottomans, this snowy-white, slightly chewy ice cream is popular in the eastern Mediterranean region. The colour comes from the sahlab and the elasticity from the mastic, while the orange blossom gives it a floral lift.

**PREP** 5 MINS, PLUS FREEZING
**COOK** 30 MINS ❖ **SERVES** 4–6

2–3 **mastic crystals**
225g (8oz) **granulated sugar**
3 tbsp **sahlab** or **cornflour**
1.2 litres (2 pints) **milk**
2 tbsp **orange blossom water**
**pistachios**, roughly chopped, to garnish

1 Using a small mortar and pestle, pound the mastic crystals with 1 teaspoon of the sugar until the mixture resembles a coarse powder. Place the sahlab and a little cold milk in a small bowl and mix to form a smooth, loose paste.

2 Place the remaining milk and the sugar in a heavy-based pan. Bring to the boil, stirring constantly, until the sugar dissolves. Stir a little milk into the sahlab mixture, then tip the mixture into the pan, whisking constantly, until it begins to thicken. Add the ground mastic, whisking constantly to disperse any lumps that may form.

3 Reduce the heat and simmer for 10–15 minutes, stirring occasionally, until the mixture is thick and coats the back of the spoon. Pour in the orange blossom water and cook, whisking, for 1–2 minutes. Remove from the heat.

4 Pour the mixture into a freezerproof container, cover with a dry kitchen towel, and set aside to cool. Remove the towel, cover the container with foil, and place it in the freezer. Leave it to set, beating it at intervals to break up the ice crystals. Alternatively, pour the cooled liquid into the bowl of an ice-cream maker and churn according to the instructions.

5 To serve, remove the ice cream from the freezer and allow to sit out for 5–10 minutes so it is easier to scoop. Do not leave at room temperature for too long as it is a fast-melting ice cream. Serve the ice cream on its own or topped with a sprinkling of pistachios.

# lenguas de gato

*spain*

These thin crisp biscuits, translated as "cats' tongues", are delicious with ice cream and also to dip into a cup of hot chocolate.

**PREP** 20 MINS ❖ **COOK** 12 MINS ❖ **MAKES** 18

175ml (6fl oz) **double cream** or **whipping cream**
3 tbsp **caster sugar**
1 tsp **vanilla extract**
4 **egg whites**, whisked to soft peaks
150g (5½oz) **plain flour**
**butter**, for greasing

1 Preheat the oven to 190°C (375°F/Gas 5). Beat the cream with the sugar and vanilla extract until it has thickened slightly. Carefully fold in the beaten egg whites. Sprinkle the flour over the mixture, a little at a time, continuing to fold until combined.

2 Lightly grease a baking tray. Using a piping bag, lay down finger-width strips of the mixture, at least 1 finger-width apart, as the mixture will spread during baking. Bake for 10–12 minutes, or until golden. The centres should still be soft. Leave to cool slightly.

3 Using a palette knife, carefully lift the biscuits off the baking tray and place on a wire rack to cool. Serve when the biscuits have cooled completely.

**prepare ahead**

These biscuits can be made several days in advance and stored in an airtight container. If they become soft, bake for a few minutes in a gentle oven to crisp up again.

# cantucci

*· tuscany ·*

Crisp, crunchy, and twice-baked, these almond biscuits from Tuscany are ideal for dipping in glasses of vin santo after a meal.

**PREP** 10 MINS, PLUS COOLING
**COOK** 40 MINS ❖ **MAKES** 32

oil, for greasing
3 large **eggs**, and 2 large **yolks**, beaten
350g (12oz) **plain flour**, plus extra
   for dusting
150g (5½oz) **caster sugar**
150g (5½oz) whole **almonds**, roughly
   chopped and toasted
2 tsp **baking powder**
finely grated zest of 1 **orange**

1 Preheat the oven to 190°C (375°F/Gas 5) and grease a large baking sheet. Place 2 tablespoons of the beaten egg in a separate bowl and set aside.

2 Place the flour, sugar, almonds, baking powder, and orange zest in a large bowl and stir together. Make a well in the centre, add the eggs, and mix until a dough forms.

3 Shape the dough into a ball, then cut in half. On a lightly floured surface, roll out the dough halves into 2 logs, each 5cm (2in) wide and 2.5cm (1in) high. Place on a baking sheet, flatten slightly, and brush the tops with the reserved egg mixture.

4 Bake for 20 minutes, or until lightly browned on top and the centres are baked through. Remove from the oven and increase the temperature to 200°C (400°F/ Gas 6).

5 Cut the logs diagonally into 1cm (½in) slices. Return the slices to the baking sheet and bake for a further 8 minutes, or until golden. Leave the biscuits to cool on the baking sheets for 5 minutes, then transfer to wire racks to cool completely.

### prepare ahead

The dough can be prepared up to step 3, covered with cling film, and refrigerated for up to 2 days before baking.

### cook's tip

These biscuits are good with a glass of vin santo for dunking, or with coffee or tea. Leftovers can be stored in an airtight container for up to 5 days.

# biscotti di pistacchio e arancia

*· italy ·*

These fragrant pistachio and orange biscotti are delicious served either with coffee or dipped in a glass of sweet dessert wine. Substitute the pistachios with other nuts, if you like.

**PREP** 15 MINS ❖ **COOK** 40-45 MINS
**MAKES** 25-30

100g (3½oz) whole **pistachios**, shelled
225g (8oz) **self-raising flour**, plus extra
   for dusting
100g (3½oz) **caster sugar**
finely grated zest of 1 **orange**
2 **eggs**
1 tsp **vanilla extract**
50g (1¾oz) **unsalted butter**, melted
   and cooled

1 Preheat the oven to 180°C (350°F/Gas 4). Spread the pistachios on an unlined baking sheet. Bake for 5–10 minutes. Allow to cool, rub in a clean kitchen towel to remove the skin, then roughly chop.

2 In a bowl, mix the flour, sugar, orange zest, and pistachios. In a separate bowl, whisk together the eggs, vanilla extract, and butter. Mix the wet and dry ingredients together to make a dough.

3 Turn out the dough onto a floured surface and form into 2 logs, each 20cm (8in) long by 7cm (3in) wide. Place on a baking sheet lined with silicone paper and bake for 20 minutes in the centre of the oven. Cool slightly, then cut diagonally into 3–5cm (1¼–2in) thick slices with a serrated knife.

4 Return the slices to the baking sheet and bake for a further 15 minutes, turning once after 10 minutes, until golden and hard to the touch.

# torta di mandorle all'arancia

## *sicily*

Almond and citrus trees thrive in Sicily where there are numerous favourite family recipes for a *torta*, a cake involving almonds and oranges. This scrumptious moist dessert is made using olive oil, another local ingredient, rather than butter.

**PREP** 15 MINS ❖ **COOK** 1 HR ❖ **SERVES** 6-8

### ingredients

3 **eggs**, separated

140g (5oz) **caster sugar**

juice and grated zest of 1 large unwaxed **orange**

a few drops of **vanilla extract**

4 tbsp **extra virgin olive oil**

6 tbsp **vin santo** or other sweet dessert wine, such as Muscatel

115g (4oz) ground **almonds**

60g (2oz) **plain flour**

2 tsp **baking powder**

### for the orange glaze

115g (4oz) **caster sugar** or **icing sugar**

juice and finely grated zest of 1 large unwaxed **orange**

2 tbsp **amaretto liqueur**

1 heaped tbsp flaked **almonds**

1 tbsp shredded **orange peel** (optional), (see p281)

1 **Preheat the oven** to 180°C (350°F/Gas 4). Line a 20cm (8in) loose bottom tin with baking parchment. Beat the egg yolks with the sugar until pale and fluffy. Add the orange juice and zest, and the vanilla. Add the olive oil and wine to the mixture, and beat well.

2 **Place the ground almonds** in a mixing bowl, then sift in the flour and baking powder. Mix well.

3 **Whisk the egg whites** until stiff peaks form. Add the almonds and flour to the orange mixture, then fold in the whites. Pour into the tin. Bake for 40–50 minutes, until the cake is risen and golden and a skewer inserted in the middle comes out clean. Cover with foil if it starts to brown too quickly. Remove from the oven and leave to cool. Release from the tin and place on a plate.

4 **For the orange glaze**, heat the sugar and orange juice over a medium-high heat until it comes almost to the boil. Reduce the heat, and bubble up for 5–8 minutes, until reduced and syrupy. Stir in the liqueur and zest, and bubble up for 2 more minutes, then remove from the heat.

5 **Put the flaked almonds** in a saucer, pour over a little syrup, and stir to coat. Set aside. Make several holes in the cake with a skewer, spoon over the syrup, and leave to cool. Decorate with the caramelized almonds. If you like, scatter over the orange peel.

# crostata di ricotta

### ❖ *italy* ❖

Fresh curd cheese is mixed with candied peel and almonds, and baked in a sweet lemony pastry crust in this classic Italian cheesecake.

**PREP** 35-40 MINS, PLUS CHILLING
**COOK** 1-1¼ HRS ❖ **SERVES** 8-10

175g (6oz) **unsalted butter**, plus extra for greasing
250g (9oz) **plain flour**, plus extra for dusting
finely grated zest of 1 **lemon**
50g (1¾oz) **caster sugar**
4 **egg yolks**, plus 1 egg, beaten, for glazing
pinch of **salt**

### For the filling

1.25kg (2¾lb) **ricotta cheese**
100g (3½oz) **caster sugar**
1 tbsp **plain flour**
pinch of **salt**
finely grated zest of 1 **orange**
2 tbsp chopped **candied orange peel**
1 tsp **vanilla extract**
45g (1½oz) **sultanas**
30g (1oz) **flaked almonds**
4 **egg yolks**

1 Pound the butter between 2 sheets of baking parchment using a rolling pin to soften it. Sift the flour onto a clean work surface and make a well in the centre. Place the lemon zest, sugar, butter, egg yolks, and salt into the well. With your fingertips, work all the ingredients together until they are mixed well. Draw in the flour and press the dough into a ball.

2 On a floured surface, knead the dough for 1–2 minutes, until very smooth. Shape into a ball, wrap in cling film, and chill for 30 minutes. Grease a 23–25cm (9–10in) round springform cake tin. Flour the work surface and roll out three-quarters of the dough to make a 35–37cm (14–15in) round. Roll the round around the rolling pin, then drape over the tin. Press it into the bottom of the tin and up the sides. Trim the excess dough. Chill the shell, with the dough and trimmings, for 15 minutes.

3 To make the filling, place the ricotta in a large bowl and beat in the sugar, flour, and salt. Add the orange zest, candied peel, vanilla extract, sultanas, almonds, and egg yolks. Beat the mixture to combine. Spoon

the filling into the pastry shell. Tap the tin on the work surface to remove any air pockets. Smooth the top of the filling using the back of a wooden spoon.

4 Press the trimmings into the remaining dough and roll it out to a 25cm (10in) round on a floured surface. Cut into strips about 1cm (½in) wide, and place them on the top in a crisscross fashion. Trim off the hanging ends, so that the strips are even with the edge of the pastry shell.

5 Moisten the ends of the strips with the egg glaze, then seal them to the edge. Brush the lattice with the glaze and chill the cake for 15–30 minutes, until firm. Preheat the oven to 180°C (350°F/Gas 4), and place a baking sheet near the bottom of the oven.

6 Place the cake on the baking sheet and bake for 1–1¼ hours, until the top is firm and golden brown. Leave to cool in its tin until just warm. Remove the sides of the tin and cool completely. Then transfer to a plate, cut into wedges, and serve at room temperature.

### prepare ahead

The crostata can be made 1 day ahead and kept refrigerated, though the texture will not be as light.

### cook's tip

This traditional Italian version of cheesecake uses ricotta for a light texture and taste. The ricotta must be fresh and of the very best quality for perfect results, so buy it from an Italian delicatessen, if you can.

# tarte aux pignons

### ❖ *provence* ❖

This delicious tart is a traditional festive dessert with a rich ground almond and candied fruit filling topped with delicate pine nuts.

**PREP** 50 MINS, PLUS RESTING AND MACERATING
**COOK** 35-40 MINS ❖ **SERVES** 4-6

### For the shortcrust pastry

60g (2oz) **unsalted butter**
125g (4½oz) **plain flour**
¼ tsp **salt**
1 tbsp **caster sugar**
½ **egg yolk**

### For the filling

2 tbsp **raisins**
3 tbsp **rum**
125g (4½oz) soft **unsalted butter**, plus extra for greasing
115g (4oz) **caster sugar**
115g (4oz) ground **almonds**
2 large **eggs**
200g (7oz) **candied fruit**, diced
100g (3½oz) **pine nuts**

1 For the dough, place the butter in a bowl and beat with a spoon until creamy. Sift the flour onto a clean work surface and make a well in the centre. Add the salt, sugar, and 3 tablespoons cold water to the well and mix into the flour. Add the egg yolk and butter.

2 Work the ingredients together to make a soft dough. Flatten it gently with the palm of your hand against the work surface, then gather it together and flatten it again. Form it into a ball, line a clean cloth with flour, and wrap the dough. Leave to rest in a cool place for at least 2 hours or overnight.

3 For the filling, put the raisins in a cup, add the rum, and leave for 4 hours or overnight. Preheat the oven to 200°C (400°F/Gas 6). Butter a 23cm (9in) loose-bottomed tart tin. In a bowl, mix together the sugar, almonds, and butter. Beat in the eggs, one at a time, then stir in the raisins (with any remaining rum) and the candied fruit.

4 Roll out the dough thinly on a floured surface. Lift onto the tin and press in lightly. Prick the pastry case a few times with a fork. Spoon the filling into the case and smooth down with the back of the spoon. Sprinkle over the pine nuts and bake for 35–40 minutes. Leave to cool in the tin before turning out and serving.

# tarte au citron

*✧ provence ✧*

Deliciously pretty little lemon tarts are a great way to round off a special meal. You can use the same method to make orange tarts. Simply replace the lemons with 2 oranges.

**PREP** 30 MINS, PLUS MAKING PASTRY
**COOK** 30 MINS ❖ **MAKES** 6 TARTS

2 portions **shortcrust pastry** (see p298)
**soft butter**, for greasing

### For the filling
grated zest and juice of 2 **lemons**
2 medium **eggs**
2 medium **egg yolks**
200ml (7fl oz) **double cream**
150g (5½oz) **caster sugar**

### For the lemon topping
1 small **lemon**
5 tbsp **caster sugar**

1 Preheat the oven to 180°C (350°F/Gas 4). Use soft butter to grease 6 individual loose-bottomed, fluted tartlet tins.

2 Roll out the pastry dough thinly on a floured work surface. Lift onto the tins and press the dough into them lightly with your fingers without stretching the dough. Prick each pastry case with fork, line with baking parchment, and fill with dried beans.. Bake blind for 10 minutes. Take the pastry cases out of the oven, remove the beans, and leave the pastry cases to cool, then trim off the excess pastry. Set aside.

3 Increase the oven temperature to 200°C (400°F/Gas 6). For the filling, combine the lemon zest and juice, eggs, and yolks in a bowl. Whisk until slightly frothy. Add the cream and sugar, and whisk vigorously. Spoon the filling into the pastry cases. Bake for 18–20 minutes until just set.

4 Meanwhile, prepare the lemon topping. Thinly slice the lemon. Put the sugar in a saucepan with 200ml (7fl oz) cold water. Stir over a medium heat until the sugar has dissolved, then bubble up for 3 minutes. Add the lemon slices and simmer gently for 15 minutes. Lift out the slices and drain on a rack placed over a plate. Decorate each tart with a caramelized lemon slice. Serve warm.

### cook's tip

To make a large tart to serve 6, use a loose-bottomed 30cm (12in) tart tin. Gently press the pastry into the tin, then prick with a fork, line with baking parchment, and fill with dried beans. Bake blind for 15 minutes. Once filled, bake for 30–40 minutes until just set. To finish, decorate the top with the caramelized lemon slices.

# castagnaccio

*✧ tuscany ✧*

Chestnut flour gives this interesting Tuscan cake a dense yet moist texture. It keeps in an airtight container for 3 days.

**PREP** 25 MINS ❖ **COOK** 50-60 MINS
**SERVES** 6-8

1 tbsp **olive oil**, plus extra for greasing
50g (1¾oz) **raisins**
25g (scant 1oz) **flaked almonds**
30g (1oz) **pine nuts**
300g (10oz) **chestnut flour**
25g (scant 1oz) **caster sugar**
pinch of **salt**
400ml (14fl oz) **milk** or **water**
1 tbsp finely chopped **rosemary leaves**
zest of 1 **orange**

1 Preheat the oven to 180°C (350°F/Gas 4). Grease a 20cm (8in) round springform cake tin and line the base with baking parchment. Cover the raisins with warm water and leave for 5 minutes to plump up. Drain.

2 Place the almonds and pine nuts on a baking tray and bake for 5–10 minutes until lightly browned. Sift the chestnut flour into a large bowl, then add the sugar and salt.

3 Using a balloon whisk, gradually whisk in the milk to produce a thick, smooth batter. Whisk in the olive oil, pour the batter into the tin, and scatter over the raisins, rosemary, orange zest, and nuts.

4 Bake in the centre of the oven for 50–60 minutes until the surface is dry and the edges slightly browned. The cake will not rise much. Leave in the tin for 10 minutes, then carefully turn out onto a wire rack and leave to cool completely. Remove the baking parchment and serve.

### cook's tip

Chestnut flour is available from Italian delis, health food stores, or online.

# pastel de santiago

❖ *s p a i n* ❖

This lemony almond sponge is baked in a crisp shell of cinnamon-flavoured pastry lightened with soft white pork lard, which is often used instead of butter in Spain to make cookies and pastries.

**PREP** 25 MINS, PLUS CHILLING AND COOLING
**COOK** 20-25 MINS ❖ **SERVES** 6-8

### For the pastry
100g (3½oz) **lard**
100g (3½oz) **caster sugar**
1 **egg yolk**
200g (7oz) **plain flour**, plus extra for dusting
1 tsp ground **cinnamon**
**icing sugar**, for dusting

### For the filling
8 **eggs**
500g (1lb 2oz) **caster sugar**
500g (1lb 2oz) ground **almonds**
juice and finely grated zest of 1 **lemon**

1 For the pastry, beat the lard with the sugar until light and fluffy. Beat in the egg yolk, sprinkle in a little flour and the cinnamon, then work in the remaining flour until you have a slightly soft ball of dough. Cover with cling film and set aside for 30 minutes, until firm.

2 Preheat the oven to 200°C (400°F/Gas 6). On a lightly floured surface, roll out the pastry thinly using a floured rolling pin. Line a 22 x 5cm (8½ x 2in) round baking tin with the pastry. Prick the base with a fork, cover with baking parchment, and weigh down with baking beans or rice grains.

3 Bake blind for 8–10 minutes to set the pastry. Remove the parchment and bake for 1–2 minutes more. Set aside to cool.

4 For the filling, whisk the eggs until light and fluffy. Sprinkle in the sugar, a spoon at a time. Continue to beat until doubled in volume. Gently fold in the almonds and lemon juice and zest without overworking the mix and collapsing the air bubbles.

5 Spoon the mixture into the pastry case, filling it almost to the top, leaving a little edge of the pastry. Bake for 45–50 minutes, until the topping is well-risen, firm, and nut-brown. Allow to cool before unmoulding. Dust with icing sugar before serving. You can also decorate the top with a cut-out of a scallop shell – the pilgrim's emblem.

## cook's tip

The tart is named as a mark of respect for St James the apostle, whose sanctuary at Santiago de Compostella ranks with Rome and Jerusalem as a destination for pilgrims. The lemon in the filling is for the sorrow of Good Friday and the almonds from the Jordan Valley serve as a reminder of the Holy Land.

# m'hanncha

### ❖ *north africa* ❖

Translated in Arabic as "snake", an apt description as it is coiled like one, this Moroccan pastry is best served warm with a glass of mint tea.

**PREP** 1 HR, PLUS CHILLING
**COOK** 30-35 MINS ❖ **SERVES** 6-8

### For the pastry

125g (4½oz) **filo sheets**, about 6 sheets

60g (2oz) **unsalted butter**, melted, plus extra for greasing

1 **egg yolk**, beaten with 1 tbsp water

### For the filling

350g (12oz) ground **almonds**

225g (8oz) **caster sugar**

60g (2oz) **icing sugar**

1 tbsp ground **cinnamon**

4 tbsp **orange blossom water**

### For the topping

2–3 tbsp **icing sugar**

2 tsp ground **cinnamon**

1 Preheat the oven to 180°C (350°F/Gas 4). Place the ingredients for the filling in a bowl with 3 tablespoons of cold water and work them with your hands to form a stiff paste. Add a little more water if required. Take lumps of the paste and roll them on a flat surface to form fingers about 2cm (¾in) thick. Cover and chill for 30 minutes.

2 Line a baking sheet with lightly greased baking parchment. Place a filo sheet on the work surface, with the longer side nearest to you. Lightly brush it with a little butter, then place some almond fingers, end to end, along the edge nearest to you.

3 Roll up the edge over the filling, tuck in the ends, and roll the sheet into a long, thin tube. Gently push both ends of the tube towards the centre, so that it creases like an accordion. Place in the middle of the baking sheet. Carefully, curve it into a tight coil. Repeat the process with the remaining sheets, curving each tube around the inner coils so the pastry resembles a coiled snake. Brush the top with the egg wash and bake for 30–35 minutes, until crisp and lightly browned.

4 Sprinkle the pastry liberally with icing sugar, then sprinkle the cinnamon to form thin lines leading from the centre to the outer rim, like the spokes of a wheel. Serve in generous portions while still warm.

# cannoli

### ❖ *sicily* ❖

Literally translated as "little tubes", these crisp pastries, filled with glacé fruits and ricotta cheese, are a Sicilian speciality.

**PREP** 30 MINS, PLUS COOLING
**COOK** 20 MINS ❖ **MAKES** 16

### For the pastry

175g (6oz) **plain flour**, plus extra for rolling and dusting

pinch of **salt**

60g (2oz) **unsalted butter**

45g (1½oz) **caster sugar**

1 **egg**, beaten

2–3 tbsp **dry white wine** or **Marsala**

1 **egg white**, lightly beaten

**oil**, for deep-frying

**icing sugar**, for dusting

### For the filling

60g (2oz) **dark chocolate**, grated or very finely chopped

350g (12oz) **ricotta cheese**

60g (2oz) **icing sugar**, plus extra for dusting

finely grated zest of 1 **orange**

60g (2oz) chopped **glacé fruits** or **candied citrus peel**

1 For the pastry, sift the flour and salt into a bowl and rub in the butter. Stir in the sugar and egg, then add enough wine to make a soft dough. Knead until smooth.

2 On a lightly floured work surface, roll out the pastry thinly and cut into 16 squares, each measuring roughly 7.5cm (3in). Dust 4 cannoli moulds with flour and wrap a pastry square loosely around each on the diagonal, dampening the edges with the egg white and pressing them together to seal.

3 Heat the oil in a pan to 180°C (350°F) and deep-fry for 3–4 minutes, or until the pastry is golden and crisp. Drain on a plate lined with kitchen paper. When cool enough to handle, carefully twist the metal tubes to pull them out of the pastry. Cook 3 more batches in the same way.

4 For the filling, mix all the ingredients together. When the pastry tubes are cold, pipe or spoon the filling into them. Dust with icing sugar to serve.

### cook's note

Although cannoli moulds are available from kitchen stores, short lengths of stainless steel tubing, 15cm (6in) long and 2cm (½in) in diameter, from a hardware shop, work equally well.

# nuts

You cannot cook Mediterranean fare without such favourites as almonds, hazelnuts, pine nuts, and pistachios. Store small amounts in sealed plastic bags.

**Pine nuts** are used widely in the Middle East, for savoury kibbeh, sweet baklava, and other dishes.

**Almonds are** nutritious, versatile, and popular. Raw or toasted, they make an ideal snack, and a moreish nibble with a little sea salt. Blanched almonds thicken sauces and soups, whilst ground almonds replace flour *alla italiana* in cakes and pastries. Sweet almond paste is a favourite in Sicily, and in Morocco where it is used liberally in savoury dishes. Hazelnuts are popular in Italy and the Middle East for a number of sweet recipes. Pine nuts may be hard to extract from their tight cones, but they have a creamy texture, a fresh nutty taste, and are delicious in pilafs, salads, and classic Italian and Provençal biscuits.

**Hazelnuts** are traditionally used in northern Italian confectionery, and to make gianduja, a classic chocolate speciality.

**Pistachios**, the most moreish of snacks, are used in ice cream, and to flavour chocolate, halva, loukoums, and biscotti, as well as the classic Mortadella sausage.

**Marcona almonds** are round, sweet, and delicate in texture. In Spain they are lightly fried in oil, and in Italy they are used to make turrón.

# ranginak

### ❖ *middle east* ❖

This popular Arab sweetmeat, which is
a bit like date fudge cake, is prepared
for all festive occasions in the eastern
Mediterranean region and in Morocco, where
dates are offered as a mark of hospitality.

**PREP** 10 MINS ❖ **COOK** 10 MINS
**SERVES** 8-10

150g (5½oz) **walnuts**, halved lengthways
500g (1lb 2oz) soft, ready-to-eat,
  pitted **dates**
225g (8oz) **unsalted butter**
3–4 tbsp **granulated sugar**
225g (8oz) **plain flour**
1–2 tbsp finely chopped **pistachios**

1 Cut the walnut halves in half lengthways
to make quarters. Find the opening
in each date from which the stone was
extracted and stuff it with a walnut quarter.

2 Place the stuffed dates in a single
layer on a lightly greased, shallow,
23 x 18cm (9 x 7in) baking dish, packing
them close together.

3 In a small pan, melt the butter with
the sugar over a low heat, then stir in
the flour. Keep stirring until the mixture
begins to turn golden brown. Spoon the
mixture over the dates, filling in any gaps.

4 Leave the mixture to set, then sprinkle
the pistachios over the top. Cut the
cake into little squares and serve them
with tea or coffee.

### cook's tip

You can stuff the dates with blanched
almonds, a mixture of chopped nuts, or
an almond paste. Once the ranginak has
set, you can sprinkle it with desiccated
coconut, toasted pine nuts, or icing sugar.

# a taste of
# LEBANON

On the Eastern Mediterranean, at the heart of the Levant where three continents meet, Lebanon is a land where very different cultures have been coming into contact for thousands of years. Dishes go back to Roman and Phoenician times. The main influence on the cuisine is the four centuries spent under the control of the Ottoman empire. If Lebanese cooking is famous for the variety of its ingredients and spices, it is loved for the mouth-watering tastes and rich aromas of its dishes. Lebanese food is abundant and generous. Even a simple meal is preceded by nuts, pickled vegetables, and hot flat breads served with hummus redolent of tahini, with a dash of bright olive oil. Mezze might be dips and salads, tabbouleh, succulent barbecued chicken drumsticks, or tender little quails. And there's plenty more to come – a main course, then dessert, with coffee or tea.

**Hummus** is the Arabic for chickpeas – these are dried, soaked, cooked, or puréed into what we know as hummus.

**Grapes** flourish in Lebanon. The country's Bekaa valley is one of the oldest sites of wine production in the world. Lebanese wines, celebrated in the Bible for their fragrant aroma, were marketed far and wide by Phoenician traders.

Beirut, the country's capital, inhabited continuously since the 15th century BC, has undergone major reconstruction since the civil war and is once again a tourist attraction.

Sidon's Sea Castle was a fortress built by the crusaders in the 13th century on a small island connected to the mainland by a long, narrow causeway.

**Pine nuts**, often lightly toasted, are much used in savoury chicken and rice dishes, in stuffings, and to make kibbeh.

**Pomegranate seeds** and syrup are a distinctive taste of Ottoman-inspired Lebanese dishes, particularly with stewed aubergine, tomatoes, or pulses.

**Labna** is a bright, creamy soft fresh cheese made by straining yogurt. Perfect with a dribble of olive oil.

**Flat-leaf parsley**, a key herb in tabbouleh and fattoush, is used more than any other herb in Lebanon. But mint, dill, coriander and many more are also popular.

# A Lebanese meal for sharing

Lebanese people love sharing food. Mezze at home is no exception –
there won't be as many different dishes as for a special occasion
or in a restaurant, but there'll be a tempting choice. On the table are
creamy aubergine baba ganoush, khubz bread, crispy spinach and nut
pastries, herby tabbouleh, and succulent grilled chicken with a garlic
dip. Prepared fresh figs are there to refresh the palate afterwards,
with servings of sweet rose-scented milk pudding.

**Laban**

**Baba ganoush**
page 20

**Fatayer bisabanikh**
page 29

**Toum**
page 18

**Khubz**
page 257

**Muhallabia**
page 282

**Tabbouleh**
page 220

**Djaj meshwi**
page 187

# panforte

*tuscany*

This famous cake from Siena dates from the 13th century. It is quite rich, so cut thin slices to serve as a post-dinner treat.

**PREP** 30 MINS ❖ **COOK** 30 MINS
**SERVES** 12-16

115g (4oz) **whole blanched almonds**, toasted and roughly chopped

125g (4½oz) **hazelnuts**, toasted and roughly chopped

200g (7oz) **mixed candied orange** and **lemon peel**, chopped

115g (4oz) **dried figs**, roughly chopped

finely grated zest of 1 **lemon**

½ tsp ground **cinnamon**

½ tsp freshly grated **nutmeg**

¼ tsp ground **cloves**

¼ tsp **allspice**

75g (2½oz) **rice flour** or **plain flour**

30g (1oz) **unsalted butter**

140g (5oz) **caster sugar**

4 tbsp **runny honey**

**icing sugar**, for dusting

1 Line the base and sides of a 20cm (8in) round loose-bottomed cake tin with greaseproof paper, then place a disc of rice paper on top of it. Preheat the oven to 180°C (350°F/Gas 4).

2 Put the almonds, hazelnuts, candied peel, figs, lemon zest, cinnamon, nutmeg, cloves, allspice, and flour in a large bowl and mix well.

3 Put the butter, caster sugar, and honey in a pan and heat gently until melted. Pour into the fruit and nut mixture and stir to combine. Spoon into the prepared tin and, with damp hands, press down to create a smooth, even layer.

4 Bake for 30 minutes, then remove from the oven, leaving it in the tin to cool and become firm. When completely cold, remove the panforte from the tin. Peel off the greaseproof paper but leave the rice paper stuck to the bottom of the cake. Dust heavily with icing sugar and serve cut into small wedges.

# baklava

*greece*

This crispy confection, filled with chopped nuts and spices and drenched with honey syrup, has long been a favourite. It is a classic sweet pastry in Turkey and the Eastern Mediterranean.

**PREP** 50-55 MINS
**COOK** 1¼-1½ HRS ❖ **MAKES** 36

250g (9oz) shelled **unsalted pistachios**, coarsely chopped

250g (9oz) **walnuts**, coarsely chopped

250g (9oz) **caster sugar**

2 tsp ground **cinnamon**

large pinch of ground **cloves**

500g pack of **filo pastry**

250g (9oz) **unsalted butter**

250ml (9fl oz) **runny honey**

juice of 1 **lemon**

3 tbsp **orange blossom water**

1 Set aside 3–4 tablespoons of the pistachios for decoration. Place the remainder in a bowl with the walnuts, 50g (1¾oz) of the sugar, the cinnamon, and cloves. Stir to mix.

2 Preheat the oven to 180°C (350°F/Gas 4). Lay a damp kitchen towel on the work surface, unroll the filo sheets on it, and cover with a second damp towel. Melt the butter in a small saucepan. Brush a deep-sided 30 x 40cm (12 x 16in) baking tray with a little butter. Take a sheet of filo and line the tray with it, folding over one end to fit.

3 Brush the filo with butter and gently press into the corners and sides of the tin. Lay another sheet on top, brush with butter, and press into the tin as before. Continue layering and buttering each sheet, until one-third has been used. Scatter half the nut filling over the top sheet.

4 Layer another third of the filo sheets as before, then sprinkle the remaining nut filling over it. Layer the remaining sheets in the same manner. Trim off the excess with a knife. Brush with butter and pour any remaining butter on top. With a small knife, cut diagonal lines, 1cm (½in) deep, in the filo to mark out 4cm (1½in) diamond shapes. Do not press down when cutting.

5 Bake on a low shelf for 1¼–1½ hours, until golden and a skewer inserted in the centre for 30 seconds comes out clean.

6 For the syrup, place the remaining sugar and 250ml (9fl oz) cold water in a pan and heat until dissolved, stirring occasionally. Pour in the honey and stir to mix. Boil for about 25 minutes without stirring, until the syrup reaches the soft ball stage, 115°C (239°F) on a sugar thermometer. To test the syrup without a thermometer, take the pan off the heat and dip a teaspoon in the hot syrup. Let the syrup cool for a few seconds, then take a little between your finger and thumb; a soft ball should form.

7 Remove the syrup from the heat and let it cool to lukewarm. Add the lemon juice and orange blossom water. Remove the tin from the oven and immediately pour the syrup over the pastries.

8 With a sharp knife, cut along the marked lines, almost to the bottom (see cook's tip). Let the pastries cool, then cut through the marked lines completely. Carefully lift out the pastries with a palette knife and arrange on dessert plates. Sprinkle the top of each pastry with the reserved pistachios.

**prepare ahead**

The pastries can be made 5 days before serving. Store in an airtight container; the flavour will mellow.

**cook's tip**

Filo pastry is very delicate and can crumble slightly when cut. The syrup used in this recipe will help minimize this, but not stop it completely. Make sure you use a sharp, slim blade to cut the baklava, and be sure to score it first, as instructed in the recipe, for the neatest finish.

# Index

Entries in **bold** indicate ingredients.

## About the authors

### Editor-in-chief
**Marie-Pierre Moine** has over 20 years' experience in the food and wine media. Past editor of *Taste* and *TasteAnatolia* magazines, she is a food and travel writer, cookery demonstrator and consultant, a member of the UK Guild of Food Writers, and on the Committee of the Academy of Chocolate. Born and brought up in Paris, she fell in love with the Mediterranean during long childhood summers. Marie-Pierre lives in London but spends time in France and, whenever possible, visiting and revisiting various parts of the Mediterranean basin.

### Contributors
**Elisabeth Luard** is an award-winning food writer whose books include *European Peasant Cookery*, *The Food of Spain and Portugal*, *Tapas*, and *European Seasonal Dishes*. She has lived and worked in Spain, Italy, and France and brought up her own young family in a remote valley in Andalucia. She now lives in an old farmhouse in the foothills of the Cambrians in mid-Wales but continues to travel widely. She contributes regularly to newspapers, magazines, and on-line publications in the UK and US, and is Trustee Director of The Oxford Symposium on Food and Cookery.

**Ghillie Başan**, a cookery writer, author, and broadcaster, grew up in East Africa, and has a university degree in Social Anthropology and a Cordon Bleu diploma, which she combines in her work on the culinary cultures of Turkey, the Middle East, and North Africa. She has written more than 30 cookery books, numerous food and travel articles, and is the spice expert on Radio Scotland. Ghillie lives in the Scottish Highlands where she runs internationally acclaimed cookery workshops.

## Acknowledgments

### Marie-Pierre Moine would like to thank
First and foremost, my co-authors Ghillie Başan and Elisabeth Luard. I love their recipes and respect and value their expertise, knowledge, and talent. I am very grateful for their willingness to help at every stage. Like the fusion of cultures in Mediterranean cuisine, this book has been a genuine joint project. I have been very lucky in having Cressida Tuson as my handler within the DK in-house team. She remained friendly and calm throughout, and kept the leash light when the pressure came on. My sincere thanks also go to Sara Robin, Dawn Henderson, and Elizabeth Clinton. I'll restrict myself to mentioning only four of the people whose very different books about the Mediterranean I have enjoyed and learnt from over the years: Anna Del Conte, Arto der Haroutunian, Philip Mansel, and Claudia Roden. I would also like to thank Frances Fedden, Lisette Novo, the Petra Kitchen, and Emel Yuksel and Guray Erkan, who gave me the opportunity and inspiration to explore Turkey and its cuisine.

### DK would like to thank
Stuart West for new recipe photography; Will Heap and William Reavell for additonal photography; Penny Stock for photography art direction; Jane Lawrie and Nico Ghirlando for food styling; Henrietta Clancy, Beatrice Ferrante, and Kat Mead for food styling assistance; Rob Merrett, Liz Hippisley, and Wei Tang for prop styling; Uyen Luu for ingredients sourcing; Anne Fisher, Miranda Harvey, Lucy Parissi, and Kate Fenton for design assistance; Tom Morse for technical support; Steve Crozier for image retouching; Chris Gates, Sue Davie, and Jane Bamforth for recipe testing; Corinne Masciocchi for proofreading; and Bill Johncocks for the index.

All photography and artworks © Dorling Kindersley